Hannibal

1. Publius Cornelius
Scipio Africanus.

2. Young Hannibal   *3. Old Hannibal*
as Hercules.   *as Hercules.*

From Coins in the British Museum.
Photo. by R. N. Haile.

Hannibal

G. P. Baker

Cooper Square Press

First Cooper Square Press edition 1999

This Cooper Square Press paperback edition of *Hannibal* is an unabridged republication of the edition first published in New York in 1929.

Published by Cooper Square Press,
An Imprint of Rowman & Littlefield Publishers, Inc.
150 Fifth Avenue, Suite 911
New York, New York 10011

Distributed by National Book Network

Library of Congress Cataloging-in-Publication Data

Baker, G. P. (George Philip), 1879–1951
    Hannibal / G. P. Baker.
        p.   cm.
    Originally published : New York : Dodd, Mead & Company, 1929.
    Includes index.
    ISBN 0-8154-1005-0 (pbk. : alk. paper)
    1. Hannibal 247–182 B.C. 2. Punic War, 2nd, 218–201 B.C. 3. Generals—Tunisia—Carthage (Extinct city) Biography. 4. Rome— History—Republic, 265–30 B.C. 5. Carthage (Extinct city)—History.   I. Title.
DG249.B3   1999
937'.04'092—dc21
[B]   99-34894
                                                                CIP

♾™ The paper used in this publication meets the minimum requirements of American National Standard for Information Sciences—Permanence of Paper for Printed Library Materials, ANSI/NISO Z39.48-1992.
Manufactured in the United States of America.

HOC OPVS
GVLIELMO
GARTHWAITIO
DVNELMIAE
BARONETTO
EQVITI COR·
ONAE BELGICAE
INSCRIPTVM EST
QVI VT GRATIAS PATRIAE
SVAE AGAT SALVTEMQVE
COMMVNEM CIVITATIS
ADIUVET STVDIA HISTORIAE
GVBERNATIONIS ORIGINIS·
QVE ET AVCTVS DIGNITATIS
REGIAE FOVET.

PREFACE

To know what Hannibal was, what he did, and how and why he did it, is to look with more than usual intimacy into the causes and processes by which the world we know was founded. Like Alexander and Napoleon, he ranks among those half-dozen great soldiers whose work broke down barriers and cleared the way for larger ideas of civilization. The process is not often a pleasant one to those who undergo it; but much of human life—particularly beginning and ending—is naturally unpleasant.

That Hannibal should be among the most original and brilliant of these men is all the more noteworthy since the race to which he belonged was far more interested in commerce than in war. And indeed the first step towards understanding his career is to realize that all the military, political and racial issues were piled up upon the primary question of commercial monopoly. We shall begin, in this book, by glancing at the building up of the Phœnician monopoly, the failure of the effort to break it, and the steps by which the problem was changed into the question of what kind of power should rule a world in which that monopoly was fast becoming universalized. If Rome had not seized the control of the Mediterranean world, Carthage would have done so.

The actual story told in these pages suffers a little, as a mere story, by the fact that the reader knows the end before he begins. Hannibal did not destroy Rome.

The Romans destroyed Carthage. But what may now seem to us a matter of course was emphatically not such while it was happening. The struggle was desperate, hazardous, full of baffling turns of fortune—a contest in which the fierce antagonists staked their very skins upon a gamble the end of which the wisest man could not foresee. Not until one of the combatants was indubitably down, out, and disposed of for ever, could the other even credit that he had not lost. . . . If the historian were at liberty to change all the names, so that the identity of the parties was disguised, this element of excitement and hazard would suddenly become much more noticeable: indeed, it might dominate the story.

The interest of the struggle lies not least in the methods employed. Hardly anywhere else can we find so clear-cut an issue between two main modes of human activity, or a more direct collision between the power which springs from human genius exercising its gift of authoritative command, and that other which derives its strength from the close association of men in political society. . . . It did not end with Hannibal. He set going a contest which lasted long after his own defeat and death.

As the first serious attempt to unify upon a large scale the civilized states of the world, the monarchy of Alexander was sooner or later bound to influence the Romans in the government of the vast dominion they had acquired; but before that day came, the whole conception of personal government had been modified by the example of the methods employed by Hannibal. He depended very little if at all upon any forms or artificial paraphernalia of government. His power was based almost solely upon the direct personal influence he could, as a man, exert upon other men. . . . We shall see his limitations. From some points of view they were serious. But just where he ended and his method seemed to break down, it was picked up and re-applied by other men.

We know that the spiritual ancestor of Cæsar was Sulla. Now the spiritual ancestor of Sulla was Scipio Africanus. There cannot be much doubt where Sulla learnt some of his methods of leadership. And in the course of this book we shall see some reason at any rate to believe that Scipio was a direct, if unintentional, creation of Hannibal. . . . Hannibal, therefore, was one of the remote fountains of the whole stream of Roman imperial monarchy, and all that came of it. . . . It was the Carthaginian influence, far more than the Macedonian, that taught the Romans the art of creating and employing a professional army, and the methods of governing an empire of mixed nations. If they improved on the model it was because they used more freedom in adopting and blending the hints they gathered from their various predecessors.

Hannibal was thus one of the most important of the men who originated the tradition of personal government, as distinguished from collegial or senatorial. His gifts as a leader of men are historic. The influence he exercised upon later generations may profitably be compared and contrasted with that of Alexander. The features which later monarchy owed to Alexander were chiefly institutional. But those which Hannibal originated were ideas of method and of individual action; he taught the world certain conceptions of how to set about the task of dealing with men on a large scale, starting from the very beginning, and with the fewest possible presuppositions. A modern man who tried to learn from Alexander might be puzzled how to set about the task. But he would find very little difficulty in adapting the methods of Hannibal to his own use. Those methods, being applied psychology, are not limited by the circumstances of any place or period. They are as universal and eternal as mankind. To "work the oracle" on the hopes, fears, fortes, foibles and perversities of men, as Hannibal did, will be possible as long as men have nerves to be worked on. If we were to trace out the derivation of modern ideas of leadership, the most fertile and healthy of them would prove to come far more from Hannibal than from Alexander.

The world has not always thought so. The immense volume and influence of the popular story of Alexander has never been matched by any parallel romance of Hannibal. But the popular Alexander tale was a semi-mythical embroidery no more related to the real Alexander than the epic of Charlemagne is related to the real Charles the Great. And yet if great portions of Livy and Polybius have successfully survived where much else perished, their narratives of Hannibal's career may have been not the least of the attractions which recommended those pages to successive generations of more discerning readers who shared a profitable taste for the romance of actuality.

Soldier though he was, he would not have been a Phœnician had he enjoyed war for its own sake. He used military force as a means to an end. His method was not exclusively nor even principally a military method: it is applicable in an equal degree to most of the other activities of mankind. A man of his racial habit of mind would hardly have "wasted so much good material" if an alternative course had seemed possible. Increasing civilization has made other courses not only possible, but easier. The field of action for a new Hannibal would be on the stock markets and the exchanges. . . . War, in ancient civilization, was usually an attempt to hold or break the ring round an area of exchange. This was certainly the dominant motive of Carthaginian war. . . . In proportion as the exchanges of the world become mutually accessible, the expectation of war will grow less. There will always be the possibility that it may be resorted to on the Hannibalic rule of Surprise; but excluding this, the normal probability will diminish. War is a function of economic activity.

G. P. B.

Elmer, Sussex.

1929.

CONTENTS

CONTENTS

ILLUSTRATIONS

(i) Publius Cornelius Scipio Africanus

MAPS AND DIAGRAMS

CHAPTER I

PRELUDE TO STRUGGLE

I

THREE thousand eight hundred and twenty-six years before Mr. Orville Wright flew the first aeroplane, an aged Semitic Chief, with his stock and his stock-riders, rode up the eastern edge of the Arabian desert. According to the account of his descendants, he came from that city of Ur in Sumeria which archæologists even now are unearthing for us. In the eastward bend of the Euphrates, where it comes closest to the Mediterranean sea, he dwelt for two years; a land of wide plain and over-arching sky, in which a huge moon sailed in the sky at night, and the constellations were of orient magnificence. There he died; and his son succeeded him. From that son Lord Rothschild, Lord Melchett, Benedict Spinoza and Heinrich Heine all alike deduce their descent.

The Semitic migration

The old man had come clear of the war that for long had been devastating the civilization of the nearer east. He was far from being the only refugee. When, soon after his death, that famous son of his crossed the Euphrates fords with the stock, and went southwards, it was partly because no way was available north, where the Taurus and the Armenian mountains rose into snowy crests; and partly because kinsmen of the same race and language were already settling those southerly lands that lay between the desert and the sea, down to-

I

wards Egypt. Some had taken possession of the sea-coast. Phoinikoi, the Greeks afterwards called these; Pœni, the Romans; Phœnicians is the name by which they are known to us. According to their own account, an earthquake had driven them out of their own lands beside the Persian Gulf—a moral earthquake, we may presume. Abraham's explanation of his own arrival was simpler. The word of the Lord had come to him—a reason brief and conclusive.

The saga of the Hebrews was written by themselves, and they themselves survive to read it. The saga of the Phœnicians is written in the records of all the races of the Mediterranean, across all the lands from Syria to Britain, and in the faces and temperament of Cornishmen, Spaniards and Africans. Their claim to remembrance is that they were the pioneers who stand at the head of modern civilization. . . . They had their forerunners. Egyptians and Cretans may have been the first to develop the Spanish mines and to find the ocean route to Britain. But these handed nothing directly on to us. Only when the Phœnicians appeared in the Mediterranean did that tradition begin which descends in an unbroken line to Wall Street and Singapore Harbour.

II

The Phœnicians were Semites of an earlier migration than the modern Mohammedan Arabs. They belonged to the great "Canaanite" movement which began some time about the year 2300 B. C. Driven out by a cycle of dry seasons which contracted the pasturage of Arabia, the stock-raising tribes of the border took refuge in

The Phœnicians

The Canaanite Semites 2300 B. C.

neighbouring Mesopotamia. The dry cycle was not confined to Arabia. Its effects in the vast Central Asiatic steppes took a little time in becoming manifest; but they grew alarmingly visible when the steppe pastoralists with their horse-herds, fleeing west and south from encroaching drought, began to precipitate a human avalanche upon Mesopotamia. In those crowded and irrigated valleys, fed from the snows of the Armenian ranges, there was always food to be found.

We have no reason to suppose that ancient Mesopotamia welcomed the intruders with enthusiasm. But its objections were met by a surprise which in its day was as sensational as the application of the aeroplane to war. The men of the steppe let loose that mobile horse-drawn fighting car which for a thousand years remained the determining arm in warfare. The city states of Mesopotamia collapsed. Babylon itself was sacked: the mingled flood of conquest, half driving the Semites before it, half carrying them with it, ran right up to Egypt itself, which was invaded and over-run. For a time the whole of west Asiatic civilization was submerged. . . . *Their origin* But civilization was tough. It rose again out of the chaos. . . . When the dark age begins to clear, we see the exiled Egyptian princes building war-cars of their own. They returned from exile to sweep the invaders out of Egypt, and to reconquer Palestine right up to the Euphrates. The Assyrians, the Hebrews and their fellows dwelt under the iron rod of the restored Pharaohs; for the Phœnicians, Egypt had another and a better use.

The foundation of Phœnician prosperity was laid in those days when their sea-board cities were the Asiatic ports for the new and greater Egypt which arose from

the wreck of the old. Under Egyptian tutelage the
Phœnicians learnt their business as ship-builders, commercial carriers and middlemen. It was unnecessary for
them to learn the art of war. As merchants they began,
and merchants they remained.

III

The Phœnician cities gained rather than lost after the
wane of Egyptian power in Syria. . . . Tyre, Sidon
and Beirut were already settled and important communities towards the end of the Eighteenth Dynasty:
but it was only after the withdrawal of Egypt behind
her own frontiers, the fall of the Minos of Crete, the
arrival of the Phrygians and Achæans, the collapse of
the Hittites—events whose echo is in the thunders of
the *Iliad*—that the Semites stepped into the shoes of
the Hittite and the Cretan. While the Assyrian was organizing the military resistance which gave west
Asiatic civilization another thousand years of profitable
life, the Phœnician pushed out his ships to pick up the
dropped threads of the Mediterranean trade.

He brought to the task gifts by no means despicable.
His very physical type has impressed after ages with
a peculiar, half-distasteful interest. At some time during their migration, the "Canaanite" Semites must have
crossed with another racial stock, the identity of which
is somewhat of a mystery.[1] The cross gave them a thick-
ness of build and a sombre strength of mind foreign to

Rise of the Phœnician cities

[1] Possibly Hittite, including in this rather uncertain term the race which originated the Priest-States of Asia Minor. The Hebrew Theocratic State obviously
derives from this source, not from the Semitic side. The writer of Ezekiel XVI
actually attributes an Amorite-Hittite origin to Jerusalem.

the pure-bred Arab, but visible in the Assyrians as well as in the Phœnicians. . . . We may at the start dismiss from our minds any picture we may entertain of the Phœnician as a shuffling Shylock. He was of the same breed as those Sargons and Tiglath-Pilesers whose sport was lion-hunting and whose trade was war.

It is unlikely that either the Phœnician or the Assyrian lacked those amiable virtues, and even those amiable weaknesses, which are common to mankind: but they were only occasionally, if at all, visible. He was a masked man, over whose lighter qualities an impenetrable veil was cast. Fixed, firm and unalterable in resolution, supple and elusive, hard to pin, and of unbending obstinacy when pinned, he seemed specially created for the task of facing unmoved all the terrors of commercial adventuring in unknown and uncharted regions. We are not without modern illustrations of the type. The Jew still preserves it in a softened form. Like the Jew, the Phœnician had the mathematical gift which made him a good business man, swift to analyse and reckon up the factors before him, careful and accurate in his bookkeeping; he had a robustness of body and mind that could wear down the more temperamental European, a power of association so strong as to be a little too rigid and exclusive. He was like the houses he built: outwardly solid, forbidding and fortified against all men, with few doors or windows, and all his kindly intimacies hidden deep within.

He had, of course, the disadvantages of his qualities. He was of a more specialized type than the European. The very closeness and exclusiveness of his social unity made it difficult for him to impose his civilization upon

The
Phœnician
character

a strange race. He had not the political gift. An exclusively business ability often involves a mental short-
ness of sight which disqualifies its possessor from some
of the higher forms of human activity. He had little
speculative intelligence. . . . He was superstitious. He
endured with more or less patience the terrors of the
unseen forces of the universe. He never learned, as the
Greek did, to analyse and to explain them.[1]

IV

The Phœnician cities, therefore, eleven centuries before Christ, held almost a monopoly of "commercial
wealth, enterprise and manufacturing ingenuity" in a
world which lay exhausted after an age of war and tur-
moil. Homer knew the products of Sidon, the mother-
city of Phœnicia, whence all the rest were ultimately
derived. The country itself, hemmed in between mountain and sea, though small, was a rich and beautiful land
of great natural fertility, supplying abundance of suitable timber (fir, pine and cedar) for ship-building, besides the sand of Sidon and Akka, which produced the
best glass in the world; while the sea contained that
murex which yielded the noblest dye known to antiquity. Phœnicia was deeply involved in the manufac-

ture of dyed, woven and embroidered fabrics; these—
ranking among the best in the ancient world—she ex-
ported by land and sea to the most profitable markets,
and in addition had a large trade in a cheap line of house-

---

[1] This is not much modified by the fact that Zeno, the founder of Stoicism,
is said to have been a Phœnician who spoke imperfect Greek. On the other hand,
while equally true of the Assyrian, it would not be true of the Hebrew at all.

hold hardware for the less advanced of her customers. She engaged in a great land transport trade whose ramifications reached to Asia Minor, Armenia, Persia, Egypt and Abyssinia, by which last route she tapped the central African markets. But her sea-borne trade was the more important. In early times it reached the Black Sea. Her colonies and factories ringed the eastern Mediterranean and the Ægean.

The slow recovery of the Greeks, and perhaps climatic considerations, loosened the hold of the Phœnicians upon the Ægean and Northern trade. They had evolved their qualities in the sub-tropical desert. The Semite does not take well to the rainier and colder climate of Europe. Except in Spain, he has never successfully nor permanently established himself upon the northern shores of the Mediterranean. Africa, however, he has in all ages colonized with success. It belongs to the same desert zone to which he is specialized. . . . The Phœnicians accordingly maintained their hold along the Mediterranean westward, occupied Sicily, then Africa, and finally reached Spain. Gades (which, as Cadiz, has never lost its importance) was one of their earliest and most profitable colonies. They are said to have had three hundred trading establishments along the western coast of Africa, for thirty days' sail south from Tangier, by which they achieved fresh and more exclusive access to the central African market. From Gades they got into touch with the Spanish gold, silver and copper mines, and with the tin mines of Brittany, and later, of Cornwall. . . . Part of this trade was a mercantile carrying trade; but a large part of it consisted of the import of raw material and the export of

Spread of trade westward

manufactured articles. The Phœnicians were the chief
manufacturers of the age.

V

The Phœnician trade depended chiefly upon private
enterprise, and much of it hung upon priority in the
field, and lack of competition. The daring adventurers
who first built the trading factories and negotiated for
markets were not in a position to exercise any pressure
upon their customers. The Phœnician cities themselves
had no political unity which could be employed to gain
commercial advantages for their subjects. They were independent city-states as jealous of their sovereign autonomy as the later Greek cities. Such freedom seems
to be the indispensable condition for the risky work of
opening up new and distant markets.

It was natural enough, however, that the enormous
profits of Phœnician trade should attract the interested
attention of states which, though less wealthy and prosperous, possessed the peculiar advantage of political organization. A new colony from Tyre, Kart-hadasht,
"The New City" [1] (to be known to the Romans later
as *Carthago*) was founded in North Africa in the very
generation which saw Assyrian armies make their first
appearance in Phœnicia. . . . It was perfectly just that
Phœnician wealth should contribute to the defence and
policing of Asia; but it compelled the Phœnicians to
take politics a little more seriously. . . . Carthage was
founded, therefore, just when a fundamental change of

Character
of Phœ-
nician
Commerce

Founda-
tion of
Carthage
circ.
950 B. C.

[1] "New" possibly as respects the older Utica; or possibly with respect to some
earlier settlement which Carthage replaced; but very possibly as respects old Tyre
(Gsell, *Histoire Ancienne de l'Afrique du Nord* I. p. 379).

mental attitude was imminent among Phœnicians. The truth became evident that it might not be possible to continue the old practice of unsupported private enterprise for ever.

Tyre, the mother-city of Carthage, took the lead in this (perhaps hesitating and unwilling) drift into politics. A motive stronger than even the example of Assyrian conquest added its weight to the influences which moulded the views and policies of the new African colony—the advent of Greek ships. The gradual recovery of the Greeks from the dark days of Achæan and Dorian conquest was followed by a natural curiosity concerning the huge profits of the western trade. The Etruscans had already shown the way westward, and had built up a prosperous confederation of cities in Italy, a land untouched by Phœnician settlement. The Greek needed to carry out the work of discovery for himself. He obtained no help from his rivals. Fought at sight, baffled with false information, puzzled by lack of knowledge, his task was a laborious one. He burst into the western Mediterranean with all, and more than all, the feelings of Magellan entering the Pacific. . . . Magellan had at any rate the expectation of arriving home if he went on long enough around the world. The Greek had merely the melancholy prospect of falling over the edge.

The Greek menace

The city of Cumæ, just north of the Bay of Naples, was the first of a series of famous Greek colonies founded on the edge of the western Mediterranean. It was about a hundred years younger than Carthage. . . . Three quarters of a century elapsed before the Greeks began to arrive in force, but then they came thick and fast

Foundation of Cumæ circ. 850–800 B. C.

—and they came not in single ships nor in speculative enterprises, but in fighting-fleets organized and sponsored by the governments of their city-states. Corinth paved the way by building bigger and better ships than had ever been launched before from Greek yards,[1] and the fashion spread. The Sicilian [2] and South Italian cities were founded: Massilia with its many daughter settlements was established on the coast of Gaul, where, besides tapping the west European trade, it gained access to the Spanish markets; and wheresoever the Greeks settled, up sprang the walled town and the politically organized community. . . . Unless the Phœnicians could grapple with this menace, their days of prosperity were over.

The Greek cities flourished exceedingly. They bore to Ægean Hellas somewhat of the same relation that modern America bears to Europe. They were extremely rich and prosperous: they stood in the van of progress: but they had not the advantages which ancient assured stability and pure ethnic descent gave Athens and Sparta. . . . Carthage emerged by degrees as the leader against this aggressive Greek power. A glance at the map is almost enough to show the balance of advantages that made her the predestined rallying-point and secure base for the scattered Phœnician settlements. The climate was suitable: no great native power rendered her position difficult, or its maintenance expensive. The valley of the Bagradas, fertile under expert cultivation, secured the supplies of a great city. The harbour of Carthage commanded the southerly sea-route past

Impor-
tance of
Carthage

[1] About 700 B.C. according to Thucydides I. 13.
[2] Thucydides VI. 2 whose statements are accepted by Mr. Hackforth in *Camb. Anc. Hist.* IV. p. 349.

Sicily; her hold, carefully retained, upon the western Sicilian ports, gave her access to the northerly channel through the straits of Messina. She stood at the head of one of the chief overland caravan routes into Central Africa . . . But all this (which was equally true of Utica) was not the whole explanation. The men of Carthage handed down among themselves a tradition which other western Phœnician cities did not possess. When, after a thirteen-years' siege, old Tyre fell before Nebuchadnezzar, Tyrian capital and Tyrian manhood were driven over-seas; and the history of the Phœnicians became the history of Carthage.

VI

The term of Greek expansion was reached with the foundation of the town of Alalia in Corsica. By this time Carthage was ready. She had negotiated an alliance with the Etruscan power of central Italy, whose interests were similar to her own. Although the allied fleets were beaten in a fierce sea-fight off Alalia, the Greeks could not have faced another such battle, and The they evacuated Corsica. From this time onward there battle of Alalia was no further advance on the part of the Greeks. Their 525 B.C. settlements north of Cumæ were destroyed. Corsica and Campania became Etruscan. Sardinia passed into the hands of the Carthaginians. A second Pyrrhic victory forced Massilia to come to terms, and to sign a treaty of delimitation which cut off the Greeks from the Spanish markets, and secured the latter to the Phœnicians.

The battle of Alalia thus had far-reaching effects.

Not the least of its consequences was that it faced Carthage with difficulties of internal organization which she had to solve hastily and irrevocably. With no very profound experience of political life, the Phœnicians found themselves transformed from irresponsible traders into a gentile aristocracy—nay, more, an exclusive caste—cut off by great differences of race and tradition from the peoples who were fast becoming their subjects. They dared not take risks nor pass over failure. When, after military reverses in the course of their reduction of Sardinia, they cashiered both the general—Malchus—and his army, they may have shown an imprudent and impolitic severity; but at any rate the **The revolt of Malchus** irritated army returned to Carthage and carried out a prompt *coup d'état.* Ten of the obnoxious members of the government were executed.

The problems involved in this not wholly unnatural proceeding were many and serious. From military monarchy the feelings of the average Phœnician were never anything but averse.[1] In addition, Malchus had neither the organized political party nor the systematic political ideas necessary to carry out serious changes. A schism amongst the Phœnicians themselves would so clearly have been fatal that a swift reaction of feeling swept Malchus away. . . . But there were objections to the policy which had provoked the revolt. A caste which is in a minority of the population cannot afford some lux-

[1] From the account of Aristotle (*Pol.* II. 11.) it is clear that the Carthaginian constitution was an elaborately constructed aristocracy fenced with the most careful precautions for its stability. In VI. 7. Carthage is classed as an aristocratic state. In VIII. 7. it is noted that the attempt to introduce monarchy failed.

uries. It cannot risk heavy losses in war.[1] It cannot cashier a whole army composed of members of its own order. . . . The alternative, from whatsoever source suggested, was applied by the successor of Malchus in the Sardinian command. The practice of employing Phœnicians in the rank and file of the army was abandoned, and in their place mercenary troops were recruited from the independent fighting tribesmen of the Mediterranean littoral.[2]

Since, by this expedient, it became unnecessary to support and train an army in peace-time—or, indeed, to train any army at all—the resulting economies could be carried forward to the maintenance of much larger armies especially engaged for the duration of a war and dissolved at its close. Carthage thenceforward habitually placed in the field overwhelming forces which she could expend with a freedom denied to Greek commanders to whom the small available reserve of manpower was always an anxiety. . . . The commercial aristocracy of Carthage, holding the purse-strings by which such armies could be raised, definitely prevented the establishment of a military order capable of overriding its authority. As an additional precaution, a board of one hundred members was set up, to scrutinize the actions of the general commanders.

Reorganization of the army

We shall see presently how this military system in-

[1] This may have been the root of the whole trouble. The reverses in Sardinia may only imply that Malchus did not dare to face a heavy casualty roll, and so was caught in a dilemma.

[2] These were, of course, first-class fighting material; and in some cases, such as the Baleares, were experts in some special form of fighting. The availability of such troops in sufficient numbers was a very rare conjunction, dangerous to rely upon.

fluenced the course of events. Its greatest weakness was that it was a "reach-me-down" system. Carthaginian officers had to accept ready-made armies over the training of which they had no control at all: yet only those who train their own men can ever exploit to the full the advantages of that training.

With the new mercenary army the conquest of Sardinia was completed. The time was favourable. Persian conquest was reaching the Greek Asiatic cities just when the Carthaginian power began to get to grips with the Greek cities of the west.

VII

With their prosperity, and even their existence at stake, the Greeks faced east and west and fought.

Attack on Cumæ 524–520 B.C.

Cumæ was attacked by the Etruscans soon after the reduction of Sardinia. Now the struggle for Cumæ had some remarkable consequences. The military base of the Etruscans was the city of Rome on the Tiber, in central Italy, which, by tradition founded in 753 B. C., as a Latin outpost against them, they had taken over, rebuilt, fortified and turned into a strong military centre through which their land power extended southwards towards the Italian Greek cities. . . . Aristodemus, at first general and then dictator of Cumæ, after repulsing the Etruscans, carried the war north into Latium. The Latins were willing enough to receive a

Defeat of the Etruscans 509 B. C.

Greek liberator. A battle at Aricia drove the Etruscans back upon the line of the Tiber, and revolt in Rome (the historic "Expulsion of the Kings") followed. In spite of the recapture of the city by the Porsenna of

Clusium, it was no longer held as an Etruscan military base. Its walls were destroyed to make it useless to the enemy, and so Rome was left, starting upon a new and humble career as an independent republic on a small scale, while the Etruscans withdrew north of the Tiber.[1]

Meanwhile, a greater man than Aristodemus had come forward as the leader of the Sicilian Greeks—the famous Gelo.

Long before it came, no one could have doubted that Sicily was destined to be the scene of the main onslaught from Carthage. The actual fighting proved to be the least part of it, and occupied a few weeks: but the preparations took up more than thirty years. Just before the revolt of Rome and the collapse of Etruscan power in Latium, the Spartans, for their own purposes, had been attempting to block the communication between Carthage and Phœnicia, the Persian naval base in the eastern Mediterranean. Failing in a project for occupying the north African shore, the Spartan prince Dorieus joined in an attempt to break the hold of Carthage upon those strategically important western harbours of Sicily which were the key to Carthaginian power. His second failure proved not only that Carthage was too strong to be met with the forces normally available to the Greeks, but also that she would have to be fought on Sicilian soil. From this time forward, both sides were making ready in earnest for the trial of strength. If the Greeks were to have any chance of success against the new military system of Carthage, the most extensive changes would need to be made in their

Beginning of the struggle for Sicily 510 B. C.

[1] Homo, *Primitive Italy*, p. 116 et seq. pp. 123–128.

methods of organization. The interests at stake were too great for political theories, however precious, to stand in the way.

Two predecessors, Cleander and Hippocrates, had begun the work of uniting the Sicilian Greek states and organizing their military forces against the coming storm. To Gelo were due the final steps which perfected these measures of defence.[1] He gained possession of Syracuse—then a town of minor importance—recognized its strategic possibilities, and made it the chief city of Sicily. The island of Ortygia, on which Old Syracuse was built, he transformed into an impregnable citadel, building a new walled town upon the mainland. When he had finished, Syracuse was the mightiest fortress in the Hellenic world.

He was none too soon. The battle of Marathon, the preface to the Persian wars, had already been fought: and the whole power of the Persian empire was about to be hurled upon old Hellas. The Athenians and Spartans did not neglect to ask help from Gelo. He had his own country to defend, however, and could spare none.

The thundercloud of invasion burst simultaneously upon east and west. Later tradition declared that the Persian army which Xerxes poured into Hellas was a million strong, and that the Carthaginian force which landed the same year in Sicily numbered three hundred thousand men, brought in an armada of three thousand ships. . . . Tradition alleged, too, that the battle of

---

[1] That Gelo, like Sulla, was an aristocratic, not a popular dictator, seems certain: his repute, however, was very good. See the two striking testimonies given by Plutarch, *Dion.* c. V. 5, and *Timoleon.* c. XXIII. 5.

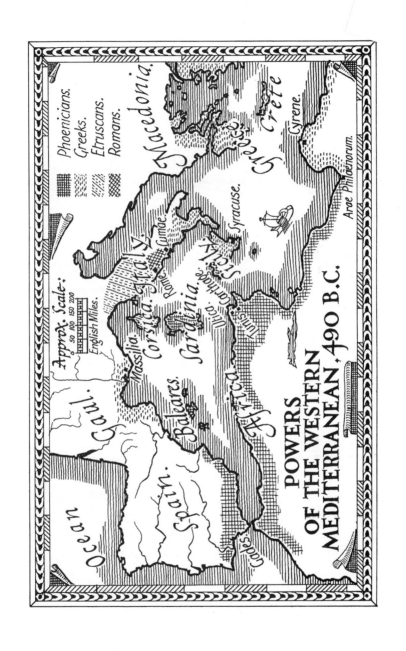

POWERS
OF THE WESTERN
MEDITERRANEAN, 490 B.C.

Phoenicians.
Greeks.
Etruscans.
Romans.

Approx. Scale:
0 50 100 150 200
English Miles.

Ocean

Gaul.

Spain.

Massilia.

Corsica.

Sardinia.

Baleares.

Africa.

Utica.
Carthage.
Tunis.

Cades.

Italy.

Rome.
Cumae.

Sicily.

Syracuse.

Macedonia.

Greece.

Crete.

Cyrene.

Arae Philaenorum.

Salamis and the battle of Himera were fought on the same day. . . . What happened at Salamis is well known. . . . At Himera, the Carthaginians were overthrown with an even greater destruction by Gelo. Their commander, Hamilcar, was among the slain.

VIII

The events of the wonderful year of Salamis were the salvation of Greek civilization; and they brought seventy years of peace and abounding prosperity to Sicily. For more than two generations after the battle of Himera, Carthage lay crippled. The Etruscans, left to bear the brunt alone, were defeated by a combined Cumæan and Syracusan fleet off Cumæ. Twenty years later, the Syracusans took from them Corsica and Elba with its iron mines. The Etruscan power gradually ebbed. Carthage could neither give nor receive aid.

The Athenian fleet and the Athenian empire—the dominating facts of those years—also kept her quiet.[1] But, far from sharing the fate of the Etruscans, Carthage was only restoring her finances, consolidating her African dominion, and awaiting her chance. No power interfered with this process, nor dared to push home the advantage won by Gelo.

Consequences of Himera

Carthage lived through that high summer of Hellenic glory until it dissolved of itself amid the fratricidal strife of Athens and Sparta. Once more the signs of change were indicated from those western harbours of

---

[1] So Thucydides makes Hermocrates say (VI. 34). Events seem to bear out the assertion: but it is not a direct statement of Thucydides.

Sicily. Egesta, in difficulties with her neighbour city
of Selinus, appealed to Carthage for help. It was cau-
tiously refused; and Egesta transferred the appeal to
Athens.

After some hesitation, seeing the possible advantages,
Athens decided to intervene in Sicily. The siege of Syracuse, the desperate defence, and the final catastrophe
which wiped out the whole Athenian expeditionary
force under the walls of Gelo's stronghold, were the
prelude to the downfall of Athenian power. The renewed appeal of Egesta to Carthage met now with a
very different response. Carthage was ready.

Athenian
disaster at
Syracuse
413 B. C.

Vast preparations ushered in the nightmare of irresistible destruction which smote Sicily. . . . Selinus and
Himera were stormed and sacked with every circumstance of sensational horror. Three years later, the advance was continued. Another immense army and fleet
invested the wealthy city of Agrigentum, then one of
the most magnificent cities in the Greek world, the
home of Empedocles the philosopher and of innumer-
able victors in the Olympic games. But Gelo and his
generation had long been dead, and an attempt by the
Syracusans to relieve Agrigentum only brought out in
full force the difficulties which are liable to confront a
democratic government in time of war. The terrible
events accompanying the evacuation of Agrigentum
and the retreat to Syracuse were at once followed by
political changes. Dionysius, who was pushed forward
now to take up the control of Hellenic Sicily, began
life as a cheap clerk. He ended it, long afterwards, a
grim political prophet who foreshadowed the necessity

Cartha-
ginian
invasion
of Sicily
409 B. C.

of that great unified State which Alexander attempted and Augustus achieved.[1]

Even a dictator could not at first make head against the Carthaginians. Dionysius was compelled to give ground and to accept terms. The Carthaginians withdrew from a Sicily which they had crushed into the dust and made tributary.

Under the leadership of Dionysius, Sicily proceeded to arise with energy from her dust. He was a hard taskmaster, but a wise one: and the deeds he did and the man he was deserve a book to themselves. He rode rough-shod over all the sectional interests and the political theories, and with a typically Hellenic admixture of craft, violence, high intelligence and brutal humour he moulded the whole fabric of Greek society in Sicily to resist the Semite. Syracuse hated Dionysius with bitterness and obeyed him with enthusiasm. An impregnable fortress, an immense army and fleet, sprang into existence as if under an enchanter's wand. He mobilized all the resources of the Greek brain. His ships were the largest that so far had ever been built: his siege engines were the most wonderful that had ever been contrived. No hustling foreman ever drove his gang more efficiently than Dionysius drove Syracuse. . . . Three years later, he struck his return blow before Carthage could put up her guard.

Autocracy of Dionysius

[1] See Grote's powerful narration of these events—a fine piece of historical writing. For Dionysius, see Prof. J. B. Bury in *Camb. Anc. Hist.* Vol. VI. Grote, a typical liberal of the old school, was unable to see Dionysius as anything but an unnecessary tyrant. The more modern historian sees him as the precursor of Alexander in military science, and a statesman of orginality and imagination.

Siege
of Motya

The siege of Motya, the Carthaginian stronghold on the west coast of Sicily, was as formidable an undertaking as any siege of Syracuse: but it was forced through with remorseless determination to final success. The defence of the city, which was held by Carthaginian citizens, gave Carthage time to mobilize. No exertions of Dionysius could prevent the skilful measures by which the Carthaginian commander evaded the Greek fleets, and poured his army, a hundred thousand strong, into Sicily. Dionysius, in the circumstances, dared not risk a stand-up fight. A defeat of the Syracusan ships in an engagement at sea cleared the way for another investment of Syracuse. But the city, as Gelo had built it and Dionysius had refortified it, defied all efforts. Pestilence broke out in the Carthaginian camp. If the Athenians had failed before Syracuse, a still worse disaster overtook the Carthaginians. . . . Such was the issue of the third siege of Syracuse.

IX

A lull of some years enabled Carthage to recover from the combined effects of war and the plague, while Dionysius was endeavouring to strengthen his position by bringing under his own control the Italian Greek cities and their resources. He felt his way as far east as the Adriatic, and as far north as Latium and Etruria. The sack of Pyrgi, the port of Etruscan Cære, and the rich temple of Leucothea, put into his hands a vast treasure of 1500 talents. There was reason for his interest so far afield. The year before the last siege of Syracuse, the city of Rome, which had spent a laborious century in fighting and negotiating the Latins into a united alli-

Dionysius
in Italy

ance, and in struggling with the Etruscan city of Veii, at last succeeded in taking and destroying the latter, with the consequence that the whole of southern Etruria fell into Roman possession. That very same year, the Gauls made their first serious entry into history by capturing the Etruscan city of Melpum in the north. It was evident that the end of the Etruscans was at hand; and nothing could be more natural than that the chief of the Sicilian and Italian Greeks should be at hand to share in the plunder. The treasure of Leucothea went far to equip Dionysius for a new Carthaginian war—a thought that must have given him much satisfaction. Fall of Etruscan power

He may have heard of the subsequent events—the march of the Gauls on Rome itself, the battle of the Allia, the sack of the unfortified city, and the flight of the Romans: but he is not likely to have taken more than a perfunctory interest in the local excitements of an obscure Italian town which was absorbed in its own parish-pump politics.

The treasure of Leucothea did no great good to Dionysius. A reopening of the war with Carthage saw him triumphant after the battle of Cabala, but so badly defeated at the succeeding battle of Cronium that he made peace, paid an indemnity which absorbed two thirds of Leucothea's treasure, and granted the Carthaginians a frontier uncomfortably near Syracuse. He waited fourteen years, and then renewed the struggle. After all but capturing Lilybæum he was outwitted and surprised by the Carthaginian fleet, and the war ended in stalemate. . . . Two years later he died, owing to the perhaps too great enthusiasm with which he cele- Death of Dionysius brated the victory of one of his plays in the Olympic competition. . . . Not many dictators have died of a successful play.

X

Up to this point, the scoring had been distinctly in favour of Carthage. The whole social fabric of Sicily was strained, distorted and weakened: and the stress had fallen with particular severity upon the pure-blooded Greek citizen and upon the ideas and traditions which constituted his Hellenism. On the other hand, Carthage remained untouched by war. In her case the stress had fallen upon mercenary armies of hired men, behind whose protection the grim Semite pursued un-ruffled his prosperous way. She had not altogether escaped the recoil of the energies she had unleashed. Plague, brought back from Syracuse, had raged in Africa with deadly effect. But, in the main, the mar-kets, the trade, and the financial resources of Carthage were entirely uninjured. At this rate, Greek Sicily would bleed to death long before Carthage. Nothing but a renovation of Hellenic life, or, alternatively, the entry into the fray of an ally with immensely greater resources of man-power, could save the Greeks from ultimate defeat.

Effects
of the
struggle
for Sicily

Reform was the first thing tried. No less a person than Plato himself had already visited Syracuse to preach the gospel of intellectual reconstruction and self-conscious Hellenism. After the death of Dionysius the elder, his brother-in-law, Dion, brought Plato back again as spiritual adviser to Dionysius the younger, who, unlike his father, was fonder of drink than of the drama. . . . Plato was not altogether a failure, though his influence was destined to work through Dion rather than through young Dionysius. The expulsion of Plato and the exile of Dion was followed by the return of the latter with arguments more forcible than words. The object of Dion was to free Sicily from the moral strangulation exerted upon it by its own means of military defence. His plan was to restore political freedom on the basis of a mixed constitution—a moderate Liberalism, as we should nowadays call it—inclusive and comprehensive rather than extreme in theory. Even before his assassination it became clear that he could not succeed. No balance of power within the State could be established. But another and an even more remarkable man stepped into his shoes—the Corinthian, Timoleon.

Policy of Dion

If it is possible for a man to be a political saint, Timoleon was one.[1] He possessed the simplicity, the sincerity, the power of working miracles, which only two or three political idealists in the world's history have shared with him. The Greeks came at last to the astonished belief—not wholly unreasonable—that Timoleon was under the especial protection of the divine powers. He came to Sicily with a forlorn hope just when it seemed as if Greek society were about to dissolve into barbarism. In a series of the most romantic and improbable adventures he captured Syracuse, received the surrender of young Dionysius, sent him to

---

[1] Plutarch's life of Timoleon ranks among his best, and is one of those which have given him an immortal reputation as the biographer of the ancient world.

Corinth to be a wonder to all beholders,[1] and almost refounded Sicilian Hellenism. He capped his feats of successful political idealism by the military triumph he won at the Crimesus, when he met and overthrew not merely a Carthaginian mercenary army, but the veritable "Sacred Band" of Carthage itself—fierce and ornate Semitic citizens who dined in camp off gold plate, and came into battle in gold and silver. He resigned his power into the hands of a restored Syracusan democracy which repaid him with a devoted affection such as few men have ever had the privilege of enjoying—especially from Greeks. Old, blind and retired, he remained a dictator without a body-guard, without a secret police, and without a privilege, who swayed his fellow-citizens purely by moral prestige. He died on the day which saw the assassination of Philip of Macedon and the accession of Alexander to the Macedonian throne. The gods who loved him did not allow the old champion of republican democracy to witness the career of the most inspired despot who ever arose in the world of ancient Hellas.

Democratic Dictatorship of Timoleon

XI

But Timoleon was a miracle worker; and after his death the normal laws of human society resumed their

---

[1] The exile of young Dionysius was almost as famous as the autocracy of his father. Though he failed as a statesman, he had much of his father's intelligence, and many stories came to be told of him. Philip of Macedon, over a bottle of wine, said: "I cannot understand how your father ever found time to write plays." Dionysius replied urbanely: "It was in those spare moments which we happier fellows spend in boozing." . . . He apparently found his true career in training choruses for theatrical productions. Everyone came to visit him; and most of those who tried to take any advantage got very much the worst of the encounter.

unpleasant sway. The very supremacy of Timoleon, however much based on moral prestige, told its own tale. Genuine Greek democracy could not hold its own in a world which was becoming more and more one in which orders needed to be sharply given and promptly obeyed.

Carthage outlived and lived down her defeat at the Crimesus, and bred a new Sacred Band, whose gold plate was not noticeably diminished. There was no Timoleon when the Carthaginians resumed their advance. After an oligarchy no more competent than the democracy had tried to save the country, and while the parties were quarrelling over which—if either—should save it, the reins of state were snatched by a man who could drive, and who dared to use the whip. *Renewed Carthaginian advance*

This man was Agathocles.

XII

Agathocles was the last throw of Hellenism, in the spirit of a man who stands to lose all, and who doubles the stakes with desperate courage. It could not be that the Hellenic civilization which had seen its ancient foe, the Persian of the east, crumble into nothing before the touch of Alexander, could fail before the western Semite with his gold plate and brazen Moloch, his mercenary armies and swarthy seamen. . . . Agathocles was a perfect type and representative of his age: the Hellene in decadence, his physical power and intellectual astuteness undiminished, but his moral gift (and Hellenism had been a spiritual principle) dying under the strain of events. As distinctly as Dionysius, Agath- *Dictatorship of Agathocles*

ocles was a popular dictator. He was a potter by trade
and a soldier by natural genius. His sympathies were
with the common people, as long as the stress of imperative necessity allowed him to indulge in any sympathies
at all. . . . But drive as he might, the reins were rot-
ten and the whip was broken and the horse was dead.

Agathocles manœuvred the Carthaginian enemy
themselves into placing in his hands the rule of Syracuse. When he threw off the mask, and showed that he
was the champion of Hellenism and not the dupe of
Carthaginian paymasters, Carthage poured a fresh army
of overwhelming strength into Sicily. Besieged in Syracuse, with no prospect but downfall and death, Agathocles proved himself a man of genius. Gathering
together what ships and men he could scrape up, he
waited for a moment when the sea was clear and flung
himself upon no less an objective than the city of Carthage itself!

XIII

Invasion
of Africa

The age which saw the incredible wonders of Alexander's career had attention still to spare for the Syracusan potter who, with none of Alexander's advantages,
led this desperate adventure against the greatest city in
the world. He had a vast audience for his impromptu
epic. Agathocles had accurately guessed the factors
which would work out in his favour. The subject
African cities were unfortified and discontented. His
aim was to destroy and dissociate. . . . Up to a certain point all the calculations of Agathocles proved
sound. The damage he did and the confusion he caused
were beyond all count or reckoning. . . . In the mean-

time the Carthaginian siege of Syracuse broke up. The commander was captured during a night assault and the army dispersed. . . . But Agathocles suffered under that fatal weakness which repeatedly hampered Greek commanders—insufficient man-power. His utmost shifts could never gain him an army large enough to face the real task—the capture of Carthage. By degrees the expedition degenerated into a buccaneering raid which, in spite of the diversion it had effected, could never hope to achieve its aim. It ended when Agathocles bolted almost alone in a small boat, leaving behind him a raging and betrayed army thirsting for his blood. . . . Most of the troops took service with the Carthaginians, and as soon as they grew accustomed to the accent of their new officers no doubt they scarcely noticed the difference.

Agathocles returned to Sicily full of enthusiastic schemes for the future. His plans, brilliant as they were, came to an abrupt end when his secretary passed him a poisoned toothpick. He was the last Sicilian Greek who upheld the ancient power of the Hellenes.

Failure and death of Agathocles 289 B. C.

Over the western Mediterranean now stretched the shadow of Carthage. She seemed inexhaustible, unconquerable and undiminished. Her power had never been greater. Yet Hellenic Sicily had been the breakwater which stayed the first force of her onslaught. Gelo and Dionysius and Timoleon and Agathocles had not fought their battles in vain.

XIV

Strangers hastened to step in. Nine years after the death of Agathocles the citizens of Tarentum called

upon his son-in-law, King Pyrrhus of Epirus, to protect them against the Romans, an obscure barbarous
people of central Italy. Pyrrhus [1] was a soldier and

**Designs of
Pyrrhus**

statesman of the new Macedonian school, trained in the
methods of Alexander. He came, bringing with him the
most striking of the military innovations brought back
by Alexander from the east—the use of war-elephants.
. . . Far more comprehensive schemes were in his mind
than he confided to the Tarentines. His purpose was
to carry out the plans begun by Dionysius and continued by Agathocles, of consolidating the whole Greek
west into a unified State which could not only with-
stand but could crush Carthage, and open up her
monopoly of the western trade. . . . It was a magnificent policy; and by the testimony of his contemporaries he was a man worthy of it.

He was too late. Unknown to him, the task was
already almost accomplished. A force greater than himself pushed him out of the way and took over the plans
of Agathocles. When he saw the Romans, he said:
"These barbarians have nothing barbarous about their
military organization." And when he had been over the
field of battle, and seen the nature of his success, he
began to entertain a suspicion of the truth. . . . He
uttered that immortal phrase: "One more such victory
and we are lost!" He found, too, that the barbarians
had nothing barbarous about their political organization. What Pyrrhus could not gain by force, his minister

---

[1] For Pyrrhus see Homo, *op. cit.* pp. 206–209 where it is vividly brought out
that his aim was the disruption of the Italian Federation headed by Rome: that
is, he was the inventor of the policy afterwards adopted by his admirer Hannibal,
just as Agathocles was the inventor of the policy afterwards followed by his
admirer Scipio Africanus.

Cineas could not gain by negotiation. The Roman Senate refused all proposals for compromise. It asserted
the principle that Rome must control the whole of
Italy. Cineas returned from Rome surprised and impressed. That which stood behind the Roman armies
was no council of village elders, but something which
aroused respect even in a cynical Greek.

Writing off, therefore, any immediate hope of controlling the resources of the Italian Greek States, Pyrrhus went to Sicily. His success there was brilliant.
Before he paused he had the Carthaginians clinging to a
last precarious foothold in besieged Lilybæum. They
noted his war-elephants, and resolved to make arrangements for acquiring some of their own.[1]

The plain fact, however, was that Sicily by itself was
not enough to furnish the means for an attack upon
Carthage. A second attempt to gain control of the resources of Italy failed when the Romans, under grim
Manius Curius Dentatus, stood against him, elephants
and all, at Beneventum, and beat him. . . . He threw
in his hand and returned to Greece, where he was killed
soon after. . . . A few years later the Romans were
masters of all Italy.

Failure of
Pyrrhus

XV

Looking across the straits of Messina was now a new,
unexpected power, which had proved victorious in the

[1] The elephants of Pyrrhus were Indian. The later Carthaginian elephants are
a famous subject of dispute. It seems clear now that they were a breed of
African elephants then wild in north-west Africa, smaller than either the
Indian or the central African elephants. See Sir H. H. Johnston, *Colonization
of Africa by Alien Races*, p. 35 f. n. Correspondence in the *Times Lit. Suppl.*
July 20th, 1916, and in the *Times* March 8th, to April 7th, 1928.

local wars of the Italian peninsula. The Carthaginians did not yet realize all that Pyrrhus had realized. To them the Romans were the inheritors of the old, friendly Etruscan power. Carthaginian fleets had hovered benignly off the coasts of Italy while Pyrrhus was on Italian soil, ready, if need be, to land troops. Old treaties linked them.[1]

But how had it come about that the unfortified city which the Gauls destroyed had become the head of a united Italy? . . . Carthage was already casting her eyes upon the Italian Greek States, her next prospective acquisition after the reduction of Sicily. . . . Rome was not a naval power. . . . All the omens pointed to the extension of Carthaginian dominion, with its rigidly exclusive commercial monopoly, up to the very coasts of Greece. Carthage might, perhaps, in days to come, return to Tyre, her mother-city, bringing her sheaves with her.

Perhaps! But what was there against it?

Carthage supreme in the western Mediterranean

[1] Carthage had also, Mr. Mattingley thinks, helped to organize the Roman monetary system for the purposes of the war (*Roman Coins.* p. 7 et seq.)

CHAPTER II

THE PROTAGONISTS ENTER THE ARENA

I

THE obstacle which stood in the way of absolute Carthaginian supremacy throughout the Mediterranean was the emergence, not so much of a new military power as of a new political method. So far as the contest had gone up to this point, the Carthaginian state with its closed caste of Phœnician aristocrats, its commercial system and its hired mercenary armies, had proved a stronger thing than the Greek political state, no matter how much this last rang the changes on Gelonian aristocratic dictatorship, Dionysian popular autocracy, the liberalism of Dion or the democracy of Timoleon. The Carthaginians were now to be confronted with a surprise. They did not at first grasp the fact that they were dealing with a new force of complex structure and unexpected character. It took time for the novelty to penetrate to their consciousness.

The situation 272 B. C.

And even now it is not an easy matter to coin a sentence that will express briefly and accurately that novelty which the Romans tabled before an astonished world. It was the discovery of the *focus* of politics. . . . There were ideals and realities which the Greeks had never been able to reconcile. Aristocracy, democracy, oligarchy, military organization and civil procedure, in the thought and practice of the Greek, remained principles either antagonistic and mutually exclusive or else

The surprise

but very imperfectly harmonized. The Roman, starting from the purely practical end, with little regard for theory, almost unconsciously found the point of relationship. The discovery was unique. Perhaps it has remained unique. All subsequent political evolution in some way springs from the original root that grew in the obscure Italian town on the Tiber.

The Roman had been forced by necessity to learn the art of reconciling the acutely antagonistic elements within his own city. He learnt it so well that it became a second nature to him. He entered upon the wider stage of the world at large in the character of a blender of men, an expert in assimilation. To say that he was in personal power a stronger man than the Phœnician would be to say too much. But if a supreme gift for diverting, directing and controlling human energy be the definition of strength—then the Roman was almost the only man of his age who possessed it at all.

II

Preliminaries:— Rhegium and Messina

As soon, therefore, as the field was cleared by the withdrawal of Pyrrhus, the clash between Rome and Carthage was quick to come. Rhegium and Messina lie opposite to one another on the Straits between Italy and Sicily. Some unemployed Campanian mercenaries of Agathocles, on the look-out for a job, fixed upon Messina. After the citizens had been thrown out with whatsoever degree of violence was necessary, the Campanians settled down with the wives and properties of their predecessors.

In the meantime the citizens of Rhegium, apprehen-

sive that Pyrrhus might quarter troops upon them, had
appealed to Rome for protection. Rome sent them a
garrison—Campanians, as it happened. . . . The Campanians gazed across the Straits at Messina, envied and
fell. So there were two very similar cases in which harmless and law-abiding towns had been violated by a law-
less soldiery. . . . The Romans, however, suffered from
that tendency to take law and order seriously which
has been a matter of complaint among later successors
of the Campanians against other communities of the
bourgeois type. . . . They could do nothing at the moment; but as soon as their hands were free, a Roman
army appeared at Rhegium. With acute prevision of
their probable fate, the Campanians elected most of
them to fall sword in hand. The few survivors were
haled off to Rome, and publicly flogged and beheaded
in the Forum. . . . Rhegium was restored to its right-
ful owners.

The Syracusans—inspired perhaps by this example
—then proceeded to attend to Messina. The alarmed
Campanians, deprived of their former allies in Rhegium, The appeal
and beaten in a fight, were pressed to extremity. Some to Rome
appealed for help to the Carthaginians. Others appealed
to Rome.

The Carthaginians had no reason for refusing an ad-
vantageous offer, and they promptly took charge of
Messina. The Romans were in a more difficult position.
Messina was not an Italian town. No possible argument could make out a justifiable case for intervention.
How could Rome, moreover, after executing the vio-
lators of Rhegium, take a benevolent interest in those
of Messina? . . . But the case for illegitimate and un-

justifiable intervention was overwhelming. Messina was
on the Straits. Carthage already held most of Sicily. As

Reasons
for Roman
inter-
vention
a jumping-off ground for an invasion of Italy, Messina
was ideal. . . . The Senate, unable to bring itself to
the perpetration of an act of cynical realism, did what
Senates have not infrequently done. . . . We do not
know what activity went on behind the scenes in Rome,
nor the identity of the scene-shifters who dressed the
stage; but when the curtain rose again it was on a most
impressive tableau. The conscientious Senate, repudiating with horror the suggestion of any illegitimate policy,
was being solemnly over-ruled by the vote of a Sovereign People. . . . After the world had gazed sufficiently
at this inspiring spectacle the curtain descended, the
Sovereign People dispersed, and the Senate prepared for
practical business.

III

The zealous moralists who had rushed to the rescue
of Messina found the ground inconveniently crowded.
When the consul Appius Claudius arrived with the
Roman forces, it was to find the Carthaginians already
in possession and a Syracusan army encamped outside.
Neither party responded with cordiality to the proposals for peaceful negotiation put forward by Appius.
Not until he had driven the Carthaginians off and had
laid siege to Syracuse, did the latter power begin to perceive the friendly and peaceable nature of his intentions.
Hiero, the acute young ruler of Syracuse, finally entered
into treaty relations with Rome which gained for his
city and his authority a long period of most valuable
protection. . . . The die was cast. Rome had taken

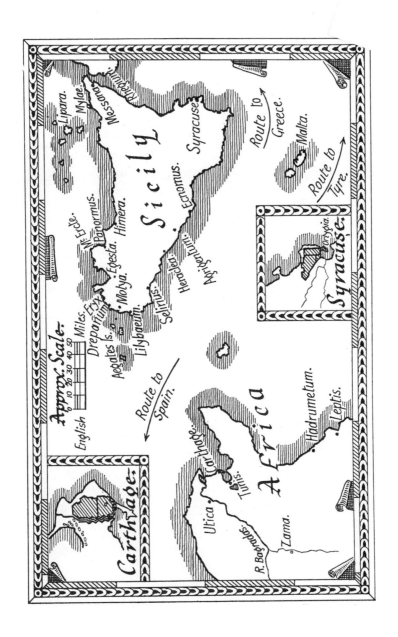

Approx. Scale.

English Miles.
0 10 20 30 40 50

Route to Spain.

Route to Greece.

Route to Tyre.

Sicily

Lipara.
Mylae.
Messana.
Syracuse.
Ecnomus.
Malta.

Mt. Ercte.
Panormus.
Himera.
Egesta.
Molya.
Eryx.
Drepanum.
Aegates Is.
Lilybaeum.
Selinus.
Heraclea.
Agrigentum.
Miles.

Syracuse.
Ortygia.

Africa

Hadrumetum.
Leptis.

Utica.
Carthage.
Tunis.
Zama.
R. Bagradas.

Carthage.

over the responsibilities of Syracuse, and was fighting for empire with the greatest power of the western Mediterranean. Two hundred years of war had slowly ground the Sicilian Greeks to earth. How would it fare with Rome? **The Romans enter Sicily 264 B. C.**

Polybius—the last but by no means the least of the great Greek historians—made comments upon the first Punic War which neatly summarize it. There were, he thought, few previous wars which lasted longer, were prepared on a more gigantic scale, were more continuous, or were subject to more surprising changes of fortune. The moral and material power of both states was at its greatest height. The first Punic War was the true trial of strength between Rome and Carthage.

IV

The first point which emerged was that Rome possessed a man-power in striking contrast with that of the contemporary Greek States. She needed no political revolution, no abnormal effort, in order to exert her military strength. For Carthage the main task now was indeed to build up an army capable of meeting the Roman in the field. Agrigentum was established as the Carthaginian base. It was in the third year of the war that the Romans invested Agrigentum. Significant changes were already visible. Dionysius probably put as great material equipment into his wars as Rome ever did; what was different was the temper, the moral tension. Rome came into the struggle with the calm which springs from the consciousness of ample reserves. She could produce not merely a new type of organization, **The New Spirit** but a large amount of it. The Greek had always been straining beyond his strength, continually harassed by the sense that he was dipping into his capital. Rome fought comfortably on her income. . . . She drew her lines around Agrigentum in a fashion that would have pulled the heart out of Sicilian Greeks. They were large, copious, ample lines, well provided with all necessary

The first trial of strength

supplies. The Carthaginian commander was soon sending urgent messages home. He had fifty thousand mouths to feed in the city. . . . Carthage came up to the scratch. Another of her vast hosts was poured into Sicily. It was beaten and broken up by the Roman investing force. The Carthaginians in Agrigentum made their way out during the following night, leaving Agrigentum to the Romans. . . . The Romans scored no mark of historic fame against the episode. It was, and it remains, one of the very minor battles of Roman history. Greeks would have counted it a second Salamis.

V

Only when Rome had proved her ability to hold and defeat Carthaginian armies was a second and more serious necessity revealed to her. From the first, Phœnician power had everywhere been based upon the naval policy

Question of Sea Power

of controlling the sea-board and then allowing the logic of the situation to develop to its natural conclusion. Even in the case of peninsular Spain and continental Africa, the policy had been effective; with islands such as Sicily and Sardinia, its success was certain. When it became clear that while Rome could take the inland Sicilian towns, Carthage could hold those of the sea-

board, and ravage the coasts of Italy into the bargain,
the inferences were too plain and too threatening to be
ignored. Encouraged by events on land, the Senate resolved to build a navy capable of meeting the Carthaginian at sea.[1]

There are probably few historical incidents more rich
in humour than this resolution. The Carthaginians certainly appreciated it. They had no objection to Rome
building as many navies as she liked. The trouble began
at the start. The standard fighting ship was the five-
banker. Not only had Rome no five-bankers, but not a
single one existed in Italy. The Senate, however, possessed a trophy in the shape of a derelict Carthaginian
five-banker which had run aground in Sicily. This was
put at the disposal of the Italian ship-builders, and an
order for one hundred was placed. The crews were
trained on land. The whole business reeked of amateur- Roman
                                                         fleet built
ism at its grossest. The navy was built. Gnæus Cornelius
Scipio had the privilege of commanding it. He sailed
with the first squadron, leaving the main fleet to follow.

---

[1] The narratives of Polybius (I, 20 et seq.) is nowadays, for various good
reasons, questioned. The exact corrections to be made are a matter allowing
some difference of opinion; but we shall probably not be far wrong in taking
it that the Romans had expert advice on naval questions from either Italian-
Greek, or Sicilian-Greek sources, probably the latter. The Carthaginian warships,
like the Athenian, were practically nothing but rams with highly trained
oarsmen and pilots, and only a small fighting crew. The naval advisers of the
Romans, having to meet these with inferior ships and badly trained oarsmen,
instructed the pilots (no doubt Sicilian Greeks) to run alongside, grapple, and
throw on board armed forces carefully calculated to outnumber the enemy.
How extremely effective this expedient at first was, can be seen by the narrative.
There is no possibility of Polybius' story being true unless the "Roman" pilots
were very highly skilled men, capable of meeting and beating Phœnician pilots
on level terms. The naval amateurism of the Romans is therefore more or less
of a "Gun-room Yarn." The old tactics of Dionysius and the Syracusan navy took
a new lease of life when Roman officers began to do the shouting and the foot-
stamping.

As he lay in Lipara, a Carthaginian squadron came quietly up. The Roman crews promptly sought refuge on shore: Scipio himself dismally surrendered: the Roman fleet was towed off. . . . The swarthy and ear-ringed seamen of Carthage must have chuckled. . . . They could do with many Roman fleets of this type—the more, the merrier.

The excellent joke of the capture of Gnæus Scipio at Lipara was, as it chanced, only the first of a series. Resuming in a mood of exaltation its voyage towards the presumably undefended coasts of Italy, the Carthaginian squadron unexpectedly ran into the main Roman fleet, which was muddling its way south. . . . The Carthaginians got off with somewhat severe damage. . . . The Roman fleet then muddled its way successfully to Messina, where it reported that it had lost its admiral. . . . The consul Duilius immediately came to take charge. . . . While he was on his way, some pessimistic spirit among the Roman seamen, contemplating the extreme improbability that they would ever get to close quarters with more than the armoured rams of the fast and well-handled Phœnician ships, thought of inventing a combined boarding bridge and hold-fast. . . . Duilius, a serious-minded man, saw no objection to the proposal. The eye of a Mediterranean seaman of the old school must have been profoundly shocked at the sight of war-ships leaving port decorated with what appeared to be derricks.

Duilius sailed to meet the Carthaginians, who were off Mylæ. Although surprised at the remarkable appearance of his ships, they were pleased to see him, and had not the slightest doubt of the result. The engage-

Battle
of Mylæ
260 B. C.

ment which followed was sensational. Coming into action with a hundred and thirty ships, led by the giant seven-banker, the Dreadnought of its day, which had once belonged to King Pyrrhus, the Carthaginians saw their first thirty ships grappled, held, and boarded by Roman legionaries. The admiral himself barely escaped in a boat when the seven-banker was taken. . . . As soon as they recovered from the shock, they pulled themselves together, got into manœuvring order, and began to employ the open tactics which, with their superior seamanship, gave them the advantage. They then found that the "ravens" worked on pivots, and could be lifted, swung and lowered in any position. After losing fifty ships, the Carthaginians gave up. They were free to withdraw; and they took advantage of the fortunate fact.

VI

The defeat of the Carthaginian fleet at Mylæ was historic. It demonstrated beyond doubt that the supremacy of Carthage at sea could be successfully challenged. To challenge it in earnest meant, of course, the destruction of the Carthaginian battle-fleet, the opening of the sea-passage to transports, and the invasion of Africa. Agathocles, in far less favourable circumstances, had proved the possibility. Such an undertaking could not be prepared in a day. . . . While it was in process of organization, the Romans gradually extended and confirmed their hold upon Sicily. The Carthaginians declined any decisive action on land.

Not until four years after the battle of Mylæ was the Roman armada ready. It arrived in the Straits three

Challenge to Carthaginian sea-power

hundred and thirty ships strong. Its course was past
Syracuse to the southern coast of Sicily—the route of
Agathocles—where, at Ecnomus, it picked up forty
thousand troops, of whom twenty thousand were the
intended expeditionary force. The Carthaginian command was well-informed: for simultaneously a fleet of
three hundred and fifty ships left Carthage, touched at
Lilybæum, and passed south, taking station at Heraclea, across the course of the Roman fleet. The passage
to Africa would need to be fought for.

Battle of
Ecnomus
256 B. C. The sea-battle of Ecnomus was fiercely fought and
desperately contested. The old, highly skilled mobile
tactics were put to a thorough test against methods invented by untrained landsmen; and the novelty, even
at the disadvantage of numbers, again beat the con-
ventions. The Roman fleet fought in a wedge; the Carthaginians, in a long line which enveloped the wedge,
broke it, and cut it into isolated parts. Employing its
"ravens," the Roman vanguard broke and dispersed the
Carthaginian centre, and then, turning back, came to
the rescue of the transports. . . . Twenty-four Roman ships were sunk in the battle. None were captured.
. . . The Carthaginians lost thirty sunk, while sixty-
four ships were captured with all hands.

Anticipating an immediate attack upon Carthage itself, the Carthaginian fleet retired upon its port. While
it was watching Carthage, the Romans made their landing elsewhere on the African coast, the army built itself a fortified base, and the fleet sailed back to Italy.

Although the Romans had paid Agathocles the sincere compliment of imitation, they had prepared their
expedition with a completeness to which his could have

laid no claim. From a purely military point of view it was perfectly successful. Carthage, crowded with refugees, her commercial interests imperilled, her commanders incapable of dealing effectively with the novel and apparently insoluble problems involved, consented to negotiate.

VII

Neither side was absolutely sincere. M. Atilius Regulus, the Roman consul, anxious to have the credit of finishing the war, gambled a little on the possibility that the Carthaginian Council would accept terms which he could submit to the Senate with a reasonable chance that they would be approved: but on these terms being laid before the Council, they were rejected with an amount of heat which indicated that the Council was seriously upset at this revelation of the spirit in which Rome was conducting the war. Since it was obvious that none of those convenient little temporary accommodations were possible which had been arranged in the past with the Sicilian Greeks, the Council, in a somewhat chastened mood, prepared to continue the struggle.

Any nation but the Carthaginian would have made a legend of what followed. Among the new recruits who signed on with their mercenary army was a Spartan named Xanthippus. If any mysterious signs betokened that this man was a god in disguise, the Carthaginians failed to observe it. They only observed that Xanthippus passed certain criticisms upon his military superiors. Called to answer for it before the War Council, the Spartan made such an impression upon the board of generals in their new mood, that they gave him a free hand to fight the war in his own way. . . . Several important consequences ensued which affected the whole subsequent course of events. Xanthippus had appreciated that the Carthaginians, although they possessed war-elephants, were ignorant of the tactical methods of employing them in the field. He proceeded to use them as no Carthaginian had ever been able to use them before; and he also invented a method of en-

Destruction of the Roman expedition

velopment by cavalry.[1] . . . The news that trickled through to Rome was confounding. Not the capture of Carthage was announced, but the tidings that two thousand fugitives, the sole survivors of the army of Regulus, were defending themselves behind the fortifications of Apsis, waiting for rescue.

Having accomplished his work, Xanthippus prudently disappeared. He left behind him his two tactical principles; and we shall presently see the very remarkable results which attended their use when Carthaginians employed them.

VIII

No Greek would have doubted that Xanthippus was one of the immortals. He flitted briefly across the firmament, leaving a trail not only of defeat but of disaster and misfortune for Rome. The Roman fleet put out to the relief of Apsis. It beat the inferior Carthaginian fleet off Heræum in Sicily, capturing a hundred and fourteen ships, made its way to Apsis, and took off the

[1] From the description of Polybius (I. 33–34) it is obvious that these tactics of Xanthippus were the starting point from which were evolved the tactics of Cannæ and Zama.

survivors of the army of Regulus. The sailing masters Wreck of the Roman fleet 255 B. C. warned the military chiefs not to sail south under Sicily on the way back. They refused to heed the advice: they were caught in the storm which the navigating officers had anticipated, and out of three hundred and sixty-four ships only eighty got to harbour.

There was hope for Carthage. She reassembled her energies, sent a new commander to Sicily, and put a new fleet of two hundred ships on the sea. But Rome capped the effort, built a new navy of two hundred and twenty ships, and appeared at Panormus with a total of three hundred. Panormus fell. The next year she re-entered African waters. . . . Some unfortunate incidents during the course of the expedition were the prelude to the catastrophe which followed. Caught in A second fleet lost 253 B.C. another storm, the fleet lost a hundred and fifty ships on its way home.

In view of such misfortunes the Senate hesitated to go on building. For a while the war flagged and dragged on land. Carthage once more held command of the sea.[1] Moreover, the news that had gradually spread concerning the events in Africa had an unsettling effect. Roman troops, who would face anything human, could not be induced to face elephants employed on the Xanthippidean system. . . . Three years later the The War renewed choice of alternatives had to be squarely met. If Rome were not to hold the sea, she must relinquish all hope of effective victory. . . . Ship-building was resumed. Overtures from Carthage were declined. . . . A last effort was made to dislodge the Semitic grip upon

[1] According to Appian *Sicil.* Frag. 1. Carthage was trying to raise a loan in Egypt about this time. (252 B.C.)

Sicily. The two great strongholds of Drepanum and Lilybæum could be taken only by a power able to cut their sea-communications. Lilybæum became the centre of the struggle.

IX

Lilybæum could not be taken. Blockade was no more successful than direct assault. Malaria wrought havoc in the Roman army, while Drepanum remained a centre from which the Carthaginians raided by land and ran the blockade by sea.[1] When Publius Claudius Pulcher attempted to destroy the Carthaginian fleet at Drepanum, the luck still continued bad. He was beaten with a loss of ninety-three ships;[2] the blockade of Lilybæum was broken, and the Roman fleet was itself shut in. The Carthaginians seized the opportunity to intercept the supply fleet which was reprovisioning the besiegers. It was driven on shore and then broken up by a storm. Lilybæum continued to hold out.

Failure of the Romans

In spite of all efforts, therefore, the Romans had failed to loosen the hold of Carthage upon Sicily. Unless the Carthaginian bases in Sicily could be taken, the island was no more permanently in Roman hands than it had been in Greek. Rome had failed, just as Dionysius and Agathocles had failed. At the suitable moment, Carthage could resume her interrupted advance. . . . The damage done by the war was enormous. The Senate might well reflect that Rome seemed to be drift-

[1] The redoubtable exploits of Hannibal "The Rhodian" told of in Polybius I. 46–47 give a vivid idea of what Phœnician seamanship really was.

[2] Polybius I. 49–51. He had only himself to thank. He was warned by the Sacred Chickens, which refused to eat before the action. The ungrateful Publius threw them overboard, with the unkind remark that if they wouldn't eat they could drink. The reader will not be surprised at the consequences.

ing in the same direction as Syracuse. The roll of citizens was down by forty thousand. But Carthage had sustained damage no less serious. She had been obliged in some cases to double her tax assessments on her subjects, and to try the expedient of raising a loan in Egypt. If she resumed her advance, it would not be just yet, nor in the old spirit.

It was at this point that Hamilcar Barca took over the command in Sicily.

Hamilcar was one of those men who arise to supply a demand. If Carthage were to maintain herself, new men and new methods were necessary: and she was capable of producing both at need. The Semitic mind —which in Assyria had produced great organizers of victory—had in the western Mediterranean only intermittently and partially applied itself to the serious study of war and statesmanship. For the most part it had concentrated upon commerce. But Carthage was locked in a life-and-death struggle with a foe whose resources were derived from conditions requiring especial study. Xanthippus was the originating mind which had given the first impulse. He had passed like some divine messenger, leaving behind him a wonderful atmosphere of fortune and stimulus. . . . Hamilcar was the man of the new era.

Hamilcar Barca appointed to Sicily

x

Let us, at this particular stage in the story, cast our eyes for a moment over the field of contest, and try to appreciate some of the difficulties with which Hamilcar had to deal. The interest which the modern reader may take in them was, in his case, sharpened by in-

Review of the situation

tense necessity. Only too plainly the Romans were introducing into the struggle some element which, measured by contemporary standards, had a power of producing abnormal results. Unless it could be isolated, identified and counteracted, the most unpleasant consequences might be impending over Carthage.

That the results were abnormal may be seen if we compare the material power of the two States. Carthage was, at this time, probably the largest and richest city in the world. Rome was a much smaller, much poorer state, well away from the main centres of civilization. Her material externals contained no secret. They were only those common to cities of the age, tinctured with the fashions and methods (now somewhat the worse from lapse of time and provincial isolation) which had been spread through Italy by the Etruscans, and by the indirect influence of the Italian Greeks. They resembled the material externals of Carthaginian and Sicilian life much as those of Bordeaux resemble those of Paris, or those of Nashville resemble those of New York. The Roman was governed by Consuls, a Senate and an Assembly; and to a stranger these institutions might seem to differ only in minor details from the **Search for a principle** Suffetes and Council of Carthage, or the Strategoi and Ecclesia of a Greek city. The minor diversity amid general resemblance which runs through the modern world ran also through the ancient. . . . The difference could only lie in principle and method.

The nature of this principle and this method was not easy to ascertain. The essential quality of the Roman discovery was its complexity. There was no simple intellectual formula behind it. It arose living from a vor-

tex of events, accidents and conditions too intricate to
be readily disentangled. . . . One practical method existed, however, by which Hamilcar could isolate and
identify the particular thing he wanted. He could apply
what we have learned to call the "method of difference." Whatsoever the principle was, it was something
fundamentally opposed to the old Carthaginian habit.
It could be found by the test that it was the most un-
Carthaginian thing about the Romans. But in order
to discern what was unCarthaginian about the Romans, let us glance for a moment at what was Carthaginian in the Carthaginians.

XI

In common with all Semites the Phœnician shared a
highly specialized character which set limits to his actions not safely to be transgressed. The broad tendency
to traditionalism so set up was reinforced by the peculiar historical qualities of the Canaanite Semites, who
in all their several branches showed certain tricks of The
mind over and above those common to their Semitic Phœnician
origin. They had a habit of travelling mentally in a mind
straight line, unless compelled by impressed forces to
change that state; and even then they were apt to return to their course with a pertinacity which in all ages
has been noted with mingled feelings by their various
critics.[1] . . . Their position as a closed caste imposed
upon them a discipline which still further exaggerated

[1] Many enraged comments on this peculiarity will be found scattered through
the Old Testament, the authors of which may be presumed to have been in a
position to judge.

this rigidity of temper. Their power was sustained much more by prudence and conservatism than by any originality of action. This negative quality in them was fixed by the almost unbroken prosperity which Carthage had enjoyed.[1] The Carthaginian had never been pressed to extremity; he hardly knew what it was to have to adapt himself to unexpected circumstances— much less to those desperate crises in which men are compelled to work miracles or perish. . . . Hence the Phœnician aristocracy of Carthage had tended to develop the habit of making the means more important than the end. Beginning by taking the end for granted so long as a certain ritual was observed, they wound up by losing sight of the alternative methods. They made sacrosanct, not the ultimate object, but the intermediate process.

The way in which this worked out in practice may be illustrated by one or two examples which must have been particularly familiar to Hamilcar Barca. The Carthaginians had very imperfectly kept pace with the advance of military science. In the days of Hamilcar Barca they had fallen hopelessly behind, as we can see by the havoc wrought by the new tactics of Pyrrhus, and the revolution created in their affairs by the advice of an obscure Spartan officer. Their commanders made sacrosanct the methods they employed, not the objects they sought to achieve. Again, it is a general testimony of all who came into contact with them that the Carthaginians had a love of money bordering upon the absurd: and if money is not an "intermediate process"

Phœnician inertia

---

[1] Aristotle (*Pol.* VIII. c. 12.) notes that up to his time Carthage had never known a revolution.

it is nothing. This mental twist was a typical Carthaginian characteristic.

Now the Greek, driven to bay, had shown the multiplicity and ingenuity of his resources. He had not hesitated to use any and every expedient he could think of, from mechanical artillery to Platonic philosophy. He adapted his means to suit his ends; and he owed the possibility of doing so to his power of analytic reasoning. The expansion of Greek art and Greek thought had proceeded simultaneously with the expansion of Greek trade, and the three were indissolubly connected. Commerce was, if not the cause, certainly the stimulus which created the habit of submitting all things to the test of rational judgment. A commercial man, more than any other kind of man, deals with practical reason. For him, all depends upon the instant application of the rational judgment. He therefore gets into the habit of judging all things upon their merits—not least, upon their merits as useful and profitable to himself.

Intellectual influence of commercial life

This effect of the commercial life had its influence upon the Phœnician, no less than upon the Greek. We shall have no difficulty, later on in this book, in tracing in Hamilcar and in Hannibal the free-thinking temper with its disregard of mere precedent and mere tradition —and there is no reason to suppose that they were unique in this respect. Driven to bay in his own turn, the Phœnician had characteristics which he could, if he chose, divert from commerce into politics and war.

XII

The Carthaginians, like the Etruscans, were a ruling caste which had settled among races inferior to them in the arts of civilization, and parted from them by deep differences of descent and character. The differences were in neither case bridged. The Roman state, on the other hand, had started with a primary core of native landed proprietors, round which in turn gathered by degrees the commercial classes and the peasant holders who formed the population of historic Rome. The differences between the classes were not too great to be bridged; and the difficulty experienced by each class in establishing any kind of exclusive dominance provided a powerful motive for bridging them. Necessity does not always make men agree. Often enough they prefer to hang separately rather than hang together. But if the original Roman had any passion at all, it was a passion for achieving his ends.[1] In later ages he became a great builder of aqueducts and constructor of roads: and this fact is an accurate symbol of his intellectual quality. He drove roads with brutal directness over hill and dale, river, gulf and morass; but only in order to arrive somewhere. His gigantic aqueducts, still a world's wonder, never had any such motive as the Egyptian pyramids; their intermediate mass was only for the purpose of carrying water where it was wanted. . . . There never was a type of man who consulted more exclusively the ultimate object he had in view. He judged things by their results: for him the proof of the pudding was in the eating. . . . He started his career in the early days of Rome by putting before himself, as his principal aim, his own survival. He bridged the differences between men in the same spirit in which he

The Roman State

Mentality of the Roman

[1] Polybius (I. 37. [7–10]) particularly remarks on this tendency in the Romans, who had to learn by experience the finer points of the process.

bridged rivers; it happened to be the most convenient way across.

The secret of the Roman thus consisted largely in the application of a psychological method to the conduct of human relationship. Dion might aim at a mixed constitution for Syracuse, and the harmony of interests and principles: but he had no method by which to achieve his aim. Timoleon's success was due to the frank abandonment of any such comprehensiveness, and a reversion to pure democracy. But Rome, without a theory, produced what Dion, with Platonic philosophy to help him, could not produce.[1] She did this, because her leaders were not philosophers, but men who understood the actual working of that uncertain engine, the human mind. The men who conducted the Roman republic knew with uncommon accuracy just that particular blend of hope, fear, affection, hostility, persuasion, terrorism, the appeal to the high motive, the middle and the low, which, as if by enchantment, will make men work together, as no single motive ever can.

We have learnt, since those days, the conception that we may master nature by learning her lessons and obeying her laws. The Roman anticipated us in this: but it was human nature that attracted his attention. The secret of successful government has a combination lock, and the Roman had discovered the combination.

The Roman secret

----

[1] The unified Italy of Augustus was evolved from at least seven original stocks (Latin, Oscan, Greek, Iapygian, Gallic, Etruscan and Ligurian) speaking as many distinct languages and inheriting at least four distinct and ancient cultures. Dion could not produce a unity out of two Greek political parties! It is fair to recollect, too, that the Roman was profoundly modified by the races he absorbed. He did not destroy them.

The weapon with which the Roman was armed was therefore an art of government, an ability to create between men a sufficient bond of unity. This unity did not spring up in men spontaneously, by any law of human nature. They did not instinctively meet together and instinctively fall upon one another's necks with suitable emotion. The unity was imposed, in the first place, and was accepted and taken to men's hearts when it proved to them its excellence. There has never been any other way of achieving it. The nations of the modern world, each of which is persuaded of its own unity, were formed by precisely such a method and no other.[1] And even so, such a unification is not permanent unless men are convinced of the benefits that are being conferred upon them.

It thus differed from the method by which, through oppressive force, a slight and merely external unity was produced amongst the subjects of Carthage, without any conscious mutual interest or any willing loyalty, and still more from the pure cash-nexus by which her mercenaries were bound to her. It was practical psychology applied to the task of inducing men to act together in harmony.

A psychological method

This was the secret that Hamilcar seized.

The importance of Hamilcar lay in that he proposed to bend back upon the Romans their own chief power. He stepped upon the stage, a new kind of Carthaginian,

---

[1] The United States form an apparent exception to this rule; and it is perhaps true that in their case the amount of compulsion was comparatively slight—no greater than General Grant could exercise.

no longer content to trudge decorously in the well-beaten track of his predecessors, but using his intelligence as a weapon. From the moment of his advent, the relation of Rome and Carthage was altered. What the Romans had done half unconsciously, he made ready to do with clear and deliberate thought.

XIV

The first step of Hamilcar was to create an impregnable military base in Sicily, and from it to initiate a new science of war. For this purpose he chose neither Drepanum nor Lilybæum, but the wild slopes of Mount Ercte. He afterwards took in the city of Eryx as his link with the sea; but his main policy was to get away into the open.

Political organization is not the only conceivable application of the psychological method. There are others. While it was still a mercenary army by which he held Mount Ercte, he introduced a new note into his relations with his men. To establish with them the same kind of relationship which a Roman consul bore to his citizen troops was indeed not possible, nor, from his point of view, either desirable or necessary; but it was possible to introduce a friendly and paternal spirit which not only attached them securely to his service, but gave him a much increased disciplinary hold over them. . . . It was not an impersonal and constitutional reciprocity that he was creating, but a personal one, centred on himself; the disciplined consciousness of free citizenship in a constitutional State, which was the source of Roman strength, he replaced by a purely military *esprit de*

Policy of Hamilcar

corps which exploited the same human qualities, with the additional advantage that it centred, not in an impersonal magistracy, but in an individual commander. The pitch of discipline so achievable allowed the introduction of one further element to which constitutional freedom is actually adverse—the idea of scientific generalship.

These expedients blended well. Once he had his army devoted to his service he could model it, adapt it and use it with freedom. His son afterwards was a man well read in the military literature of his day, when, we may remember, Alexander was dead but three quarters of a century, and Pyrrhus had conducted his campaigns within the memory of living men.[1] It is not a hazardous guess that Hamilcar was familiar with his son's favourite authors. . . . On Mount Ercte he put into practice the latest military improvements. He employed troops of every arm, as Alexander had done, compact into a small, highly paid, highly trained, manageable force, and he used them with discrimination; he developed the positioning tactics of Pyrrhus, making the ground he stood upon fight for him. Above all, he refused to be pinned to huge material fixtures. He played for those circumstances in which brains alone should count.

Once stirred to action, the Semitic mind had a robustness denied to the Persian. Through six years of careful and systematic warfare Hamilcar proved that a

(margin note: Alternative uses of psychological method)

---

[1] Pyrrhus, according to Plutarch, left memoirs in which he described his military career. An accurate—indeed, official—account of Alexander's campaigns was available in Ptolemy's History of Alexander. Hannibal was certainly much influenced by Pyrrhus.

loyal and well-treated mercenary army, directed by a mind which had studied the conditions of war, could hold its own on equal terms with the Romans. . . . Against the wonderful Roman invention of political unity, Hamilcar pitted the resource of technical specialization. *Specialization as a method*

Whether the resource would be sufficient time alone could show; and only time could demonstrate how deep might be the suspicion excited among the Carthaginian aristocracy by the plans of Hamilcar.

XV

Brought to dead-lock on their own element—the land —the Romans returned to the sea. The one flaw in Hamilcar's position was that Sicily was an island. He could be isolated by the destruction of Carthaginian sea-power. . . . The Senate still hesitated to take the responsibility of imposing the taxation and conscription necessary for naval war. . . . Prudence had much to say on this head. The political stability of Rome might have been shaken by another naval disaster.

That which the Senate would not venture to do was accordingly done by voluntary action. Private citizens organized a subscription. Those whose interest or whose patriotism guided them produced the resources which the Senate dared not ask of the state.

A fleet of two hundred ships was built and fitted out; sixty thousand men were engaged to man it; and this remarkable and unique gift was presented to the government. The pro-consul Gaius Lutatius Catulus sailed *The new Roman fleet* with this fleet in the year 241 B. C. Lilybæum and Drepanum were blockaded. The Carthaginian communications were cut.

Then came the tug of war. The relief fleet which Carthage dispatched was intercepted and brought to action. It was completely beaten at the Ægates. The control of the sea passed once more into the hands of Rome. Sicily was isolated.[1] It could only be a matter of time now before the strangle-hold closed upon Hamilcar Barca.

XVI

He recognized the meaning of the loss of sea-power, and judged it better to resign himself—though not gladly—to the inevitable consequences. He consented to negotiate the peace which Carthage elected to ask.

Battle of the Ægates 241 B. C.

The terms included the evacuation of all Sicily, and a war indemnity of twelve hundred talents to be paid by instalments over a period of twenty years. Hamilcar flatly refused to concede some of the demands made upon him, and Catulus did not press them. . . . The real nature of the peace is illuminated by several incidents. The Assembly at Rome, which had slightly exalted ideas concerning the winning of the war, at first refused to ratify the terms. A board of commissioners was sent to investigate matters upon the spot. Once they

The Peace Treaty

were in Sicily, the truth became apparent. The peace was not quite what the Assembly imagined. They obtained an increase of the war indemnity to twenty-two

[1] Polybius V. 59–61. It appears that this subscription fleet was a better one than the earlier government-built fleets. The ships were built on the model of Hannibal the Rhodian's fast blockade-runner. (*ibid*. I. 47.)

hundred talents, and the cession of all the islands—
potential naval stations for Carthage, which Hamilcar
did not want—between Sicily and Italy. . . . The Senate pulled the strings, and the Assembly sulkily ratified
the treaty, not quite understanding why it was not en-
titled to grind the Carthaginian into the dust. . . .
And indeed, why was it not?

The Senate could have told. Rome had barely struggled through to a victory which had strained her resources to the utmost limit: a victory "on points" which
did not involve the destruction nor even the permanent
crippling of Carthaginian power. . . . Hamilcar could
have divulged still more. . . . Questions of domestic
politics at Carthage had some share of responsibility for
the fact that any peace was concluded at all. There were
those who would breathe more freely when Hamilcar's
army was dissolved. . . . An island base, moreover, was
not ideal for his purposes. Since it had been his duty
to hold Sicily, he had done so; and he might conceivably have continued to do so until Carthage placed a
new fleet upon the sea. . . . But he was willing to buy
time for reorganization, and for the choice of a new
and safer base independent of all fleets and their incer-
titude, rather than drag on an indecisive war. . . . As
for grinding Carthage into the dust, he could afford to
smile at the romanticism of Italian peasants and artisans.

XVII

So, for the time being, the two formidable heavy-
weights left the arena. Rome had done far better than
the Greeks. She had actually won the whole of Sicily

Results of
the war

and ratified the success with a definitive treaty; she had torn the Carthaginian grip from the hold on those western Sicilian harbours which it had retained for six hundred years. And she had done this without being distorted or destroyed. . . . But Hamilcar had intentions for the future in which Sicily played no part.

XVIII

Birth of
Hannibal
247 B. C.

During Hamilcar's command in Sicily a son was born to him, who was named Hannibal. And this Hannibal was to grow up into the war-wizard whose fame rivalled that of Alexander, and whose story will fill most of the rest of this book.

CHAPTER III

THE CROSSING OF THE ALPS

I

No sooner had Hamilcar removed his army from Eryx to Lilybæum than he resigned his command. The general officer commanding at Lilybæum, Gisco, took over the work of returning the troops to Africa, the first step towards demobilizing and repatriating them. He embarked them in detachments at intervals, in order to give the government time to pay them off and pass them on their way home, before the new detachment arrived. . . . Gisco's correct and prudent conduct was frustrated by influences the source of which has never been made clear. . . . The government was short of money; and moreover had been persuaded that if Hamilcar's select and highly paid troops were collected at Carthage, they could be induced to accept less than was in the bond: an idea which seems very strange. Demobilization of Hamilcar's army

The pack of roaring blades who thus were gathered in the decorous commercial city of Carthage were as rough a crew of vagabundos as ever followed a Morgan to the sack of Portobello or Panama. Crime increased at such an alarming rate that the authorities hastily ordered the officers to remove their men to the town of Sicca. The vagabundos wished to leave their baggage on deposit at Carthage, expecting to return; but the government had had enough of them, and they

were turned out bag and baggage with a peremptoriness
which gave considerable offence.

At Sicca they enjoyed a care-free time which was a
great change from the strain of their recent activities
in the trenches around Eryx. Had rum then been in-
Effects of vented, the break-out might have come earlier. As it
Hamilcar's was, the more intelligent spent their leisure in reckon-
policy ing up their possible arrears of pay—with, invariably, a
magnificent balance on the right side. They trusted—
remembering the promises made to them by Hamilcar
in moments of emergency—that the government would
take the same generous view of its liabilities: an idea
which, also, seems very strange. The disillusionment began when Hanno, the general commanding in Africa,
came to visit them.

Unlike Hamilcar, Hanno was an old-fashioned Carthaginian. He was horrified at the balance-sheets presented for his inspection by the army; he protested that
such claims could not possibly be met, and he pointed
out to his audience the general distress and the heavy
taxation that prevailed in consequence of the late war.
The camp was convulsed with resentment at this per-
verse point of view. Meetings were at once held; some
Negotia- of them comparatively rational assemblages of men of
tions the same race and language—others, general meetings
of mutually incomprehensible speakers whose common
bond was the voice of honest indignation.

Hanno had his own difficulties. The army was composed of Africans, Baleares, Spaniards, Gauls and not a
few half-bred Greeks. Hanno did not know the languages of all these races; all he could do was to com-
municate with them through their officers—who in

many cases, either through misunderstanding or in malice, reported to their men remarks which were very far indeed from conveying Hanno's meaning. Finally, repudiating Hanno and all his works, the army marched back to Tunis and camped there over against Carthage. It was twenty thousand strong.

The Carthaginians realized now, too late, that they had committed very nearly every imprudence that it was possible for them to commit. They strove frantically to soothe the genie which they had incautiously raised. The vagabundos, however, were in a truly roaring and buccaneering temper. Assured that they had got their employers grovelling, they rocketed into the most extravagant demands. . . . At last, when the government, with almost hysterical plenitude, had granted everything that was asked, the army nobly consented to admit the mediation of one of its own Sicilian generals. Hamilcar the troops considered to have betrayed them—and he had certainly remained very quiet in the background—but they were willing to accept Gisco.

II

Gisco arrived at Tunis, interviewed the officers, spoke vigorous words of good sense to the men, and began to pay off the army. Now that the undertakings of Hamilcar were, however reluctantly, fulfilled, the whole trouble might have ended: but at this point was illustrated the danger of possessing a bad name. The ringleaders knew the repute of the men they were dealing with—"Punic Faith" is a byword still—and they placed no reliance there. Two of them—Spendius, an escaped

Spendius
and Matho

Roman slave, and Matho, the leader of the Africans—
had a heart-to-heart talk. Guessing that they would be
marked down for vengeance, they determined to save
themselves by wrecking the settlement. . . . It was
easy to set the Africans going. The argument that, once
the army was dispersed, they would be left alone to bear
the brunt of suppressed Carthaginian anger, went home
with only too much conviction to their minds. Such is
the evil of a reputation: and such is the devilish logic
that plunges men sea-deep in hell—for it was not destined to be much less.

The efforts to work up the storm afresh were successful. Desperadoes who feel their skins at stake will stop

**Revolt of
the Merce-
naries**

at nothing. Those who sought to restrain them were
overborne with brutal energy. The cry "Stone him!"
became the only international phrase which everyone
in the army understood. Many, both of officers and men,
suffered this ferocious vote at popular meetings. . . .
All opposition being effectively silenced, Spendius and
Matho were elected to the leadership.

Gisco's attempt to persist in his efforts at reconciliation were soon terminated. He and his staff were
promptly thrown into irons. Horrid and blasphemous
oaths of mutual fidelity were taken by the mutineers.
. . . And now the gage was cast down and the war was
afoot.

III

Matho had little difficulty in raising the tributary
African towns in general revolt. Crushing taxation and
severe repression during the war years had made the
native population as tow to the spark. It came into the

fray with an eagerness which told its own tale. Women
sold their ornaments to fill the war chest; and they filled
it full to overflowing. The towns of Utica and Hippacritæ, which refused to join the movement, were besieged. . . . And at one stroke the dumfounded Carthaginians found their world dissolved at their feet.
They were once more a single town alone against the
world.

As the historian dryly comments, they had no one
but themselves to blame.

If any hopes had been placed in the military skill of
Hanno, they were rapidly lost. That old-fashioned Carthaginian was a parade general who knew nothing of
the kind of war in which real weapons are used and
actual blood is shed. He was badly beaten at Utica, and
threw away all the opportunities presented to him. Before long, necessity taught its lesson. Hamilcar Barca
once more stepped upon the stage. He was needed.

Even though his immediate task were to destroy the
dangerous instrument which he had created, and to
restore order in Africa, the return of Hamilcar meant
the triumph of his general policy. He had discreetly
given his political opponents enough rope to hang themselves; and he came now graciously to cut them down.

The first touch of the master-hand of Hamilcar
Barca transformed the war. It had been impossible, so
far, to relieve Utica. He succeeded by one of those characteristic wizardries which his son learned from him.
At certain times the tide silted up the mouth of the
river. Hamilcar forded it at the right moment, and, as
if by a miracle, raised the siege of Utica. Spendius was
outwitted and beaten. Hamilcar swept the neighbour-

(margin: Hamilcar recalled)

(margin: Methods of Hamilcar)

ing country, bringing some towns back to their allegiance by persuasion, and some by force. Autaritus, the leader of the Gauls, joined Spendius. In a pitched battle they were defeated with a loss of ten thousand killed and four thousand prisoners.

Hamilcar was reasonable enough with his prisoners. He gave them the alternative of rejoining his army or of being sent home. In the latter case he cautioned them concerning the consequences of ever again being taken in arms against Carthage.

IV

But the logic which had created the revolt continued to operate step by step. Matho, Spendius and Autaritus were seriously alarmed at the policy of Hamilcar. Such a method of treating his prisoners would drain their men away from them like water. Punic Faith was still their fear. Their only hope lay in some measure which would create an impassable barrier to reconciliation or generosity. They fixed upon Gisco as their means. By a little adequate stage-management they arranged to receive dispatches warning them against the secret machinations of Gisco; and when the vagabundos had been worked up into a mood of roaring fury, Autaritus rose to advocate that Gisco and all other Carthaginians should be put to death. The first word of argument against this course revived the cry of "Stone him!"— and that was the end of the opposition. . . . The bodies of Gisco and his staff, horribly and deliberately mutilated, were cast into the no-man's land between the two armies.

The revolt becomes more serious

While Phœnicians were Phœnicians, a deed such as this would assuredly cut off all hope of reconciliation. The wail of horror and the demand for vengeance which came to Hamilcar from Carthage were probably unnecessary to remind him that his blood also was Semitic. Requests for the bodies for burial were refused with the warning that any herald or messenger might expect a like fate. The mutineers then took another oath to torture and kill any Carthaginian they captured, and to return handless to Carthage any ally of hers who fell into their hands—a rule which they proceeded to execute with care. Hamilcar bowed to their decision. They were not likely to beat him at any game which they elected to play.

V

His first step was to invite Hanno to join him: for he knew that these were deeds of desperate men. The war—by no choice of his—was to be a war of extermination. Henceforward all his prisoners were thrown to the elephants, who soon learned what to do with them.

Desperate the mutineers were. The stress of war now pressed in earnest. It grew worse before it grew better. The two generals could not work together. A plebiscite of the army sent Hanno home, leaving Hamilcar in sole and indisputable command. Supplies were a serious difficulty. The unexpected loss of a supply fleet pressed Carthage hard, while the mutineers were buying freely from Sicilian and Italian sources. Utica and Hippacritæ went over to the mutineers. Carthage itself was invested. . . . An appeal to Rome and Syracuse met, however, with immediate and sympathetic response.

Hamilcar sole commander

Both powers undertook to prevent their subjects from supplying the mutineers: while Rome laid no embargo upon export to Carthage.

Hamilcar was thus enabled to take up the task of relieving Carthage. He never showed greater military skill than in the ingenious methods by which he cut off the supplies of the investing army, harassed it into its lines, and all but besieged it there. All the prisoners he took were thrown to the elephants. . . . The besiegers hung on with the most desperate tenacity. When food ran out, they are said to have resorted to cannibalism. Having eaten all their available slaves, they finally faced the alternatives of fighting Hamilcar or negotiating with him. They chose the latter.

VI

It was a case of diamond cut diamond. Even now the leaders of the mutineers were not honest towards their followers: and as a direct result they were entrapped by the very Punic Faith which had been their dread. The terms on which Hamilcar agreed were that the Carthaginians might choose out of the mutineers ten men as the price of letting the rest go. This having been settled, he promptly chose the ten peace envoys and seized them. They included Spendius, Autaritus, and all the chief leaders save Matho—who, as an African, perhaps knew too much to trust himself in the serpent's den. . . . The Africans elected to fight. Forty thousand starved and demoralized men lay on the field of battle when all was over. The survivors no doubt were thrown to the elephants.

Hamilcar reduced most of the cities before moving against Tunis, where Matho still held out. There he crucified Spendius, Autaritus, and the other eight leaders within view of the walls. . . . Matho was not yet at the end of his tether. He saw signs of negligence and disorder in the Carthaginian army. A swift sortie dramatically changed the face of affairs. Spendius was rescued, and in his place the Carthaginian general, Hamilcar's colleague, was nailed to the cross. Thirty Carthaginians were slain to accompany the ghost of Spendius whithersoever its home was destined to be.

Hamilcar retreated, and Matho made the final throw of hazarding a pitched battle. In that fight the last of the African insurgents fell: Matho himself was taken. Africa, having no choice, submitted. *End of the revolt*

It is a strange story—brutal, barbaric, ferocious and bloodstained. The Romans were not ignorant of the tale: it comes down to us through them. . . . And if at any time later on we have cause to wonder at the unbending resistance of Rome and the cold endurance she showed, we may remember that it was against such mercenaries that she fought, and against the son of Hamilcar, and against his manslaying elephants.

VII

The revolt and its suppression were a point of crisis in the history of Carthage. They were perhaps partly the cause, partly the effect, and partly the accompaniment of a series of changes in the Carthaginian state which can be only imperfectly traced. The storm-cloud which hung over Africa both had its vortex in the plans and proceedings of Hamilcar Barca, and also somewhat *Hamilcar leaves for Spain 237 B. C.*

obscured their nature to succeeding generations. When it cleared, Hamilcar was on his way to Spain. . . . But in the meantime, some hidden struggle had taken place in Carthage itself.[1] To the effects of the Peace Treaty and the Revolt of the Mercenaries a third force added itself; for as soon as the revolt was over the Romans rewarded themselves for their friendly neutrality by seizing Sardinia: and in order to avoid war, which in the circumstances could not be contemplated, Carthage was compelled to pay a further heavy indemnity. Before such accumulated humiliation the power of the old Carthaginian aristocracy was shaken to its foundations.

And in more ways than one. The revolution which

Weakening of the Carthaginian aristocracy

[1] There are two stories: first, the plain straight-forward tale of Polybius (II. 1.) perfectly coherent, but written entirely from the official Roman point of view, and derived from the circle of eminent Roman statesmen and soldiers in which he moved: secondly, the less coherent account of Appian (VI. 4–6) which can hardly be reconciled with it. Polybius himself betrays the probable truth by his description (III. 8–9) of the assertions made by the historian Fabius Pictor, whose works are lost. The accounts given by Appian and Fabius are, it is evident, versions of the Carthaginian side of the story: and they amount, ravelled out, to the statements given in the text.

Difficult and imperfect though the evidence is, it leaves no doubt that Hamilcar established what we can only call a dictatorship. Livy (XXI. 3) makes Hanno speak as though Hamilcar had certainly exercised dictatorial powers. The relationship which Hamilcar and his successors bore towards Carthage was therefore peculiarly dubious and hard to describe. It varied as the strength of the opposing parties. The strange assertions—flatly disbelieved by the Romans and by Polybius—that the Carthaginian government had never ratified Hasdrubal's treaty with the Romans—may have been perfectly true. Carthaginians might well laugh, however, at the demand that they should surrender Hannibal! They had no such power! The aristocratic government at Carthage was not responsible for the actions of the Spanish Dictator, and did not necessarily endorse them: but it had to follow him and support him for all that. (Cf. Livy XXX. 16 and 22).

It may be noticed that Hamilcar's dictatorship, like those of Dionysius and Agathocles before him and of Cæsar after him, was based upon an appeal to the People. (Livy XXI. 2.) Hannibal afterwards appealed to the democracies of the Italian cities as against the pro-Roman aristocracies. See Homo, *Primitive Italy*, p. 293, instancing Livy XXIV. 2. (8–9).

darkened and concealed the face of Phœnician affairs was not only political but also—and perhaps even more —a vast operation of capital, such as we might nowadays see in oil or rubber. Hamilcar—so they asserted who should have known—though he had had all prepared for a *coup d'état* at Carthage, had, like most other men who attempted that feat, at the last moment fumbled and failed. He and his backers had at first succeeded in making his Sicilian army a self-supporting enterprise. The Peace had been forced upon him because his resources gave out. He had therefore been obliged to come to terms with the government, who, in taking over the responsibility for paying his army, seized, for political reasons, the chance of breaking it up and then went on to involve him in proceedings for intended treason. He would have fallen, as all his predecessors had fallen, but for the necessity of recalling him to power to suppress the mercenaries. But there were Carthaginians whose views of their own interests differed widely from those of the immediate governing circle. The promise of Hamilcar's military abilities—and perhaps of his private conversation—brought to his aid the protection and support of a syndicate or combine of (apparently) Spanish capitalists which we know of under the name of "Beau" Hasdrubal, its chairman or president. Hasdrubal married Hamilcar's daughter, and cast around him the powerful defences which the leader of a financial group can throw. Out of the temporary obscurity arose a new combination: a Spanish power in which Hasdrubal and his friends supplied the capital, and Hamilcar the brains and policy. . . . To those who set their faith in Hamilcar, Spain well repaid the investment.

The Coup d'état

Whatsoever the cause that sent Hamilcar to Spain, he went with quite definite intentions and with a definite policy directed to their realization.[1] . . . Many years afterwards, to illustrate his own views and prejudices, Hannibal told King Antiochus the story of his father's departure.

After the official sacrifices had been held and pronounced favourable, Hamilcar poured the libation and finished the sacred rites. He then motioned back those who stood near him, and called his little son forward. Hannibal was nine years old.

The
Oath of
Hannibal

It is through the eyes of that little boy—the sole occasion on which we ever see through them—that we learn of the kindly affection with which his famous father spoke to him. Would Hannibal go with them to Spain? . . . Not only would he go, but with a sudden burst of anxiety he implored to be taken. . . . Hamilcar led him up to the altar and made him place his hand upon the victim. He then recited, and Hannibal took, the oath that never would he be a friend of the Romans.[2] . . . That oath Hannibal felt to be binding upon him throughout his life. He grew up in an atmosphere of stern and unbending hostility to Rome and all her works; and he in turn became its representative and protagonist.

Hamilcar's career in Spain lasted nine years. In this

[1] Polybius III. 9–10. Livy XXI. 2. The problem (which we have no means of solving) is: Did Hamilcar go to Spain partly because he had failed to effect a *coup d'état* at Carthage?—or did he intend from the first to make his new power a Spanish power?

[2] Polybius III. 11. Livy XXI. 1. It was no doubt a party-oath, taken by all the associates of the Spanish dictatorship. Of precisely what motives and feelings it was built up those may say who can grope with assurance in the deep—and often dark—recesses of the Semitic mind: but we are certainly not called upon to regard it as an expression of personal hatred.

time he brought a large part of the peninsula under
Carthaginian rule, and by founding a new and richer
colonial dominion to take the place of Sicily and Sardinia, he transformed the economic position of Carthage. The city owed him too much in this respect to
quarrel with him. If there were, among the old aristocrats, a deep distrust of his methods, it was restrained
by the general appreciation of his aims. His military
plans had carefully considered objectives. Starting from
the already secure base of the Carthaginian towns in
south-western Spain, he moved north-eastward up the
river valleys towards the Ebro. He established a new advanced base and capital for his Spanish dominion at
Acra Leuca, which the Romans knew as Lucentum, not
far from Alicante and Cap la Nao; and he was drowned
in crossing a stream while on campaign.[1]

At his death, his power passed to his son-in-law, Hasdrubal, who for eight years continued Hamilcar's work.
Hasdrubal's administration saw Carthaginian rule extended up to the Ebro, and New Carthage founded to
take the place of Hamilcar's capital at Lucentum. The
splendour of New Carthage, its arsenal, its mint, and
its almost royal palace, spread wide the fame of Hasdrubal.[2]

Hamilcar in Spain (margin)

[1] Diod. XXV (frag.). Livy XXIV. 41. calls the place Castrum Album.
Gsell: *op. cit.* III. p. 131.

[2] Polybius II. 13. Appian VI. 6. Livy XXI. 2. The latter indicates that it was
by Hasdrubal's invitation that Hannibal went to Spain. (XXI. 3.) This would
be in 229 B.C. when Hannibal was certainly "little more than a boy." But
in XXI. 4. Hannibal is alleged to have served three years under Hasdrubal,
which would make the date 224 B.C.—Finally, Hannibal himself (XXX. 37. Polybius II. 1. XV. 19.) says that he left Carthage when he was nine years old, *i. e.*, in
238 B.C. when Hamilcar set out for Spain. This last is no doubt the truth. The
tradition of Hasdrubal's "invitation" probably refers to a formal nomination of his
successor, possibly in 224 B.C.

The suggestion of purpose in these conquests did not
escape keen and interested eyes. It may possibly have
been the influence of the commercial port of Massilia

which in 231 B. C. stirred the Romans to send a mission
of inquiry to Spain. Hamilcar received it with bland
courtesy and with convincing explanations of the need
that Carthage should be able to pay her war indemnities.[1] But the advance of Hasdrubal to the Ebro stirred
up fresh apprehensions. A Roman embassy five years
later needed more serious treatment. That very astute
diplomatist entered into an undertaking (which probably he had no serious intention of observing longer
than it suited him to do so) not to cross the Ebro.

The north-eastern push was, in fact, bringing the
Carthaginians within tolerably close striking-distance
of Massilia and the trade routes through Gaul. For some
seventy years past—largely, no doubt, owing to the wars
—the tin trade had to a steadily increasing extent been
diverted from the sea-route to that through Massilia.[2]
Any project of securing the Garonne, or even the Rhone
valley, and recapturing the northern tin trade, was
stopped by the agreement, which in achieving this end
rendered any idea of a Carthaginian invasion of Italy
—never very likely—practically impossible. That a Carthaginian army could pass direct from Spain, through
Gaul, over the Rhone and Alps, into Italy, was not a
probability to be seriously entertained.

Hannibal was eighteen years old when his father died
—too young for supreme responsibility. He was twenty-
six, and an experienced soldier, when the assassination of

[1] Gsell, op. cit. III, p. 135 quoting Dion Cassius frag. 46 edit. Melber.
[2] Tarn, Hellenistic Civilization, p. 204.

Hasdrubal left him the natural and intended successor of his sister's husband.

The power which had grown up in Spain was a remarkable and unusual one. Carthage had externalized and thrown off a dictatorship—almost a monarchy—which functioned without changing the ancient institutions of the city itself, and, as far as we can see, almost without interfering with them. . . . What had been isolated was the "initiative," the direction of the high policy of the Carthaginian state. A general staff had been organized in Spain, equipped no longer with one of the old type of mercenary armies, but with a highly disciplined and permanent striking force,[1] and furnished with a financial system which, instead of being dependent upon Carthage, and therefore under her control, was actually the source from which the economic position of Carthage had been restored, and thus exercised a controlling influence over her.[2] . . . Men stumbled over the name by which such a system should be called. One version was that young Hannibal had been made a King. Another explained that Hasdrubal had attempted to found a monarchy, but had been restrained by the aristocratic party at Carthage. Rome ignored these ideas. She took account of nothing

The Spanish Dictatorship

[1] For the military philosophy of such a striking force see the summary of Marshal Saxe's views, given by Captain Liddell Hart in *Great Captains Unveiled*. pp. 42–46.

[2] It is perhaps a commonplace that Spain was "the El Dorado of the ancient world" but the general reader, who only knows modern Spain, may underrate its wealth. At any rate, according to tradition, Hamilcar found the simple natives using feeding troughs and wine jars of silver. Besides gold, silver and lead, the country produced grain, wine, the finest olive oil, wax, honey, dye-stuffs and cinnabar, and a race of hefty white savages who may be commended to those who think that the white man was created christianized and civilized. See Strabo at length. c. 137 et seq. Diodorus V. 2 et seq.

but the formal political heads of the Carthaginian state, with which she had formally concluded treaties.

These formal political heads of the state took no steps regarding the succession to Hasdrubal. When the news came that Hannibal had been elected by the army [1] to fill his place, the choice was accepted [2] as a matter of course. . . . So the matter stood. The Romans had no comment to make.

VIII

None other of the world's famous men entered quite so suddenly and so unexpectedly upon his career as did Hannibal, the son of Hamilcar Barca. . . . With a little preliminary flicker there burst out in Spain the dazzling light of a new star; and men watched its increase with a kind of stupefaction. . . . And yet there were men then, and there are men still, to think that the brilliance of Hannibal was no more than the reflected light of Hamilcar Barca.

He had already plenty of practical experience gained under the careful tuition of his predecessors. Although young, he was a reputable and trusted soldier. His personal gifts made him popular with the army,[3] his deft handling of his new power settled him firmly in office.

He was at once in touch with the leaders of his party in Carthage, who took advantage of the occasion to

---

[1] *i. e.*, by the Carthaginian officers who staffed and led it.

[2] Polybius III. 13. Appian VI. 8. Livy XXI. 3.

[3] Livy XXI. 4. speaks of his likeness to Hamilcar; his piercing eyes, stern countenance, inflexible resolution; his courage, physical temperance, plain tastes in food and dress; only his horses and his arms marked him from other men. Livy mentions with horror his religious scepticism and his Richelieu-like subtlety.

remind their new chief of their importance. On the amount of support they could give him, his position might largely depend. It was very necessary, therefore, that he should support them to the utmost of his power. All of which he seems to have appreciated.

His own view was that the time was ripe for the realization of his father's aims. He perhaps foresaw the possibility that his own youth and apparent inexperience might tempt his political enemies into opposition which, even though it might be successfully repressed, would waste time, money and effort even to the extent of crippling his resources. Hamilcar's experience afforded a warning. The sound policy was to seize the initiative himself, and to keep it.

Both his friends and his foes no doubt were prepared to contemplate without undue surprise a project for the completion of the conquest of Spain, and even for the extension of Carthaginian dominion over the Pyrenees and down to the Rhone, where it would take in those valuable overland trade-routes that found their port in Massilia. At Hannibal's accession to command the prospect shaped to some such end, and his first vigorous actions were perfectly consistent with it. The wisdom of giving no excuse for Roman action before he was ready would be readily understood. No one could reasonably detect any meaning other than this in the two years of campaigning by which he ordered and settled the last of the Spanish tribes south of the Ebro: nor could there be anything surprising in the fact that he was surveying the route through Gaul. Even if Hamilcar and Hasdrubal had already had their intelligence service at

Forward Policy decided upon

Ostensible aims

work,[1] the negotiations with the Gallic tribes would need to be fresh and recent. Not only were changes constantly in progress, but the Celtic temperament was not one to be bound by old and half-forgotten undertakings.

There was similarly no need to look beyond such a program for an explanation of the care with which he cultivated his officers and the native Spaniards. In whatsoever field his campaigns were to be, he would need the absolute confidence of his men. If, after two seasons' work, he could rest assured that he had under him a well-disciplined army, and a Spain that fed out of his hand —that was certainly no evidence that his intentions were directed to any objective other than Gaul.

IX

Such intentions spurred Rome to diplomatic precautions which Hannibal promptly twisted to suit his own ends. A local quarrel was in progress at Saguntum, an obscure city well south of the Ebro. The Saguntines, having involved themselves rather seriously with a neighbouring tribe, appealed to Rome; and Rome, thinking the opportunity good, officially notified Hannibal that Saguntum was under Roman protection.

Now the agreement between Hasdrubal and the Romans, which defined the Ebro as the northerly limit of Carthaginian dominion, had tacitly confirmed to

Roman intervention

[1] Polybius (III. 14) seems to imply that Hamilcar had the scheme fully worked out before he died. It is questionable whether the full information of the route which Hannibal possessed (see III. 48) could have been acquired in only three years. The Romans found a party of Carthaginians in Liguria during the year 230 B.C. while Hamilcar was still alive.

Carthage all that lay south of the river. But even omitting this consideration, the Roman action was an obvious violation of the war-settlement. Nothing could have suited Hannibal better. He received the envoys and discussed the position with acrid candour. For him to give way implied the complete collapse of Carthaginian prestige in Spain. Accordingly he meant to fight. Since Rome, through the Sicilian harbours, could throw an army into Africa long before he could arrive to protect Carthage, it was by no means clear to the envoys that his attitude was more than bluff. The real truth never for a moment dawned upon them.

Meanwhile the word was passed to his party at Carthage. Its members were primed with the full facts concerning this crowning instance of Roman insolence, and the call was given for a united front.

The Senate had an Illyrian problem upon its hands. It was convinced that the state of the negotiations with Hannibal allowed it to deal with this difficulty before any serious demand upon its attention would be made from Spain. Then came the first surprise. As soon as the consul L. Æmilius Paulus had left with his army for Illyria, Hannibal invested Saguntum.

X

Timed to a nicety, the siege of Saguntum enabled Hannibal to create at Carthage the united front he wanted. Saguntum was stormed, his personal prestige was established, Carthaginian power was vindicated in the eyes of the world, and a vast treasure went to fill

Saguntum seized.

his war chest, to line the purses of the mercenaries, and to stampede public opinion at home.[1]

Roman plenipotentiaries were soon at Carthage. They met a hostile audience which was exalted with hope, enraged at the ultimatum they came to deliver, and furious over the memory of Sardinia and the war indemnities. The aristocratic party, left to itself, might prudently have restrained the storm; but the treasures of

Roman ulti-matum Spain had done their work. The ultimatum took the form of a demand for the surrender of Hannibal. In reply, the Carthaginian Council blew off steam by an embittered argument over the validity and meaning of the treaties. The plenipotentiaries declined argument.[2]

A dramatic scene ended the conference. Modern nations deliver ultimatums in documentary form. The senior Roman envoy presented no document; he performed a ritual. Pointing to the fold of his cloak, he said:

"Here are peace and war. Which shall I leave you?"

The acting suffete answered: "Leave which you like."

"Then I leave war."

Many voices answered: "War we take!"

On these terms they separated.[3]

XI

All was ready. When the dispatch reached Hannibal and he knew that Africa had lined up with Spain, he

[1] Polybius III. 17. From various hints, it is doubtful if the plunder of Saguntum came to much. A good deal of what purported to be the treasure of Saguntum probably came out of the Spanish exchequer.

[2] Polybius III. 20. 21. Gsell (*op. cit.* III. 137–139) makes out a very strong case in favour of the Carthaginians.

[3] Polybius III. 33.

had nothing to do but to start. Favourable assurances from the Gallic chiefs along the route had arrived, and were ready for publication. Elaborate precautionary measures had been made against his possibly prolonged absence. His Spanish infantry had enjoyed a long furlough during the winter. His last action was to give his brother Hasdrubal a commission as deputy governor of Spain, with careful instructions. . . . He crossed the Ebro, and at the passes of the Pyrenees said farewell, sent back his heavy baggage, and with his expeditionary force of some sixty thousand men took the road into Gaul.

The start for Gaul

The Senate acted with vigour. Promptly upon receiving the report of its plenipotentiaries it set the levy on foot. One army was commissioned for Spain, under Publius Cornelius Scipio, in order to hold Hannibal there. Another, under Tiberius Sempronius Longus, was destined for Africa; and by the preparations he began at Lilybæum it was clear that the African campaign would be formidable. Scipio left Pisa by sea on his passage to Spain. It was already known that Hannibal had crossed the Ebro.

Scipio landed at the mouth of the Rhone, intending to deal with the Carthaginian army at his leisure. There was ample time, for the news had just reached him that Hannibal was over the Pyrenees. His cavalry reconnaissance, however, confirmed an incredible report that the Carthaginians were actually at this moment crossing the Rhone! The cavalry had driven in the Numidian horse, and ridden right up to Hannibal's camp. Scipio at once re-embarked his baggage, prepared for active service, and advanced with all speed to establish touch.

... When he reached the crossing at Tarascon, the Carthaginians had gone. . . . Hannibal had bought up all the boats available, as well as a large quantity of lumber. In two days he had an immense flotilla collected. As there was prospect of resistance from some of the local tribes, he threw a force across the stream higher up, on rafts, turned the position, got his vanguard over, and secured the passage. He next ferried over his main body. It was then that he heard of Scipio's proximity. By desperate efforts the elephants, thirty-seven in number, were floated across. Under cover of a cavalry screen, he got his army upon the march, himself bringing up the rear with the elephants and the cavalry. . . . When Scipio arrived at the crossing three days later, the birds had flown!

Hannibal over the Rhone

The consul needed to think out his best course of action. By degrees the truth was emerging. Hannibal was not engaged in a conquest of the Rhone valley and the overland trade routes, but in a high-speed invasion of Italy itself! Scipio was one of the most intelligent of the Romans, but the conception struck him with astonishment. He finally decided to send on his army to Spain, while he himself made a dash to catch Hannibal on his emergence from the Alpine passes on the Italian side. Roman troops were available, engaged in more or less desultory operations against the Cisalpine Gauls, who were restless. He knew enough of the Alps to suspect that these troops would be sufficient to hold the survivors of Hannibal's men who managed to get through —if any managed to get through at all. The season was late, and Scipio, travelling alone, could arrive in time if Hannibal took the lower and the longer passes; while if

Attempt to intercept Hannibal

he took the higher and the shorter, the probabilities
were that he never could make the passage. . . . The
calculation was quite sound. . . . Scipio set sail again
for Pisa.

XII

While Scipio was upon his way, Hannibal was struggling with the difficulties of transporting an army
across the mountains. He had full information of his
route, and knew what he was doing.[1] Far more serious
than any physical obstacle was the problem of the attitude of the local powers. Organization and preparation could overcome merely material difficulties, but the
diplomatic question remained a delicate one.

It had probably been arranged beforehand that he
should purchase a free road to the foot of the pass by
employing his troops to decide a local political contest.
The candidate who had engaged his support repaid the
assistance by supplying the army with weapons and
rations, and above all with suitable clothing and foot-
wear for the mountains. He moreover provided a rear-
guard to protect the Carthaginian march: for it was
here that the army had to run the gauntlet of a hostile
opposition. The powerful tribe of the Allobroges dogged
the Carthaginians for a hundred miles up to the foot
of the pass. Once the army was in the pass, the friendly
rear-guard turned back, for Hannibal was comparatively safe.[2]

Passage of the Alps

---

[1] Polybius III. 48. where this point is particularly stressed.

[2] Polybius III. 49. The exact route of Hannibal is not yet agreed. Colonel
Dodge (*Hannibal* p. viii-ix) remarks that he found 350 treatises on the subject,
and there are more now. Kromayer and Veith (*Schlachtenatlas*, Part I Sheet 3)
give five different routes according to twenty different authorities: Mont Cenis,

The Allobroges were soon left behind. They did their best to waylay and break up the long tenuous line that was mounting the pass: but their chance had gone. Other and more questionable hosts were encountered further up. Led off the track by effusive but false guides; trapped into a spot where the local sportsmen could roll down rocks on the army; compelled to bivouac in the open, Hannibal fought his way up to the summit. . . . Only isolated parties hung on their flank now, keeping well away from the elephants. At the summit, Hannibal rested the army for two days.

It had been a difficult march. The casualties had been very numerous. Some of the missing men and beasts came struggling in during the halt. But at any rate the summit was reached.

XIII

The mercenaries were somewhat depressed at finding themselves upon an Alpine Col, with snow on the ground. Hannibal showed them their goal. There, far below them, extending to a blue horizon, stretched the Padane plain, and beyond it was Rome. He pointed out to them the direction in which Rome lay. Cheered by this, the army began the descent. It was, if anything, worse than the ascent. The road was exceedingly steep and narrow. A stumble was fatal, and a step off the path was a step into eternity. At last they met complete

The descent

Little St. Bernard, Great St. Bernard, Mont Genevre, and the Col Argentière: to which may be added a sixth, the Col de la Traversette, brilliantly advocated by the late Mr. Cecil Torr (*Hannibal crosses the Alps*, 2nd Edition, 1925.) The argument at present seems to be between the last three—and probably most sportsmen would like to back Mr. Torr's route.

check. A landslide had nearly covered the path. Men might slip by, but for the pack-animals and the elephants passage was impossible. Fresh snow had fallen, and rested upon a frozen underlayer on which men slipped, and in which animals stuck fast.

Hannibal had the ridge cleared of snow. Then working all day, the army proceeded to cut a path,[1] and get the mules and horses down, below the snow, out at pasture. . . . The elephants took longer. Three days of work by the Africans was necessary before the path could be made fit for elephants. Finally, nearly dead from starvation (for the great beasts could find no food above the snow-line) they were got down. Three more days saw them out of the pass and in the Italian peninsula.

XIV

The mighty deed had been accomplished! . . . Hannibal had crossed the Alps!

It was, of course, not simply the passage of the Alps that struck the world with an astonishment which has not yet died out. Gaulish tribes had made the passage often enough. . . . The Latins themselves, in long past days, had come into Italy across the mountain barrier. . . . But Hannibal's passage was no drift of migrating tribes. He was a civilized soldier, who in five months had transported an organized expeditionary force of

The passage achieved

---

[1] It was here that, according to Livy, Hannibal cleared his path by breaking up the rock with vinegar. This story is now generally left alone by historians. Colonel Hennebert (*Histoire d'Annibal* Vol. II. B^k V ch. iv.) discusses at length a theory that the vinegar was the Greek "oxus" and produced some of the results of an explosive. Polybius does not mention the story, which in any case is not necessary to the narrative and may be omitted without loss.

all arms, including elephants, from the south of Spain, through the Pyrenees, over the Rhone, across the Alps, into the Italian peninsula; and who in doing so had prevented any knowledge of his ultimate intention from transpiring, had slipped past a Roman army, and had arrived at his destination with time to rest, recuperate and refit. He had crossed the Alps in fifteen days.

The
casualties

The feat had been a tremendous one. He had had all his movements and objective to plan throughout; few precedents, and very little experience of any definite use to him, existed for his guidance. . . . The speed of his march and the difficulties he had encountered had produced a casualty list which might well stagger a modern general. He had lost fourteen thousand men in the passage of the Pyrenees and the march through Gaul. Starting from the Rhone with forty-six thousand men, he had lost twenty thousand in the passage of the Alps. . . . The twenty-six thousand who remained were battered, bearded, weary and unwashed.[1] But—and this was the remarkable part—their *moral* was unimpaired. He knew how to maintain it. He marked his arrival in Italy by an address to his bearded desperadoes. His own philosophy of life he never expounded to the world: but he provided them with one which impressed them.

Hannibal's
Speech

They must (he told them) conquer or die: or else have the pleasing experience of falling alive into the hands of the Romans. The reward of victory would not

---

[1] Polybius III. 60. Livy XXI. 38. tells us that L. Cincius Alimentus, who was a prisoner of war with the Carthaginians, recorded that he heard Hannibal say that he had lost thirty-six thousand men since crossing the Rhone. The number twenty-six thousand, as the force with which Hannibal entered Italy, was copied by Polybius from Hannibal's own inscription in the Temple of Juno Lacinia (III. 56). It is therefore official.

be a little booty, but the treasure of Rome itself. To die in battle was one of the least painful of deaths. But to be beaten, and live, would be the most miserable fate that could befall them. There was no retreat over the road they had come. Victory or death must be their watchword. . . . And if they made up their minds to this, victory it would be, for no men who fought in such a mood had ever failed.

The desperadoes saw the point. They had faith in him. They washed, they shaved, they sharpened their weapons and prepared to conquer or to die.[1]

XV

So much for them. But Hannibal himself had designs which he never for a moment thought of divulging to such men. He had no expectation of conquering Italy with an army of twenty-six thousand men. In all his actions so far he had shown the most alert appreciation of sound information, and had taken the utmost care to acquire it. He must have had a sufficiently accurate knowledge of the military resources of Rome. The Senate could call upon the services of nearly seven hundred and fifty thousand robust citizens and allies.[2] The huge war indemnities which had been exacted from Carthage could not all have vanished into thin air. In the face of such facts as these, the hope of conquering Rome with Hannibal's immediately available forces would have been a wild one. . . . He never had any such hope. . . .

The task before him

[1] Polybius III. 63.
[2] 748,300—These figures came from Fabius Pictor, a contemporary, who copied the official register. Homo, *op. cit.* pp. 232–234 and authorities there quoted.

His aim was to disrupt and destroy the political union of Italy. His warfare had political objectives.[1] As soon as he had demonstrated that this unity, which rested upon appeal to the interests, the faith and the social sense of men, could be torn apart by appeal to their fear, their doubt and their selfishness, he would have as much help as he wanted: perhaps more than he needed.

So now the force was unloosed which would test the strength of the political principles of Rome.

[1] Homo, *op. cit.* pp. 239–243; 291–293.

CHAPTER IV

THE ENTRY INTO ITALY

I

In the meantime, Publius Cornelius Scipio was hastening back by sea to catch the Carthaginians on their emergence from the mountains. He landed at Pisa, and picked up the somewhat battered remnants of the two corps of Manlius and Atilius. By the time he reached Placentia, Hannibal had taken Turin by storm, as a warning to the Gauls, and was advancing eastward, trusting to the impression he had produced to bring the Gallic tribes over to his side. Scipio crossed the Padus and seized a crossing on the Ticinus, threw over a bridge and fortified a bridge-head beyond it. He then advanced to a position five miles from Hannibal's camp. A cavalry reconnaissance of the Carthaginians, advancing north, met the Roman cavalry moving south, and the Romans were driven back; Scipio himself was wounded. The contact revealed Hannibal's cavalry strength and the difficulty which the Romans would find in dealing with it. The retreat began that night. The Ticinus was recrossed, and the army retired towards Placentia. Hannibal was quick on their heels. He captured the detachment left behind to disconnect the bridge; but on learning how long a start Scipio had obtained he made no attempt to cross. He would have needed to force the passage of the Padus against Roman opposition. Instead, he turned back, went two days' march up the Padus, crossed

Hannibal's advance

The Roman retreat

87

by a pontoon bridge, and found that Scipio had taken position on high ground west of the Trebia, covering Placentia.

This did not last long. It was necessary at all costs to preserve free communication, for rescue was on the way. The African expedition was being broken up post-haste, and the troops from Sicily were on the road northward. Scipio determined to continue his retreat. He crossed the Trebia at night, seeking better ground. Only a delay on the part of Hannibal's Numidian cavalry, who spent too long in looting the Roman camp, saved the consul. His rear-guard was caught and captured; but the crossing was safely effected.

The arrival of T. Sempronius Longus with the Sicilian legions seemed to change the situation, Scipio, who had been in touch with Hannibal, was in favour of caution; Longus, who had not been, was all for cheery vigour. . . . The state of affairs was in fact somewhat arguable. Hannibal, who did not like the cautious neutrality of the majority of the Gallic population, tried the experiment of a little judicious frightfulness. The expedient answered admirably. Longus pointed out to his colleague that the best way of securing the loyalty of the country-side was to protect it. Scipio doubted the wisdom of attempting to do so. Longus thereupon sent a force upon his own responsibility. . . . The difference of opinion was not without justification; but the trouble was that although neither of the consuls was wrong, both of them could not be right.

The protecting force drove in the raiders, and was repulsed by reinforcements from the Carthaginian camp. After skirmishing and indecisive fighting the ac-

Arrival
of Longus

tion petered out. . . . But Hannibal had learned all that he wished to know. From the various results, he picked out the one that suited him.

He saw so clearly the right course for the Romans to adopt, that he scarcely dared to hope for the success of the plan which he now put into operation. He intended to try to exploit the mood of Longus, and to force a general engagement. He had everything to gain from a quick and decisive battle. After inspecting the ground between the two armies, he satisfied himself that a stream, deeply cut between two banks, with a bed thickly massed with undergrowth, would serve his purpose. He called for volunteers. That night, a thousand footmen and a thousand horse quietly took position in the bed of the stream, and settled down in concealment.

II

The first thing in the morning, he was ready. With that intense sympathy with human foible and human weakness which he always showed, he had ordered large fires to be made, and oil to be served out. His troops equipped themselves in comfort, oiled their limbs, had an ample and early breakfast, and sat down to wait.

While these preparations were on foot he sent out his Numidian light horse with definite orders to draw the Romans after them. They experienced no difficulty in carrying out their orders. They came skirmishing back through the waters of the Trebia not only with the Roman cavalry and light infantry close upon them, but with the confident Sempronius Longus and the legions following. As soon as the Romans had waded

Battle of the Trebia (Dec. 218 B. C.)

the river Hannibal kept them there by sending in his own light infantry. He then proceeded to take ground in force with the whole of his heavy troops.

The season was winter. Snow was falling, a bitter wind was blowing over the raw marsh country between Alps and Apennines; the river was swollen breast-high by over-night rains. The Romans had been brought out of camp before breakfast; they had waded the Trebia; they were famished, frozen and fatigued, and in this state they confronted troops warm, well-fed, oiled against the weather, and perfectly fresh.

The Romans drawn across the river

Longus signalled his cavalry to break off what he saw to be their futile engagement with the Numidians. The two cavalry screens broke and passed to take ground on the wings. The two light infantry lines then engaged. The advantage was so much with the Carthaginians that Longus ordered his own men to pass back to the rear. Hannibal's, however, passed to the wings: and this second screen was thus stripped away to confront the legions with the African and Spanish infantry, headed with elephants.

The weight of heavy cavalry which was massed upon the two Carthaginian wings now drove the Roman cavalry off the field. The Carthaginian light infantry, following, enveloped the Roman flanks; the Numidians came round still further; the envelopment was complete when the men concealed in the bed of the stream broke cover and attacked the legions in the rear. . . . Only the foremost of the three Roman infantry lines held its ground. Amid the chaos that ensued it stood firm against the Africans and Spaniards; it repulsed even the elephants; more by courage than by physical strength,

Destruction of the Roman army

Livy says, it formed square ten thousand strong and cut its way out of the trap it was in. . . . It fought its way towards the road to Placentia and made good its retreat.[1] . . . It left thirty thousand men behind it, some on the field, some thronging after it as best they could, some scattering over the country, some breasting the Trebia, in most cases to be swept away by the current; some to be caught by the enemy as they stood hesitating to face that icy passage. But the most part of the army perished on the banks of the river, before the elephants and the Gaulish cavalry.

The pursuit did not pass the river. The Carthaginian losses were small, and Hannibal elected to lose no more men than he could avoid.

During the night, many stragglers ferried themselves across the Trebia on rafts. A storm was up, and the Carthaginians did not interfere. Scipio evacuated the camp, and retreated upon Placentia, whence he retired to Cremona.

III

The news of the battle of the Trebia, and the continued retreat of the armies, created in Rome a panic-stricken conviction that all must be lost. . . . Hannibal was expected to march straight upon the city. Longus had reported his defeat with reserve. The first

Panic at Rome

[1] There seems to be some doubt how it got to Placentia. Both Livy and Polybius seem to think that it did not need to cross the Trebia. This has thrown the whole facts of the battle of the Trebia into debate. For the view that the battle was fought on the right bank, see Colonel MacDougall's *Campaigns of Hannibal* (1858) Ch. I. The late Dr. Henderson (*Eng. Hist. Rev.* 1898, pp. 128-131) remarked that Mommsen's left bank site for the battle was now almost universally rejected. Nevertheless Mr. How, writing a year later, voted for it; and the present writer adds his pebble. All the various topographical possibilities are shown in the map in Kromayer and Veith's *Schlachtenatlas*.

news seemed to mean that he had been prevented by weather from securing the victory he had earned. . . . But the real facts soon were known. . . . He himself arrived at the height of the panic, after running the gauntlet of the enemy cavalry which was loose over the country. . . . He came partly on official business. It was his duty to hold the elections. His presence seems to have calmed popular feeling, for the elections passed off without trouble. . . . Possibly the elections themselves, by preoccupying the public mind with familiar passions, diverted thought. . . . In addition, time passed without the arrival of Hannibal.

Even the defeat at the Trebia, and the revolt of Cisalpine Gaul which followed, were not sufficient to convey any moral to the political parties at Rome. The conviction still remained with them that the public safety could be amply secured through the men who represented their political interests. . . . The consular elections therefore followed the usual party lines. Gnæus Servilius Geminus was the Senatorial nominee: and Gaius Flaminius Nepos was elected by the popular party.

The
Consular
elections

No more undistinguished person could never have been placed in the Curule chair than Gnæus Servilius; and the distinction which may be allowed to Flaminius belonged much more to the forum than to the field. . . . Flaminius certainly possessed character. Perhaps only an actual test would demonstrate precisely what kind of character it was.

Flaminius had a history which is by no means irrelevant to the story of his brief subsequent career. Four years earlier he had been consul during the war in Cisalpine Gaul. . . . It was one of those years in which strange things happen and other strange things are imagined. The earthquake which overthrew the Colossus of Rhodes was felt in Italy. Strange lights were seen in the sky, and three moons together. . . . Later generations have seen similar phenomena, and have attributed them to such causes as seismic disturbances. . . . Men who live in continual risk are liable to add to their practical precautions the most particular care about outward signs, auguries and portents; and the high nervous organization of the Romans made them especially careful on this head. . . . The fact that a vulture alighted in the middle of the Forum was enough to upset them. . . . They are not to be blamed: for we can never be too careful. It is probable that Flaminius did not blame his countrymen. . . . The trouble began when the augurs decided that something must be wrong with the consular elections. We have no reason to suppose that Flaminius would have experienced any lack of sympathy if they had found the fault nearer home: but his religious faith suffered when they attributed the appearance of three moons to a flaw in his title to the consulship.[1]

Gaius Flaminius Nepos

A courier was soon on the road to request Flaminius and his colleague to return home. He arrived on the eve of a serious battle. Flaminius evidently had private information. He persuaded his colleague to defer opening the letters until after the battle. . . . By good luck

[1] Flaminius, when tribune, had advocated distributing and settling with colonists the waste lands around Ariminum which were leased as pasturage to great senatorial landholders. He doubtless at this juncture recollected his indiscretion, and may have surmised that it had not been forgotten by the augural college either.

rather than by military genius, they won it. . . . Flaminius drew up his troops in dangerously restricted ground, with insufficient space for manœuvring. The substantial victory achieved was due to the skill of his officers and the quality of his men.

The letters were then opened, and found to contain orders of recall. . . . P. Furius Philo, the other consul,
Embarrassing antecedents of Flaminius was ready to obey: but Flaminius checked him. The mere fact that they had won that battle was clearly a disproof of the allegations of the augurs. His colleague prudently withdrew. Flaminius proceeded to conduct the war to the end. He took good care, by a generous distribution of the spoils of victory, to convince his troops that they had a consul who deserved to possess a sound title to office.

This was the beginning of a feud which increased with the passage of time. In spite of the popular support he received, he was compelled to resign office. The Senate refused him a triumph. His consulship nevertheless left him a senator; and he avenged himself by supporting a bill of the tribune, Gaius Claudius, restricting the rights of senators to take part in shipborne commerce. As the only senator in favour of this measure he received a large amount of publicity which was wholly to his benefit. He had after all nothing to lose from his fellow-senators, and he had much to gain from popular applause. His policy was successful in returning him to the consulship this winter, after the great defeat on the Trebia.[1]

[1] Polybius II. 32. Zonaras 8. Orosius IV. 13. Livy XXI. 63. Plutarch (in *Marcellus* c. IV. 4.) observes that the Romans attributed their success not to carnal weapons but to their religious faith. Flaminius does not seem to have disputed this principle. His objection was to the personal application.

IV

The Roman elector may possibly be excused for a feeling that these exciting domestic issues took precedence of the prosaic fact that a Carthaginian general had just defeated a Roman army in Cisalpine Gaul— a fact which would in due course be put into its right perspective. . . . The excitement grew when, promptly upon the election of Flaminius, more portents were observed by the augurs. . . . When a six-months' old child of free parents was reported to have shouted *Io Triumphe* in the vegetable market, while in the Forum Boarium an ox climbed of its own accord up the staircase to the third story of a house, Flaminius anticipated that these incidents would once more be held to disprove that the *vox populi* was the *vox dei* as far as his consulship was concerned. He left the city privately, and reached the front before he was missed.

The Augurs

He was not mistaken. The indignation of senators at his disappearance was deep and by no means silent. They had, they said, an atheist at the head of the state. Messengers were sent after him to bring him back— by force, if necessary—to discharge his solemn religious duties. Flaminius was obdurate. He declined to return. He took over the legions of Sempronius Longus and Scipio, and made ready for business,[1] leaving Gnæus Servilius to defend his country, if he wanted to, on the altars of Latium and Rome.

Trouble between Flaminius and the Senate

[1] Livy XXI. 63. For more portents, see *ibid*. XXII. 1., where the defensive ceremonies are described.

V

Hannibal was moving. His situation in Cisalpine Gaul was an uncomfortable one; the Gauls did no more than barely tolerate him, and had no enthusiasm for the presence of an army in their own country. The only condition on which they could achieve any feeling of cordiality was the prospect of carrying the war south into the rich lands of Etruria and Campania. Hannibal intended to cross the Apennines into Etruria at the first possible moment. Before he started, he addressed all his prisoners of war who were of cities allied to Rome. He told them that he had come into Italy, not as their enemy, but as their friend, to liberate them from the bonds of Roman dominion. . . . He asked them to spread this news among their countrymen, and to join the cause he represented. He then set them all free. . . . They appear to have made no remark. Whether they quite understood his meaning was uncertain then, and is not much clearer now.

Hannibal advances south

That Hannibal would march south was, of course, certain; but no man could tell by what route he would come. . . . His intentions were so doubtful that every road was watched, and every available man employed as an observer. The consul Servilius was at Ariminum guarding the port and the road junction down the eastern coast. Flaminius took up his position at Arretium in central Italy, covering the road to Rome, and ready to march whithersoever required. Servilius had the smaller army, but he was the more dangerous man, since he left more to his officers and attempted less himself. The army of Flaminius was stronger; but then its commander was a man of more distinct interest to Hannibal, for Flaminius, as we have seen, indulged in the luxury of an individuality.

While they waited and watched Hannibal marched steadily down the road from Placentia to Ariminum, his cavalry swelled by a powerful corps of Gallic troopers. On his right hand was the line of the Apennines, every pass observed and patrolled. At first it seemed as if he intended to attack Servilius or to give him the go-by and to follow the coast-road southward; but when he was near Forli he wheeled suddenly to the right, took a very short and very difficult pass which no Roman had thought it worth while to watch, and was in Etruria before he could be stopped or even expected.

If he knew enough to take this road, he must have known enough to appreciate its danger, and must deliberately have elected to run the risk. The mountains were successfully crossed. The flooded state of the country on the opposite side was the really serious difficulty. . . . For four days and three nights the Carthaginian army struggled through the mud and the water, the redoubtable Spaniards and the Africans leading the way, the Gauls following, and the Numidian horse bringing up the rear, with instructions to keep the Gauls moving. . . . In that army of thrice-tried and tested professional soldiers the formidable Gauls were the weakest spot. . . . Lack of sleep was the severest hardship of all. . . . They might very easily have perished in that march. Hannibal himself rode upon the last surviving elephant, but he did not escape the dangers of four days' exposure in a swamp. Strain, and lack of sleep, malaria and damp told upon him to such

He moves against Flaminius

a degree that in the absence of proper medical treatment he completely lost the sight of one eye. When they emerged near Fæsulæ, with the loss of many men and beasts, he pitched camp and sent out to reconnoitre. . . . It had been an expensive short cut into Etruria.

His scouts located the Roman army ahead in the vicinity of Arretium.

His arrival in Etruria

Hannibal's first step was to acquire accurate information concerning the country, and also concerning the mentality of his opponent. He soon learned the facts. He did not, perhaps, learn that Flaminius was an atheist who defied the gods; but he certainly learned that he was a hasty, self-confident man, with more assurance than brains—which, the Senate would have thought, amounted to much the same thing. And it was on this foundation—which had most surely and certainly been presented to him by the Roman people acting in their constitutional function as electors—that Hannibal built up the battle of Trasumennus and the destruction of Gaius Flaminius Nepos. It was not a heroic epic, but a psychological drama.

VI

Leaving the Roman army at Arretium upon his left, Hannibal turned to Fæsulæ. Thence he cut a wide swath of destruction through the rich central districts of Etruria, perhaps the first scientific devastation they had ever known. From the camp the consul and his army could behold the spectacle. So much the historians tell us. They do not clothe the outline of the picture with the details that would bring home its full human meaning to us. . . . Perhaps it never occurred to them

The Devastation of Etruria

that a generation would exist which, though interested in their story, would not be able, from personal experience, to supply the familiar—too familiar—commonplaces they tactfully omitted. . . . The bullock carts which carried the first seized household-gods of Etruria south, amid the crowds of penniless and ruined refugees, saved but a trifling part of all that went up in fire and smoke to signal to the army at Arretium the remainder of the story. The brief phrases of historians are usually but algebraic formulæ in the calculus of human pain.

Flaminius had never meant to stand idly by, much less to look supine upon a picture such as this. He felt it to be a personal reflection upon himself. The question was how to deal with the situation. A policy of devastation is never easy to deal with from the military point of view. . . . It was now that the second element in his temperament, his undue self-confidence, began to operate. His advisers counselled caution. It would, they thought, be best to wait for the arrival of Servilius, and for the two armies to operate upon a common plan; meanwhile, they could check the devastation of Etruria with light troops. . . . Flaminius rejected this with vehemence, and ordered immediate action. . . . His officers greeted his decision with considerable reserve. They probably knew the consul's military attainments. But it was popular with the troops.

Feelings of Flaminius

Portents are more often remembered afterwards than noted at the time. When Flaminius mounted his horse, it is alleged to have thrown him. A message was brought —possibly at the instigation of the officers—that the standards could not be pulled up out of the ground. . . . Flaminius seems to have suspected the secular

Hesitation of the officers

origin of this divine intimation, for he turned upon the messenger: "And possibly you also have a dispatch from the Senate forbidding me to fight? . . . If you are trembling too much to pull up the standards, *dig* them up." . . . After this, the standards seem to have come out of the ground meekly enough: and the army moved off in column of route.

Hannibal, after passing south-eastwards from Fæsulæ towards Clusium, on the road to Rome, wasting the country as he went, now turned suddenly eastward and took the road that leads along the northern shore of Lake Trasumennus. Such a route would lead him to Perugia and so into Umbria. To do this, he cut across the line of march by which the consul was coming down from Arretium. Never was a coast trailed more effectively. The country lent itself to the tactics at which he was most expert: and he relied (not without reason) upon the temperament of Flaminius. The road by the lake-side was close-hemmed between the water and the hills. Some distance along it a valley ran suddenly up into the mountains, ending in a steep hill, and lined with ridges of lower

Lake Trasu- mennus

height affording excellent cover. . . . Hannibal, with the Libyan and Spanish infantry, camped on the steep hill. His light infantry he sent on to take cover behind the ridges. The Numidian horse and the Gauls remained concealed near the point where the road debouched into the valley.

In these positions the Carthaginian army quietly spent the night.

Flaminius arrived on the banks of the lake at sunset, and pitched camp. He moved early the next morning.

A thick fog hung over the lake, and visibility was bad. Flaminius took the narrow road without any previous examination of the ground. . . . As soon as the Consul had cleared the road and was in the valley, Hannibal ordered the trap to be sprung.[1]

VII

The battle of Lake Trasumennus was an elaborate construction which depended for its success upon a large number of factors. Had any of them failed, Hannibal himself might have been caught in his own trap. But none of them failed. The Carthaginian forces, being above the level of the mist, could see one another, and time their movements. The Romans did not even see what struck them. Fighting began while they were still in column of march, and they were never brought into any tactical order at all. The vanguard, some six thousand men, continued to advance until they were detached from the main body, which was in inextricable confusion behind them.

Flaminius himself played a gallant but hopeless part. He made himself the centre of the desperate struggle which for three hours raged in the mist. When at last he was slain, even the personal prowess of Roman and Latin peasants could hold out no longer. Many were driven into the lake, whither the cavalry followed them. The mist rose to show the scene of disaster. The vanguard, at last perceiving what had happened, took up its standards and made the best of its way from the

The Trap

[1] M. Caspari, in *Eng. Hist. Rev.* 1910 p. 414 discusses the topography of the battle.

field. It gained a village near by; but was rounded up by Maharbal's cavalry, and compelled to surrender. . . . About a thousand men escaped from the battle of Lake Trasumennus. No military force was ever more effectively destroyed.

Destruction of the Roman army

Fifteen thousand men fell in that valley. The prisoners amounted to another fifteen thousand, of which six thousand were accounted for by the almost undamaged vanguard. . . . Hannibal's action with respect to these latter became a matter of controversy. The terms on which they surrendered are uncertain. . . . He declared that Maharbal had no authority from him to grant terms. According to Polybius, the terms were only that their lives should be spared. Livy tells us that the terms were that they should be allowed to depart with one garment apiece. . . . The Latin allies, according to Hannibal's settled policy, were set free.

The Carthaginian losses were fifteen hundred,[1] for the most part Gauls.

VIII

The rumours of the defeat at Trasumennus could not be prevented from reaching Rome. Women were soon in the streets inquiring of those whom they met what news there was. The Forum was as crowded as on an election day; and the crowd set towards the Comitium and the Senate house. . . . At sunset, the prætor, M. Pomponius, made the brief official announcement: "We

---

[1] Livy places Hannibal's losses at 2500 besides those who afterwards died of wounds received in the battle (XXII. 7). He gives the authority of Fabius for his own figures. The body of Flaminius was never found.

have been defeated in a great battle." . . . This was all the definite information that could be obtained; but the people gathered from unofficial sources, and took home with them, the news that the consul had been killed, the greater part of the army lost, and those that had escaped were either wandering in Etruria or were prisoners of war.

The historian is perhaps right in thinking that those who fell in the battle did not suffer more than the relatives at home who waited with suspense to hear the detailed tidings. An army which has been wiped out as thoroughly as that of Flaminius has no official reports to send; and Hannibal was certainly in no position to furnish information, even if he had been willing to do so. For several days large crowds, containing more women than men, waited at each of the gates to intercept new-comers. All who arrived were eagerly questioned; and it was not possible to get them away from the inquirers, especially if they were personally known, until the last detail had been repeated. Then, by the expression of the hearers and by the friends congratulating or consoling, one might guess whether the news were good or bad: but after such a disaster it must have been for the most part ill news. . . . Still, the historian has two strange stories to tell: of the mother who met her son safe and sound at the gate, and died of joy in his arms; and of that other, who sat mourning him in her house, and died when she saw him on the threshold. . . .

The prætors kept the Senate in continual session for several days, debating the steps to be taken. Before any decision had been reached, further unpleasant news arrived. Servilius, hearing that his colleague was on the

The news in Rome

march after Hannibal, had sent him four thousand cavalry under G. Centenius the pro-prætor. Hannibal, getting wind of their approach after the battle, sent Maharbal with a mobile column of light infantry and cavalry. Defeated, with the loss of half his men, Centenius took refuge on a hill, where his force was surrounded and obliged to capitulate.

Defeat of Centenius

The defeat of Centenius, though a small matter compared with the disaster of Trasumennus, seems to have turned the scale among the senators. It was determined to appoint a dictator. There were constitutional difficulties in the way. A dictator was a nominated magistrate, selected by the consuls, who resigned their joint power into his hands; he could not validly be elected by the Assembly. One consul was dead; the other was isolated at Ariminum, and could not be reached. To circumvent the difficulty, the Assembly elected a special magistrate with dictatorial powers, a pro-dictator. The man chosen for the office was Quintus Fabius Maximus. . . . An ordinary dictator appointed his own Master of the Horse. Fabius received his from the Assembly. M. Minucius Rufus was elected. . . . Fabius received the commission from the Senate (who held the purse strings) to repair the fortifications of the city, place garrisons in any place he thought good, and to destroy bridges at his discretion.

A Dictator appointed

The fight was now for Rome itself. They could no longer defend Italy.

CHAPTER V

QUINTUS FABIUS AND THE ARISTOCRATIC
DICTATORSHIP

I

WE may suppose that Hannibal, according to his invariable custom, acquainted himself in detail with the temperament and character of his new opponent, the the pro-dictator. He must have learnt some facts of the highest interest. If any man embodied the most typical and irritating virtues of the Roman, that man was Fabius. If any man concentrated in himself the qualities of that Rome which Hannibal had sworn to destroy; if there were anywhere a single individual who was the incarnation in its most offensive form of the moral atmosphere of that state which Hannibal had conquered Spain, crossed Gaul, surmounted the Alps, and invaded Italy in order to pulverize into the dust from which she sprang—Fabius was that man. The Wizard who was weaving his spells over Rome might well gaze intently on the figure of the pro-dictator. Fabius was the test for him. If some divine Creator could have sought diligently, in every corner of the universe, to find and collect and mould into human shape the strange, recondite, peculiar qualities which had been omitted from the composition of Hannibal—qualities on which his steel would not bite and his intelligence would not work —Fabius might have been the wondrous result. . . . It was a very wondrous result, indeed.

Quintus Fabius Maximus pro-dictator

II

Quintus Fabius was descended from a very old patrician family, which had occupied high offices in the State. He traced a divine descent from Hercules. The high aristocratic blood which ran in his veins did not touch him with any of those romantic qualities which we have learnt, since his day, to regard as aristocratic. As a boy he had been nicknamed Ovicula, the Little Sheep, on account of his extreme mildness and his highly developed instinct for following his leader. He had, in fact, been a preternaturally slow, solemn and obtuse child, backward in his lessons and entirely free from any decided individuality. . . . Some thought him stupid. . . . As he grew older, these very mediocre characteristics hardened into a character that was by no means mediocre. He grew into a man sane and balanced in judgment, free from any of those impatiences which hurry irritable men into petty mistakes; a man cautious in making his decisions, impossible to shift from them when they had been made, loyal to his colleagues—that is to say, a man with a kind of genius for entering into satisfactory and profitable relationship with others. . . . He was a man born for that kind of political society in which it is necessary to work with other men, and to act by common agreement.

He showed this in his appreciation of the importance of political government; the physical discipline—common to the Roman aristocrats of his age—under which he held himself, and the care with which he cultivated that art of oratory which, though it may in later times

Character of Fabius

His peculiar gifts

have become a literary exercise, was still a living art
directed towards the persuasion of his fellow-citizens.
. . . His public speaking is reported to have been terse,
plain and of good sense.

Such was the man whom the Assembly elected to
take control of the destinies of Rome.

III

Fabius at once began by convoking the Senate and
raising the question of religion. He expressed the opinion
that the fault of Flaminius lay more in neglect of religion
than in bad generalship: and he desired that an inquiry
should be made of the Divine Powers as to the necessary
measures to be taken. It was accordingly resolved that
the Sibylline Books should be consulted—a step usually
taken only in the gravest emergency.

This was a policy which showed much understanding.
It dealt with several serious difficulties at once. The most
essential task was to restore public confidence and to
tighten the reins of discipline: and the first step towards
them was to stop all talk of signs and portents, and inevitable destiny and the wrath of the gods. . . . To
switch the emphasis to religion enabled the government
moreover to soften any disheartening impression that
might have been created by two serious military failures.
. . . Finally, a strict observance of the religious forms
was a convenient method by which some control could
be kept over the vagaries of the Assembly.

The appropriate authorities accordingly proceeded to

The
religious
question

Sibylline
Books
consulted

examine the Sibylline Books,[1] and reported to the Senate
the enlightening information that a vow made to Mars
for the prosperity of the war had not been carried out in
a satisfactory manner. This discovery put matters on
a new basis. Evidently the recent reverses had not been
due to military causes. The recommendations of the
decemvirs included Games in honour of Dios Pater,
the building of two temples, a *lectisternium* with in-
tercessions, and a Sacred Spring. Since (rather incon-
sistently) the dictator would be engaged with military
affairs, the prætor was commissioned to superintend the
due performance of the religious ceremonies.

The recommendations were carried out with scrupu-
lous care. The Games were held at a cost of 333,333⅓
ases; 300 oxen were sacrificed to Dios Pater, the vows for
the Sacred Spring were made, and the intercession held.
The country people crowded into Rome to walk in the
processions. Then the *lectisternium* was held, at which
the figures of the gods—twelve in all—were set up and
feasted by the contributions offered. The dictator
undertook a temple to Venus Erycina; the prætor, one
to Mens.

Everyone seems to have been the better for these
solemnities. They afforded a convenient break or inter-
lude, and some expression to pent-up feeling. Moreover,
the portents were now officially neutralized. As Fabius
correctly told the people, the object of these religious

**Religious
steps
taken**

---

[1] Whether these "Sibylline Books" ever really existed is a question. "Consulting the Sibylline Books" may very likely have been only a technical formula
for appointing a commission to report on the steps to be taken; their report
would take the form of an imaginary quotation from books that did not
physically exist. We all know what happened when at last it became necessary
to produce them!

actions was to free them from fear by spreading a consciousness of divine protection.

IV

Any practical success for which Fabius hoped, he expected to come through somewhat different means. He was careful from the first to consult the appropriate authorities at each stage of his proceedings. The Senate authorized him to take over the troops of Gnæus Servilius, and to raise further forces at his discretion from amongst the allies. For the rest it gave him a free hand to act as he thought expedient. He decided to raise two additional legions. These were enrolled by Minucius, and instructed to assemble at Tibur; while the legions from Ariminum were directed to join him.

The plans of Fabius were based upon a number of sound and reasonable expectations. Hannibal was cut off from reinforcements, and from any permanent possibility of reprovisioning his army. The very devastations he committed would destroy his power of living upon the country. A war of exhaustion could have but one end. The Carthaginian would no doubt have everything his own way if he were allowed to force a decision; he had already proved how dangerous his tactics could be in a war of pitched battles. The object of Fabius was therefore to restrict and hamper the movements of Hannibal, while he allowed the natural course of events to mature. The cost might be enormous; but it would in any case be less than the cost involved in losing another such army as that which fell at Lake Trasumennus. . . . If Fabius fought a pitched battle, he intended it to

Plans of Fabius

be in circumstances which would make victory a foregone conclusion.

Instructions were sent to the population of the districts through which Hannibal was expected to march, to abandon their houses, destroy their crops and stores, and to take refuge in the fortresses. Inhabitants of unfortified towns were similarly to remove to the protection of those that were better defended.

It was certainly a war of exhaustion for which Fabius was preparing.

V

Near Ocriculum he met Gnæus Servilius and the army from Ariminum. Before they met, he sent to command the consul to dismiss his lictors. Both the Romans and the allies, who had almost forgotten the meaning of a military dictatorship, were deeply impressed to see a consul, without his official escort, and doubtless on foot, approach to surrender his command. . . . He was dispatched to Ostia to organize a fleet to protect the coasts of Italy from the Carthaginian fleet, which was intercepting the supplies sent to the army in Spain.

The Pro-Dictator in charge

Returning and picking up the new legions at Tibur, Fabius advanced to Præneste, cut across country, and struck the Via Latina, the main highway south-eastward, by which he proceeded in pursuit of Hannibal. He went with every military precaution.

Hannibal, after his victories over Flaminius and Centenius, had continued upon his way straight into Umbria. The march from Perugia brought him to Spoletium, the great fortified colony which dominated southern Umbria and the roads leading north from

Rome to Fanum Fortunæ on the Adriatic coast, and to Ariminum. His path was marked by the complete devastation of the country. To Spoletium he laid a test siege. The decisive repulse he met with gave him a standard by which to measure the difficulty he would encounter in a siege of far mightier Rome. Turning east again, he recrossed the Apennines into Picenum. In the rich territory of Hatria he halted to rest and refresh his troops, who were much in need of recuperation. He had time on his hands. At Rome they were busy in electing Fabius and in carrying out their religious precautions.

Hannibal's circuit (i) Picenum

Hatria brought him into touch with the sea. He accordingly sent a report of his actions to Carthage. But it was at Hatria that he first showed signs of one of the serious limitations under which he was working. The Libyan infantry needed a complete re-equipment. He solved the problem by re-arming them with Roman weapons and equipments taken from the enemy. The plan was not without it risks. It involved a new system of drill and tactics for men who had been trained upon a different model—a hazardous experiment in the middle of a critical campaign. After a thorough rest, he began to advance southward. He devastated the whole eastern slope of the Apennines down to Apulia. He was at Arpi when at length Fabius appeared along the Via Latina, and pitched camp upon the high ground near Aece.

Hannibal's immediate offer of battle met with no response. Aware that he now had to deal with an opponent who must be taken seriously, he retired into his lines.

The advent of Fabius meant that the first stage of

the war was over. Hannibal would now have to work for his results. It was followed by a prolonged struggle for position. All efforts to entrap, trick or surprise Fabius were failures. The pro-dictator kept to high ground, never lost sight of the Carthaginians, and never closed with them. His troops were confined to camp, except when they went foraging, and then they went in force, and over appointed ground. A flying division of cavalry and light infantry watched over the Roman army, and cut off Carthaginian stragglers. By success in small skirmishes Fabius restored to his men the confidence they had lost in dealing with Hannibal's professional soldiers. . . .

Fabius in touch with Hannibal

These tactics gave Hannibal much to think of. That they did not destroy his fighting force—the aim of all serious military measures—may be true enough; they did not prevent him from going whither he would, nor from devastating the country. He carried his destructive activities across the peninsula as far westward as Beneventum and Telesia. But they quietly drained his strength and kept him on guard; and they kept the Roman army intact against the day when slip or chance should suddenly present the opportunity of fighting in favourable circumstances.

Such a slip was not long in coming.

The weakness of the Fabian policy was its cost, which gave Hannibal the opportunity to convince the allies that Rome could afford them no adequate protection. This point of view found its expression in Minucius, the Master of the Horse. His criticisms, both private and public, grew more and more pointed. They found listeners who were disposed to agree. . . . The diffi-

Opposition to the Fabian policy

culty was that Hannibal was presenting the Romans with a genuine dilemma; they had to choose the least of two evils, and the critics of Fabius could not grasp the conception that while the objections to his policy might be very serious, the objections to any other policy were more serious still. . . . It was necessary for them to learn this by experience—the bitterest, as the most convincing method of acquiring knowledge. . . . That the popular party would feel doubts concerning the wisdom of an aristocratic commander whose policy involved so much suffering to the people, was a foregone conclusion.

VI

Hannibal now heard from emissaries whom he had sent into Campania. Three Campanians, taken prisoners at Trasumennus, and set free in pursuance of his policy of liberating all Roman allies, had been persuaded to ascertain for him the state of opinion there, and the amount of support he might expect. They reported that if he would enter Campania there was a prospect that he might gain possession of Capua. . . . He was undecided. Their status was hardly sufficient to make their assurances more than an expression of personal opinion, which might or might not be accurate. Apparently they arrived in person to confirm their messages. He finally made up his mind to act upon their advice: warning them plainly that they must prove its soundness by results.

His plan, based upon the counsel of men who knew the country, was to enter Latium and to occupy

Hannibal's Circuit (ii) Round to Casinum

Casinum, a town on the Rapido, a tributary of the
Liris, where the Via Latina bent eastwards. At Casinum
he could block the Via Latina, watch the parallel coast-
road, the Via Appia, prevent help reaching Campania
from Rome, and force Fabius either to fight or to remain passive. His guide, misapprehending his Carthaginian accent, led him by Allifæ, Callifæ, across the
Vulturnus to Cales, and down to the plain of Stella. This
position bore no resemblance to anything that Hannibal
had been given to understand. It was a narrow pass surrounded by high mountains. He made inquiries. The
guide assured him that this was Casilinum, on the road
to Capua.

The mistake

The error was catastrophic. So enraged was Hannibal
that the Carthaginian in him revealed itself. He ordered
the guide to be flogged and crucified as a warning to
others. But he could not by any such means undo what
had been done. Fabius had passed the Vulturnus on a
parallel course to the northward and marched along the
spur of Mount Massicus, cutting Hannibal off from
Latium and from Casinum. Hannibal's plan had gone
completely wrong.

Hannibal
shut up in
Campania

Fabius was a good deal surprised at the turn of events;
for Hannibal was now cooped into Campania with
singularly little prospect of ever being able to get out.
Unless he elected to remain there indefinitely, the only
egress was by three easily defensible passes. . . . Had
Hannibal executed his original plan, he would have secured in Campania a free hand to persuade or terrorize
the allied cities into those secessions from Rome on
which he counted as the first real step to victory. As it

was, the army of Fabius, perfectly intact, was on Mount Massicus, watching. No secessions took place.[1]

Their absence was not due to lack of the typical Carthaginian methods of persuasion. The rich Falernian land between Cales and the sea was devastated down to the coast. The Roman army, beholding the smoke go up from that doomed countryside, murmured deep and loud. Fabius was not to be moved by murmurs. He held his hand.

The policy of the dictator made him dangerously unpopular. The army was generally in favour of bolder measures: and the criticisms of Minucius voiced its opinions. Minucius observed that the dictator had chosen an excellent seat from which to view the devastation of Italy. He remarked that the earth was becoming an unsafe place for a commander as cautious as Fabius, and he gently surmised that the dictator might find it safer to get off it. These acidities Fabius met with the milk of his usual mildness. Livy tells us that if a plebiscite could have been taken the army would have voted for superseding the dictator. . . . Fabius nevertheless made no change whatever in his proceedings, aware though he was that the feeling in the army was reflected in the feeling at Rome.

Unpleasantnesses among the Romans

VII

The summer wore through. The devastation of Campania, though it had shaken opinion in Rome, had

---

[1] Livy XXII. 13. The action of Hannibal certainly does call for some such explanation as Livy gives us. The plan of occupying Casinum seems rational and probable.

had no other result. There were no political defections. Fabius and his army stood intact, and Hannibal was as far as ever from the results he was seeking. He could not winter in Campania. The land produced luxuries rather than necessities; the corn available would not have lasted the Carthaginian army through the winter. The long-deferred issue had therefore to be met.

The dictator's system of intelligence kept him informed. Every probability indicated that Hannibal's retreat would naturally be by the same route as his entrance, through the pass of Mount Callicula. . . . Premature action might have driven him to some ingenuity with which it would be difficult to cope. As soon as he began to move (and not before) Fabius sent Minucius to hold the throat of the Appian Way at Terracina, in case of any sudden change in Hannibal's plans. Fabius himself occupied Mount Callicula and threw a garrison into Casilinum. . . . How wisely he had judged could be seen by the first contact of the armies. The impetuosity of the Roman cavalry, once it was unleashed, involved it in a needless reverse. . . . As soon as it was certain that the pass of Mount Callicula was really the route chosen by Hannibal, Minucius was recalled to rejoin the dictator, and the reunited force held the pass in its full strength.

Hannibal's situation was extraordinarily difficult. The Fabian tactics were coming to their full fruition. The battle which was impending would take place with every conceivable advantage on the Roman side. It was impossible for Fabius to lose. . . . Nevertheless, it was possible for Hannibal to extricate himself without fighting, though it is highly unlikely that a soldier, after

Hannibal's difficulties

surveying the position, would have staked a single penny upon such an event.

The Carthaginian army was now upon the move, filling the whole road between the two Roman positions. Hannibal's first test was to see whether Fabius could be lured into any tactical error. An attack by cavalry and light infantry led to an unsatisfactory conclusion. Fabius had his men tight in hand. They repulsed skirmishers, but did not leave their position. . . . The prospect was to the last degree serious. The only alternative seemed to be to abandon all attempts to force a way through the pass, and to cut across the mountains. . . . Hannibal saw that his own entangling methods were being used against him. He would be caught in narrow defiles with very little hope of getting out of them. It was in this hopeless situation that he evolved the most famous and improbable of all his famous expedients. It was quickly thought of and swiftly employed.

He is caught by Fabius

Night fell. When the troops had eaten, and all was quiet, the ruse developed. . . . The Romans distinctly saw the Carthaginian army begin to mount the hill-side by torchlight. It was unmistakably the rapid and excited march of men in haste. The troops who blocked the pass saw the line of light above them, and, considering that their position had been turned, they proceeded to climb the hill in order to keep in touch with this new movement. Fabius himself could put no meaning upon the Carthaginian proceedings, and kept close. In the meantime the Roman troops on the hill had reached the line of the supposed Carthaginian march, and found, to their surprise, that it consisted chiefly of frightened oxen with flaming faggots tied to their horns. . . .

The break out of Campania

There were Carthaginian light infantry about; but as neither side had much eagerness for an engagement at night, and the cattle ran in between them, both held off. . . . Day dawned, and revealed the Carthaginian rear-guard disappearing up the pass that had been left open!

VIII

Not only was Hannibal through, but with almost insulting dexterity he extricated the force which he had detached to drive the cattle. With the earliest dawn these light infantrymen were overtaken by a stronger force of Romans, and would have been cut off had not the Spanish infantry, who formed the Carthaginian rear-guard, been on the watch. . . . The Spaniards, mountaineers born, were expert fighters on such ground. They repulsed the heavier Roman infantry with loss, brought in their stragglers, and made a clean and workmanlike finish to one of the most remarkable military operations ever carried out.

The ingenuity of the Carthaginian was in respect of magnitude matched by the stolidity of the dictator.

Fabius keeps his temper

Neither sarcasm nor even ridicule could make the latter budge from his chosen policy. He proceeded to dog Hannibal over the pass and back into Samnium. The Carthaginian turned north, devastating the country as he went. He seemed to be marching upon Rome. Fabius followed him, keeping to the high ground. But when Hannibal reached the Via Latina he turned east to Apulia. Finally he settled at Gerunium. Fabius entrenched himself at Larinum, not far off.

The second chapter of Hannibal's adventures in Italy had closed.

At Gerunium he began to accumulate supplies. The town was transformed into a depot, while the troops were quartered ouside the walls.

Meanwhile, Fabius returned to Rome to celebrate a necessary sacrifice; in other words, to report and justify his actions. Not the popular party alone, but the Senate also, felt the most serious doubts concerning the Fabian policy. . . . It was alleged that Hannibal, in his devastations, systematically spared the property of Fabius, who was presumably in secret collusion with the enemy. . . . Fabius replied to the charge by an action more effective than any words. . . . He had entered into negotiations with Hannibal for an exchange of prisoners, of whom the Carthaginian had 247 the more. As these needed to be ransomed, he had passed the matter on to the Senate. The Senate declined to find the necessary money. Fabius thereupon ordered some of the incriminated property spared by Hannibal to be sold, and himself paid the ransoms. . . . When, afterwards, most of the prisoners so released offered to repay the money, he declined to receive it.

Fabius in trouble

Before he left for Rome, he had a serious interview with his Master of the Horse. He impressed upon Minucius, both as a commander and as a friend, that it was imperative to rely upon caution rather than luck. There was no luck knocking about loose in the neighbourhood of Hannibal, as Tiberius Longus and Flaminius Nepos had discovered to their cost. Minucius must not think that the events of the summer had been fruitless. Even to have held their ground was a great gain. . . .

Fabius and Minucius

Minucius, however, remained of his old opinion still.

IX

As soon as Minucius was left to his own discretion, he waited awhile to see if Hannibal would attack him in the favorable position established by Fabius; but when Hannibal proved far too prudent to undertake any such romantic enterprise, Minucius marched down into the lower country. . . . Hannibal was willing to meet him half-way. . . . Minucius succeeded in driving the Carthaginians from a point of advantage, and entrenched himself there. As he made no further movement, Hannibal resumed his principal occupation of gathering supplies. . . . Minucius therefore marched right up to the Carthaginian position, and at the same time raided the foraging parties. Hannibal was not strong enough to fight,[1] and needed to send for Hasdrubal from Gerunium. The advent of Hasdrubal caused the prompt retirement of Minucius. . . . Hannibal returned to Gerunium.

This action, indecisive as it was, had disastrous results upon the political position of Fabius. Minucius sent off a prompt dispatch to announce a glorious victory— news which raised the enthusiasm of Rome to fever heat, and caused the dictator considerable apprehension. He knew Hannibal's gift for creating a fatal atmosphere of over-confidence. . . . His disbelief in any glorious victory, and his firm statement that he dreaded such vic-

Alleged glorious victories of Minucius

---

[1] Hannibal was resting his cavalry horses in view of next year's operations— Polybius III. 94.

tories more than failures, did not add to his popularity.
. . . A motion was brought forward in the Assembly
to give Minucius equal powers with the dictator,[1] and
to request the latter to name a consul.

Such a proposal was, of course, a method of superseding Fabius. As he had been especially appointed by
the Assembly, it had a right to vary his powers; though
it could not have influenced the conditions under which
a regular dictator held his tenure of office. . . . Fabius
thought it best to avoid meeting the Assembly. . . .
But even in the Senate he found a hostile audience.
When he tried to make clear the military quality of the
Carthaginian army, and—since he was among friends—
expressed the view that the disasters of the last two
years were due to rashness and bad generalship, he was Fabius
coldly received. In the comparative privacy of the coldly
received in
Senate, at least, he seemed temporarily to have forgotten the Senate
those clear principles of religion which he had so well
defined earlier in the year, for he asserted the alarming
doctrine that Fortune plays a far smaller part in war
than brains and military skill. Perhaps he made his case
still worse by observing that it was a truer victory to
have preserved an army from humiliating defeat, than
to have slaughtered thousands of the enemy. Finally, he
demanded that his Master of the Horse should be
cashiered for disobedience to orders.

Socrates, when he asked to be kept in the Prytaneum
at the public expense, cannot have shown greater moral
courage than Quintus Fabius when he asked for the

---

[1] According to Plutarch, *Fabius.* c IX., the motion was a protective one,
made because Fabius was believed to intend to call Minucius to account for disobedience to orders.

cashiering of Minucius. . . . It says much for the
Senate that it contemplated him with indulgence, even
if it did not grant his request. . . . The dictator accepted defeat, by nominating M. Atilius Regulus as
consul; and as he did not wish to enter upon any personal argument, he left Rome to rejoin the army, the
night before the poll was taken.

When it came to the point, the Assembly showed some
hesitation in over-riding the authority of the dictator.
The senators, though they had collectively been none
too warm in his favour, did not come forward to lead
the popular movement against him. . . . Vague popular feeling passed into definite action only when it found
a representative in the person of Gaius Terentius Varro.

Gaius
Terentius
Varro

X

The Roman historians, with such excellent material
before them, would have been more than human if they
had not decorated the character of Varro with those
dramatic ornaments which make him the splendid foil
of Quintus Fabius. . . . The legend [1] is that he was the
son of a butcher who was in a small way of trade, and
that as a boy he helped his father in the business. The
elder Varro got on in life, and left his son the money
which enabled him to aspire to a political career. . . .
The son rose to importance and notoriety by his systematic patronage of the lowest class of citizen, and by
embittered attacks upon the property and character of

[1] Livy (XXII. 25.) hardly calls it more than this. He speaks as if the antecedents of Varro were not certainly known, and came down by prejudiced
witness—which is likely enough.

the respectable classes. . . . Whether or not this account accurately represents the career of Varro, it no doubt accurately represents the view taken of him by his political opponents; and this is the main point which, in view of the subsequent events, we need to note. . . . The intervention of Varro turned the scale against the dictator. The motion before the Assembly was carried, and the Senate confirmed it.

Minucius made Co-Dictator

Fabius was on his way when he received the dispatch notifying him of the new decree. He took it with impassive philosophy. He was the only person who did not regard it as a studied insult.

Minucius was by now in an exalted state of mind which boded no great good.[1] To settle the method by which the divided command could be worked was the first business. Fabius absolutely refused to accept the proposal that each should hold the command on alternate days. Finally, they divided the army between them. In these circumstances, Minucius insisted on separate camps and complete freedom of action. Fabius retained his old position on the higher ground, while Minucius occupied ground lower down nearer the Carthaginians.

Hannibal, who was thoroughly informed of all these events, saw the general action he so much needed brought appreciably nearer. Minucius resolved to fight. All that remained was to provide him with a suitable occasion. The ground was bare, barren and treeless. It offered no apparent concealment of any kind. Hannibal began by sending the Numidian cavalry to seize a small hill half-way between the two camps. He had no diffi-

The trapping of Minucius

---

[1] Fabius took the liberty of reminding him that Hannibal, not Fabius, was the person he had to fight.

culty in drawing the light troops of Minucius into action; and then by judicious feeding of reserves he brought by degrees the whole force of Minucius upon the scene. As soon as it was completely involved, Hannibal sprang his trap. . . . The night before, strong detachments of horse and foot had been concealed in the hollows which were common in the district; and Hannibal had relied upon the battle evolving direct from the first advance of the Numidians, so that no examination of the ground by the Romans would take place beforehand. He had been perfectly justified in his expectation. Minucius had walked into an ambuscade without any inspection of the ground. He was completely surrounded by the Carthaginians.

Minucius would have shared the fate of Longus and of Flaminius, had not Fabius come to the rescue. The dictator had anticipated trouble, and had kept his troops under arms, himself taking up a post of observation whence he could see all that passed. His advance changed the face of the battle. The broken ranks were restored; and Hannibal prudently ordered a retirement. . . . It was his first actual contact with the legions of Fabius, and he is said to have remarked: "That cloud on the mountains has broken in storm at last!"

Fabius to
the rescue

XI

Fabius made no adverse comments. Minucius, however, had evidently received a shock which deeply affected his views. He resigned his separate command and handed back his troops to Fabius. The dictator received the erring sheep with his usual stolid good humour. An unfortunate day ended in general reunion and reconciliation.

The result of this day's work was the sudden and complete rehabilitation of Fabius and his policy in the eyes of the army. . . . For this he had exclusively to thank his own patience and silence. . . . His term of office was drawing to its natural end. He transferred his command to the consuls, who continued, for the remainder of the year, to follow his methods of harassing and skirmishing without venturing on a general engagement. They were so successful that Hannibal, finding himself in difficulties over the question of supplies, is said to have contemplated the idea of returning to Cisalpine Gaul. He was restrained partly by the moral effect of such a retreat; and partly by the encouraging news of the consular elections at Rome.

End of the Dictatorship

CHAPTER VI

VARRO, AND THE POLICY OF THE POPULARES

I

By the time the elections came round the war seemed to have drifted into stalemate. To those who fought in it, and who had no means of foreseeing the future, its prospects must have seemed obscure, and were certainly controversial. A review of the general situation will perhaps demonstrate the real difficulty which was felt in making definite decisions of policy.

Problems of the War

Hannibal's hopes had not been realized. The only conditions in which he could hope for ultimate success involved the break-up of the Roman hegemony in Italy. No such event had happened, and none so far, was even probable. . . . Even the succession of brilliant victories exemplified at the Trebia and at Lake Trasumennus had ceased, smothered under the Fabian tactics. . . . But Hannibal's chances were by no means gone. He still possessed an army which was capable of winning decisive battles. It is true that his communications with Spain had been cut: but then he was in sea-communication with Carthage. It is true also that Gnæus Scipio's Spanish campaigns had resulted in an increase of Roman prestige; but then the war was not likely to be decided in Spain. It would presumably be decided in Italy.

All these facts could be read in two ways. They might be held to mean—as Fabius held them to mean—that a war of battles was to the advantage of Hannibal; for one or two decisive victories might yet start the political land-slide that would strip Rome of her allies, and leave her open to military defeat. A war of exhaustion was for the same reason to the advantage of Rome. If it were merely a question who could last longest in a test of endurance, the answer would not be Hannibal. . . . But they might he held to mean that if the defection of the allies had not yet happened, it never would happen: and that it was now waste of time to aim at safeguarding a political position which was not in danger. It could be argued against Fabius that he had hesitated at the very critical moment: that is to say, just when the results of the battles of Trebia and Trasumennus had proved ineffective to bring the allies over to Hannibal, and when rapid and resolute action was called for. . . . The systematic ravaging of Italy was now the real danger. Rome could put into the field a dozen men for every man of Hannibal's. It might be far cheaper in the long run to overwhelm Hannibal with the weight of numbers, and to crush him at any cost. . . . His dexterities had their limit. They would not avail against a knock-out blow delivered with all the force at the command of the Roman government, once it set itself the task. . . . But if the destruction of life and property continued indefinitely, the power to deal that blow might be lost. . . .

These two methods of viewing the facts [1] were founded on two different abstract conceptions. . . .

Alternative readings

The party views

---

[1] They are expressed in two speeches which Livy puts into the mouths of Fabius (XXII. 39) and Herennius (XXII. 34). While these may be merely Livy's own ideas, they are too self-consistent and intrinsically probable to be lightly dismissed. They may be—and probably are—skilful dramatizations of material historical in substance if not in form.

The policy of Fabius depended on the theory that brains could outwit numbers. It is easy to recognize this as an aristocratic theory. The policy of the Populares depended on the belief that force of numbers could drown the greatest skill. This is equally recognizable as a democratic theory. There was no way of deciding which opinion was right, save an actual test.

II

The consular elections were the field on which the battle between these two policies was fought. As the time approached the Senate directed the prætor urbanus to write to the consuls Servilius and Atilius Regulus, asking one of them to return to conduct the elections. The prætor was to fix any day suitable to their convenience. The consuls, however, did not think it wise to leave the army at such a time, and thought it better that the elections should be held by an *interrex*. The Senate did not accept this suggestion. It requested the consuls to nominate a dictator. L. Veturius Philo was nominated. The augurs found the nomination invalid on religious grounds: and the dictator resigned. The

Beginning of the Elections Senate then appointed *interreges*, G. Claudius Cento and P. Cornelius Asina, both of them of the aristocratic party.

This was the signal for a storm. The Populares charged the Senate with having purposely manœuvred the control of the elections into its own hands. A modern historian is more concerned to observe the ultimate results of events than to defend the Senate from such a charge. The intense bitterness of feeling with which the elections was fought is illustrated in the speech which Livy puts into the mouth of Q. Bæbius Herennius. He not only accused the Senate of attempting to control the elections, but he went further. He charged it with having deliberately caused the war,[1] and with having as deliberately protracted it, for the political ends of the oligarchy. The old patriciate and the new nobility were all hand in glove. Minucius had made it abundantly clear that a successful decision could be reached if sufficient forces were employed. But the full force of Rome had never been employed against Hannibal. . . . He reminded the Assembly that one consulship belonged by law to a plebeian, and he exhorted it to elect a man who would force a quick end to the war.

Election of Varro

There is every sign that some speech of this kind swept the Assembly off its feet. The aristocratic party had put forward five candidates, three patricians and two plebeians. The Populares voted solid for Varro. The five candidates, having their party vote divided amongst them, did not poll the minimum number of votes required to elect any of them. Varro therefore stood triumphant, with the right, as consul, to superintend the election of his prospective colleague! The tables had been turned!

The Senate was not beaten yet, however.

As the other consul should, in accordance with the constitutional custom, be a patrician, the aristocratic party at once looked about for a candidate whom they would not have dared to run in open competition. They

---

[1] The same accusation is made in the speech of the tribune Metilius, Plut. *Fabius* c. VIII. 3–4.

pitched upon Lucius Æmilius Paulus. . . . Now
Paulus had a past. . . . Three years earlier, he had been
mixed up in an unsavoury case in which a public inquiry was held into the mysterious disappearance of
certain spoils of war. He had been acquitted; but the
conduct of the inquiry had left him with plentiful lack
of enthusiasm for the Populares. . . . His friends, appreciating his feelings, gently but firmly pushed him
into the consulship. . . . A man somewhat indifferent,
somewhat embittered, but capable of obstinacy if he
were sufficiently annoyed, was just the man they
wanted. . . . They wanted an effective drag upon the
wheels of Varro.

**Election
of L.
Æmilius
Paulus**

III

The result of the election was in effect a victory for
the Populares; and from this time forward it became
a matter of course that the policy of forcing a swift
end to the war would have its way. Great preparations
were made. Eight legions were made ready. This was
twice the normal strength of a Roman army.[1] . . . To
feed it, the Senate departed from the rule it had hitherto
observed. When the Neapolitans had offered a voluntary
gift of bullion, the Senate had accepted one golden bowl
as a mark of appreciation, but had declined the rest. An
offer from Pæstum had been similarly declined. But
when Hiero of Syracuse offered half a million measures

**Victory
of the
Populares**

[1] Polybius III. 107. Livy XXII. 36. It appears that instead of two armies
each commanded by a consul, a double army, commanded by both consuls
jointly, was organized. Eight Roman legions of extra strength were raised (*i. e.*,
of 5000 infantry and 300 cavalry each, instead of 4000 infantry and
200 cavalry). The allies contributed eight similar legions, but with double the
number of cavalry. The total comes to 87,200 men: that is, 80,000 infantry and
7200 cavalry.

of Sicilian wheat and barley, a golden statue of Victory weighing over two hundred pounds, and a body of archers and slingers, the gift was too valuable to refuse. The statue was consecrated in the Capitoline temple, for luck, and the men and supplies were employed.

A certain degree of nervousness showed itself from the start. In addition to the official oath by which the legionaries were sworn in, the old customary oath taken voluntarily between themselves by the men of each century was changed into a formal oath before the military tribunes.

The preparations occupied the whole of the first half of the year. The troops were still in Rome when Hannibal made the first move. He left Gerunium and seized the fortress of Cannæ, where the Romans had a supply depot. . . . The old consuls, who were under orders to refrain from a general action, reported that their instructions were now impossible, and that the allies were wavering. The Senate replied that a decisive action should be fought as soon as the whole Roman force was assembled.

The consuls left Rome with their antagonistic policies violently defined. Varro had assured the Assembly that the war would come to an end the day he saw the enemy. Paulus said that he should suit his actions to circum- Differences stances. . . . He is alleged to have told Fabius that if Consuls anything went wrong, he would face the foe more readily than his fellow-citizens. . . . There is nothing inconsistent in the story that he assured his troops, on the other hand, that they could not fail. There had been reasons for former defeats; there was no reason at all for defeat now. . . . The Senate (we can see) might conceivably, after the event, emphasize the doubts it had entertained on the subject of a quick decision; but there is plenty of evidence that it really had entertained doubts. . . . While the assurances of Paulus to the army might be true, they did not touch the whole truth. They did not take account of the newness of some of the Roman levies, the tried and trained quality of Hannibal's professional troops, and the wizardry of Hannibal himself. . . . The opposite points of view remained equally valid, and equally undemonstrable by any argument save the cold test of events.

IV

Cannæ

The consuls took ground and dug in some six miles distant from Hannibal, but on the opposite bank of the river.[1] As it was good going for cavalry, Æmilius counselled prudence. Varro, however, when his turn came to command, moved nearer to Hannibal. He had to fight to achieve his new ground, and the day closed with the armies practically in contact. When, the next day, Æmilius took over, he did not judge the new situation to be favourable either for fighting or retreating.

Hannibal's own view coincided with that of Æmilius. In addressing his men he pointed out to them that with their superiority in cavalry they could not possibly have obtained ground more favourable if a decisive battle were to be fought. . . . They saw this themselves. . . . He advised them, therefore, to thank the gods, and

---

[1] See the *Schlachtenatlas*, which shows all the various ideas from time to time entertained by historians concerning the topographical details of the battle. The real truth was established by Mr. Strachan-Davidson (*Selections from Polybius*, and maps and notes therein).

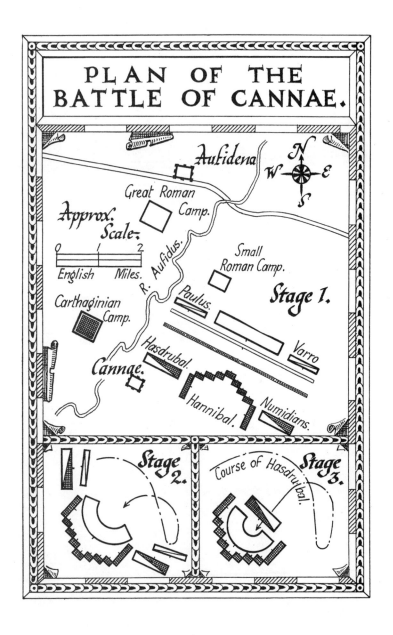

PLAN OF THE
BATTLE OF CANNAE.

Aufidena

N
W — E
S

Great Roman Camp.

Approx. Scale.

0   2

English   Miles.

R. Aufidus.

Small Roman Camp.

Paulus.

Stage 1.

Carthaginian Camp.

Varro

Hasdrubal.

Cannae.

Hannibal.

Numidians.

Stage 2.

Stage 3.

Course of Hasdrubal.

not to forget him, who had manœuvred the Roman army into this position; for the decisive battle, which would put Italy into their power, was now at hand, and there was no getting out of it.

Æmilius partially met the difficulties by throwing one third of his forces south-eastwards across the river Aufidus, where they acted as a threat to Hannibal's foragers. Hannibal crossed to the left bank and took position for battle. Æmilius did not move, believing that the Carthaginians could not retain their place long, for lack of supplies. . . . Hannibal was too wise to at- **The first** tempt to attack the Roman entrenchments, but it was **manœuvres** necessary to get the Romans to move. He sent the Numidian cavalry to drive in the enemy foragers. They did so, and carried their raid right up to the Roman en- trenched camp on the left bank of the Aufidus—a pro- ceeding intensely irritating to the Romans. The impa- tience of the latter grew greater; and in no one was it so great as in Varro.

By this time the nerves of the Romans were thoroughly on edge. As the daily reports came in, the city could think of nothing but the impending test. The crisis had the effect of stripping a mask off the temper of the whole people; and behind the confidence and urgency they had shown was revealed the deep moral impression which Hannibal had made upon them. Every sign and augury was seized upon as a prop to faith or an excuse for apprehension. Vows were made, prayers offered. . . . Nothing was too trifling to be thrown into the delicate balance of hope and fear. . . . The very eagerness of the army told its own tale. The men could not, would not wait. As Polybius pregnantly says, when a resolution is once taken, nothing tortures men like the wait before it can be executed.

Anxiety
at Rome

Hannibal, however, was in a very different mood. The story—which, true or false, records the tension—is that he rode out with his staff to survey the Roman position. There were 87,200 men in the Roman army, mostly foot. Against these, the Carthaginian could bring at most 50,000, of which one fifth were cavalry. . . . One Gisco remarked, uneasily, that it was astonishing to see so many men. . . . Hannibal replied seriously: "There is something still more astonishing which you have not noticed. . . . Not one of them is named Gisco." . . . Possibly the Carthaginians were as nervous as the Romans; at any rate, this made them laugh. . . . And when a general jests on the eve of battle, it is certainly a historical fact of the highest interest.

V

The turn to command was with Varro. He proceeded to come to grips with the situation. In spite of the dissent of Æmilius, he crossed the Aufidus and took position there, in front of the smaller advanced post which had already been established.

Varro
takes
ground

The marshalling was in the customary Roman fashion. The companies were ranged in three lines; but much more closely packed than usual, and the front line was deeper in file. . . . This was a clear hint of Varro's intention to smash his way through by brute force, and no doubt it was not lost on Hannibal. . . . The Roman cavalry, under Æmilius, were on the right, close to the river. . . . Varro led the allied horse on the left, out in the open plain. . . . But—and this too no doubt was not lost on Hannibal—Varro had taken ground too close to the river, and had left Æmilius too little room. . . . The crowding of the Roman cavalry was a tactical error of some importance, though whether it was the decisive error a modern critic is not quite in a position to judge. . . . The men who could have told us never lived to do so. . . . A reserve corps 10,000 strong was left behind in the entrenched camp, with orders to advance as and when required.

Hannibal had the advantage of being able to make his distributions to suit a surveyed position. He crossed the river at two places, and arranged his line. . . . From the evidence of the subsequent events it must have been arranged in a very purposeful way, with clear warning of all that might be expected of it. . . . He put his Gallic and Spanish cavalry close to the river opposite Æmilius: then, in the centre, a deep narrow column of Libyan infantry, a shallow long line of the Spanish and Gallic infantry, and a second deep narrow column of the Libyans; then came the Numidian horse out on the plain opposite Varro. *Dispositions of Hannibal*

If the modern reader, without foreknowledge of all that followed, can guess what these dispositions meant, he is wiser than Gaius Terentius Varro. . . . For although Hannibal may have improvised as the day wore on, he did not improvise his main dispositions. The arrangements he first directed in the morning were the trap that caught the Roman army.

VI

There was a little skirmishing of the light troops, testing all these dispositions; and as a result the battle opened with a rush on the Carthaginian left. The Roman *equites* were the flower of their class, and came to grips without hesitation. . . . But they were penned in, in a comparatively narrow space, between the river and the mass of their own infantry. There was no chance to manœuvre. They met full and square the whirlwind onslaught of the best heavy cavalry in Europe; they were borne away like straws by the torrential force of weight and numbers, and swept off the field. . . . Most went down fighting. Some—Æmilius with them—were thrown among the infantry. Those that got loose were caught and cut down by a terrible pursuit that gave no quarter.

Before this was over, Hannibal had pinned the Roman centre by advancing his own. The Numidians, out in the plain, kept Varro's wing busy in their own way. They would neither stand a charge nor drive one home, but hovered about indeterminately and elusively. In the meantime the centres got to business. . . . Hannibal's attack was an unusual one. His long line of Spaniards and Gauls bulged forward like a cresent. . . . Against this, the Roman infantry prepared to deal their knock-out blow.

Some points concerning the battle of Cannæ can never be known with precision. The tale, as Polybius tells it, is that the Spanish bulge, struck by the irresistible advance of the enormous Roman centre, began to cave in; and it caved in by degrees, till the Roman centre

Charge of Hasdrubal

Advance of the Roman infantry

was sucked as if into a funnel. The Romans went on, insensibly crowding closer, and the bulge gave way before them, until the two deep columns of Libyan infantry, facing inward, became two long lines enveloping the Roman flanks. . . . The astonishing feat had been performed of causing the Roman centre to envelop itself with a force little more than half its numbers!

Seventy thousand men, enveloped by forty thousand, could in normal circumstances have broken out of the trap by sheer brute force. But the Wizard had not finished yet. While the Roman centre was making its first ponderous efforts to adjust itself to fighting on three fronts, Hasdrubal and the Gaulish cavalry came galloping back from the pursuit. They swerved first to the other wing. . . . Varro's men scattered without waiting for them to close. . . . Sending the Numidians to keep them scattering, Hasdrubal wheeled now upon the rear of the Roman centre.

Return of the Carthaginian Cavalry

It was the tremendous arrival of Hasdrubal upon the Roman rear that decided Cannæ. The central Roman command was by now disorganized. Completely encircled, crowded tight, without intelligent direction to guide it, the great mass of Roman infantry fell fighting to the last before foes who even now were far fewer in number than themselves. Before long it was a blind struggle, every man for himself. No perfectly coherent tale of the ending of the battle of Cannæ has come down to us. The inconsistencies and contradictions of the narratives betray only too clearly the record of desperate men who had but partial and confused views of the nightmare which they survived. . . .

VII

Ill news travels fast. The news that reached Rome convulsed the anxious and waiting city as if it had been the last trump and the rolling up of the heavens as a scroll. . . . It was disaster; it was doom. To the **The news** actual men and women there, it had a side long since **in Rome** dimmed and softened by the blurring of the years— the death of sons, of brothers, of husbands. . . . The first reports spoke of the complete annihilation of the Roman army. The Wizard had breathed on it, and it had disappeared.

The Roman was not always a good man in prosperity. He might be—he often was—in his days of prosperity a bully, a blackguard and a brute. But he was a good man to be near when things went wrong. The Senate took hold with promptitude. . . . The habits of centuries, the dry decorum, the meticulous adherence to law and convention, the mutual reliance which saved any man from that sense of isolation which is the headspring of fear—all these things bore their fruit. . . . The Senate met in circumstances calculated to shake the strongest nerve. Nothing was definitely known. Their fellow-citizens had proceeded to take everything for **The** granted, and, assuming in the absence of information **Senate** to the contrary that their kinsmen were among the slain, were filling the city with that terrible lamentation for the dead which was one of the most nerve-racking primitive customs of humanity. In the midst of those collective emotions which can wrap men round and oppress them like approaching thunder and earthquake, Quintus Fabius rose to speak the refreshing words of cool common sense. He suggested that mounted scouts should be sent to collect information. As there were few of the magistrates left in the city, the Senators themselves must take over the task of calming public opinion. He advised that the women should be kept indoors, lamentations forbidden and silence imposed. All information should go before the prætors, and private persons should wait at home for any news affecting them to be officially communicated. All egress from Rome should be stopped. People must understand that safety lay in the fortifications of Rome. When calm was restored, the Senate could resume its sitting.

This was agreed to without discussion. The Senate promptly adjourned; the crowd outside the Senate house was cleared from the Forum, and the senators dispersed on their mission.

Time brings its revenges. Fabius, a short time before the most unpopular man in Rome, was now the most revered. To the awful glory of the prophet whose solitary voice has been proved by catastrophe to be the voice of truth he added the moral halo of the man who refrains from reminding his audience that he told them so. He uttered no recriminations. He took the lead in the urgent tasks of the day with mild and benevolent courage. The mere fact that he did so went far to determine the spirit in which the Romans accepted the lesson of the battle of Cannæ.

The people

VIII

When the senators reassembled, there was substantial business before the house. Varro's dispatch had arrived.

The consul reported that his colleague, L. Æmilius
Paulus, was killed, and that the army was destroyed.
He himself was at Canusium collecting the fugitives,
of whom there were about 10,000. Hannibal was still
at Cannæ, negotiating for the ransom of the prisoners.
. . . Appended to this, apparently, was the list of
casualties.

This was something definite, which could be dealt
with. The news that Hannibal was still at Cannæ was
of the utmost importance. Hitherto, it seems to have
been taken for granted that he would march direct
upon Rome. Certainly no army stood in his way. . . .
There was time in hand.

Varro's
dispatch

The casualty list was at once published. It plunged
the whole city into mourning: but now a mourning
of a more rational kind. The great festival of Ceres,
which was close at hand, was automatically suspended,
since practically every family in Rome was affected,
and no one in mourning was competent to celebrate the
festival. In order to prevent the total cessation of the
religious life of the city, the Senate accompanied the
publication by a resolution limiting mourning to thirty
days.

On top of this a new and unexpected dispatch came
in—this time from the pro-prætor in Sicily. His report
was bad. A Carthaginian fleet had appeared, and was
devastating Syracusan territory. On preparing to
render assistance, the pro-prætor found that another
fleet was off the Ægates, ready to sail against Lilybæum
and the Roman province as soon as his back was turned.
. . . He concluded by informing the Senate that they
must send help if Sicily was to be retained.

The inevitable sense created by these two dispatches, that the bottom was falling out of the world they knew, was increased by the religious scandals to which the attention of the Senate was called by conscience-stricken vigilants. Two of the Vestal Virgins had broken their vows, and what was worse, a man in priestly orders was involved. The somewhat distracted but patient Senate put this too on its agenda, and proceeded to deal with the cumulation of military defeat abroad and sacrilege at home. M. Claudius Marcellus, who commanded the fleet at Ostia, was ordered to send fifteen hundred men to garrison Rome. The third marine legion he was ordered to take to Canusium to replace the consul; and the consul at Canusium was recalled home. *Religious troubles*

The two Vestal Virgins might alternatively be considered either the dreadful origin or the happy explanation of the disasters which had happened to their country. They could, however—unlike Hannibal—be treated with sufficient severity. One of the two killed herself; the other was condemned to the full legal penalty—burial alive. The priest was publicly flogged by the Pontifex Maximus, and died under the infliction. The decemvirs were ordered to consult the sacred books. Their report led to strange and exceptional expiatory sacrifices. A Greek man and woman and a Gaulish man and woman were solemnly immured alive in a sacrificial vault in the cattle market. A commissioner—Q. Fabius Pictor, the historian—was in addition dispatched to consult the oracle of Delphi concerning the proper forms of expiation.

These extraordinary measures no doubt had the effect they were calculated to produce. Their solemnity and *Public opinion quieted* their horror awed panic-stricken and primitive-minded men into a general impression that the occasion was being dealt with in a manner fully commensurate with its importance. The Senate then took steps to satisfy its own sense of the necessities of the occasion. M. Claudius Marcellus started for Canusium. The Senate nominated a dictator—M. Junius—a levy was ordered, and by including for service even the conscripts who were below the legal age, four legions were raised. The allied cities were directed to make equivalent levies in accordance with the terms of their treaties. The equipments were put in hand. The temples were stripped of their trophies to hasten the process of equipment. It proved necessary to take exceptional measures in order to raise the Roman levy to full force. Eight thousand slaves were enrolled as voluntary recruits. Even in the stress of such terrible days it was prudently recollected that these, if taken prisoners of war, could be ransomed at a lower charge than freemen born.

Such were the earliest measures of emergency taken by the Senate.

IX

Details
of the
battle

What had happened at Cannæ meanwhile was revealed by degrees, in so far as it ever was revealed at all. Varro had owed his life to his position on the left wing, which had room to scatter and ride before the onslaught of Hasdrubal. Æmilius Paulus, who had been thrown in among the infantry, maintained to the last such resistance as he could manage to organize out of chaos. He and his dismounted cavalrymen were at last scattered, and those who could do so found their horses

and rode off the lost field. Gnæus Cornelius Lentulus
was the man who told the last news concerning the
consul. Æmilius, badly battered and covered with blood,
was sitting on a boulder when Lentulus came galloping
by. Lentulus knew him, reined up, and offered his horse.
The conversation which followed, whether true or
legendary (and it could at the best have come only from
the account of Lentulus himself) is famous. Æmilius
refused the horse. He preferred to fall with his men;
and he declined to face his fellow-countrymen after such
a defeat, or to excuse his own share in it at any other
man's cost. . . . At this point the rout and pursuit
overtook them. Æmilius, unrecognized by the enemy,
was shot down: Lentulus got away in the confusion: and
this was the end of Lucius Æmilius Paulus.

Death of
Paulus

On the field of Cannæ therefore fell one consul, two
quæstors, twenty-nine military tribunes, several men
of consular or prætorian rank (including Minucius)
eighty men who were senators, or eligible for the Senate;
and of the rank and file and lower officers an indeter-
minate number between fifty thousand and seventy
thousand—but probably nearer the smaller than the
greater figure.[1]

X

Night fell over a shambles amid which some small
unorganized groups persisted. The Roman camps were
still untaken. The men in the main camp got into communication with those in the advanced camp, but no
concerted action could be agreed upon. During the

[1] Livy XXII. 49. Strachan-Davidson, *op. cit.* p. 205 f. n.

night, however, a strong body from the latter sallied out and made its way to Canusium.

Had Hannibal possessed sufficient reserves, he might have rounded up practically the whole Roman army. But his men were exhausted, as well they might be. His commanders, in congratulating him, put before him this point of view, and advised that the men should rest until the following day. Maharbal alone dissented. His words have been often repeated. "To show you what has been won today, I foretell that in five days' time you will be celebrating your victory in the Capitol. Follow me; they will know you are come before they know you are coming."

All the world thought so. All the world expected Hannibal to march upon Rome. But the cool realism of Hannibal was not disturbed by this African flamboyance. He approved Maharbal's zeal, but answered quietly that his plans must be thought out at leisure.

Maharbal replied, in words even more famous: "The gods have not given every gift to one man. You know how to win victory, Hannibal; but you do not know how to use it."

All the world thought so. Titus Livius believed that this one day's delay saved Rome. . . . The world has had two thousand years to reflect over the problem; and it has gradually come to agree with the opinion which Hannibal formed in a much shorter time. . . . Moreover among the Carthaginian corps-commanders at the time Maharbal was in a minority of one.[1]

---

[1] Livy XXII. 51. The question whether Hannibal ought to have marched upon Rome is of course a famous historical problem. Hannibal's own opinion should be conclusive; but a good deal depends upon our view of what Hannibal

The next morning they went over the field of battle.
Cannæ is one of the few battles of antiquity of which
we get any of those details that fix it in the dry light
which the modern mind demands to give it reality. It
was no romantic dream. It was war in its full substance
and horror: "a ghastly sight even for an enemy." There
lay all those thousands of Romans, footmen and horsemen together as chance had mingled them in the struggle
or the flight. Some, tormented by their wounds, which
were nipped by the cold of the morning, raised themselves, covered with blood, from amongst the dead
around them. These were at once finished off by the
enemy. Some lay disabled with their thighs or knees
gashed, but still alive. These bared their throats and bade
their foes extinguish what life they still had left. Some
were found with their heads buried in the earth. These,
apparently, had suffocated themselves by making holes
in the ground and then heaping the earth over their
faces. A Numidian was dragged alive from beneath a
Roman who, unable to use his weapons, had torn him
with his teeth, and died while doing so.

The Battlefield

On such events, by such men, prepared to face death
and torment, and to inflict them,—men, generation
after generation, soon forgotten and obliterated—
Roman government was built up. . . . The fact has a
meaning; and perhaps, many generations hence, wiser
men than we or they will explain it with a clearness that
still eludes us. . . . If there be no divine event to which

purposed. In the past it has usually been assumed as a matter of course that he
hoped to destroy Rome and triumph over her dust. . . . Modern writers as
widely separated as the German Kromayer and the Frenchman Gsell take another view. There are signs that Hannibal was a wiser and a more civilized man
than he has been thought to be; and the more civilized we ourselves become the
more clearly we discern them.

the whole creation moves, then man is a very quaint animal. . . . He has sometimes seen as much himself.

XI

When the battlefield had been stripped, the Carthaginians turned their attention to the Roman camps. The water was cut off from the smaller camp; whereupon the exhausted garrison offered surrender on terms which Hannibal granted. About 5700 men fell into his hands. In the meantime 4200 men escaped from the **Prisoners** larger camp and made their way to Canusium. The rest surrendered on the same terms as the others. With another 2000 who were rounded up in Cannæ village, Hannibal must have had 17,300 prisoners.[1] At Canusium some 5500 men were gathered. The inhabitants gave them shelter; there was perhaps not much else to give; but a wealthy Apulian lady helped them with food and clothes.

A motley, disorganized, ragged and starving mob of Romans, thrown upon their own resources, proceeded by a kind of natural instinct to form a government. The young officers who were mingled with the rout were the sons of some of the leading men of Rome: young Fabius, son of the dictator, was among them. Publius Scipio, however, son of the consul who commanded at the Trebia, was chosen together with Appius Claudius to take command. A small amateur senate of subalterns at once sat to discuss the situation. It must have seemed to them very dark. Not much imagination was necessary to

[1] Ultimately; while a total of 14,500 escaped. (Strachan-Davidson, *loc. cit.* following Livy.)

form a mental picture of what was presumably even then taking place—the march of Hannibal upon an unprotected Rome: the collapse of the Roman state: the sack of the city, and the end of the story. To most of those at Canusium it must have seemed highly questionable whether they would ever see their homes and families again.

Men who make history usually do so in virture of an almost fantastic confidence. Scipio was a man destined to make history; and he appears to have opened the proceedings of his amateur senate by addressing it on the subject of How They were to Win the War. The proceedings received a sudden check by the rising of P. Furius Philus, who informed the youthful Patres that this prospect was rather remote, since L. Cæcilius Metellus and others were already planning to leave Italy and take service with some foreign King. **Publius Scipio at Canusium**

This news was worse than depressing: it was alarming. Men vary a good deal in the way in which they react to fear. The amateur senate dismally suggested calling a general assembly to discuss the matter. Scipio was spurred to instant action. It was no job for an assembly. Deeds, not words, were wanted. Calling for those to come with him who would, he set off with a few followers to find Metellus. He burst in upon the pessimists while they were still talking, and held his drawn sword over their heads. There he repeated his own oath of allegiance. "I solemnly swear that I will not abandon the Roman respublica, nor permit any other Roman citizen to do so; and if I knowingly break this oath, O Jupiter Optimus Maximus, visit me, my house, my kindred, my estate with utter destruction. . . . I de- **Scipio and Metellus**

mand that you, L. Metellus, and all here present, take
this oath. Whosoever will not swear, let him know that
this sword is drawn against him."

They were intimidated; perhaps they were ashamed;
very likely they were much encouraged; for they all
took the oath, and put themselves into the hands of
Scipio.

XII

Varro had ridden off the field of Cannæ with fifty
horsemen, and had reached Venusia. There, by degrees,
some 4500 men, both horse and foot, joined him. They
were befriended by the citizens, and provided with
quarters and equipment. Scipio and Appius Claudius,
on hearing that the consul survived, and was at Venusia,
sent to ask what forces he had, and whether he intended
that the concentration should be at Venusia or Canusium. The consul naturally decided on the latter, and
moved his forces thither. Canusium is five or six miles
from Cannæ; Venusia is thirty. . . . Moreover, Canusium was on the road to Rome. . . . Hence, thanks to
the young men, Varro could write to the Senate from
Canusium, reporting himself there with a force ten
thousand strong; which was very much more creditable
than at one time he could have ventured to hope.

Æmilius Paulus need not have worried over the prospect of facing his fellow-citizens. . . . Men are in the
habit of lamenting the disasters and tragedies that darken
their days; but they should remember that they give
Providence every encouragement to chastise them. They
are never so good nor so wise as in adversity. . . . It was
a sobered and subdued Varro who walked his horse to the

Varro's
reception
at Rome

gates of Rome, revolving in his mind his explanations of the great change that had come over his views. . . . His fellow-citizens had also changed. He was perhaps surprised to find himself met by the Senate and People of Rome in procession, and to be voted solemn thanks because in this crisis he had not despaired of the State.

XIII

As Livy says, if he had been the commander-in-chief of the Carthaginians, there was no torture that would not have been inflicted upon him.

CHAPTER VII

THE MORROW OF CANNÆ

I

THE morrow of Cannæ was a grand and a critical moment. The hour had struck! . . . Now was the time when, pushing aside all the childish hopes and ignorant enthusiasms of his followers, who knew no better, Hannibal himself, the Wizard himself, might look forth to observe the day. . . . Now, for the first time, he might with serious expectation hope to see the signs heralding the political earthquake which would bring Rome down into the dust. . . . If there were any weakness, any cowardice, any doubt—this was the hour when the results would be manifest.

Effects of Cannæ

Varro had spoken truly in his surprising statement to the Senate that Hannibal was negotiating for the ransom of the prisoners. If ever there were a time when Rome might, if she had chosen, have come to an understanding with Hannibal, it was just after Cannæ. The Wizard was perfectly amenable; he was even amiable. He made no attempt to wipe out the Roman survivors at Canusium. He offered to negotiate over the prisoners. More—he sent a special representative, Carthalo, to speak to the Senate respecting peace. He showed a spirit even more friendly than that which Pyrrhus had shown; and with less need, for Cannæ was no Pyrrhic victory.

The Senate refuses compromise

But the Senate knew that he was no Pyrrhus. It refused to ransom the prisoners. It refused to receive the

survivors of Cannæ honourably back in Rome. It ran
Carthalo straight off Roman ground, back to his master.
It definitely rejected the hand held out to it. The Wizard,
after crossing the Alps, had given out the slogan, "Victory or Death." Now, after Cannæ, the Roman Senate
took up that slogan itself. Victory or death it most
surely should be.

II

Hannibal lost no time in laying his results before the
Council at Carthage. . . . Mago, his younger brother,
proceeded to Africa in person. The interview between
Mago and the Council was sufficiently interesting and
dramatic to be preserved by Roman annalists and
through them—doubtless in an imperfect form—it has
come down to us.

Mago went on business. His task was to lay before
Carthage the excellent proposition that was now represented by the enterprise in Italy, and, if not exactly to
offer his fellow-countrymen a seat on the board, at any
rate to raise more capital and to indicate the value of
the investment. His report was therefore glowing; and
not without reason. Since arriving in Italy Hannibal
had fought and won three great pitched battles against Mago at
the main armies of Rome; two of these armies he had Carthage
completely destroyed. He had faced six commanders-in-
chief, four of them consuls, two a dictator and his
Master of the Horse. The most reputed and admired of
the Roman generals had won his reputation by the novel
expedient of never fighting a battle (a gibe that has
clung to Quintus Fabius Cunctator ever since!). Hannibal had killed two hundred thousand men, and taken

fifty thousand prisoners. The whole of southern Italy —Brutians and Apulians, together with a large part of the Samnites and Lucanians—had gone over to him. Capua, next to Rome the greatest city in Italy, was in his hands. For these great victories, thanks should be given to the gods.

Mago had not come without his bag of samples. He now proceeded to open it, and turn it out—and he heaped upon the pavement a peck or so of golden rings: part of the regalia which was worn by the highest class of Roman *equites*. He explained what they were.

Finally he pointed out that the nearer Hannibal was to complete success, the more it was to their interest to see that he was enabled to achieve it. He was in the midst of a distant hostile country. Immense quantities of supplies and money had been consumed. The battles which had destroyed Roman armies had seriously diminished his own. Reinforcements, money and supplies were needed for the men who could show the results he had illustrated.

His Report

Such was the report Mago submitted. It was accurate.

III

The enthusiasm with which the Carthaginians heard this account of the state of affairs in Italy was natural enough. They were not told—and perhaps they did not wish to hear—the other side of the case. Capua, Acerræ and Nuceria, on the main military road through Campania, had indeed gone over to Hannibal; but Nola, no unimportant strategic point on the same road, had not. . . . Neapolis, Puteoli and Cumæ, the Greek sea-

ports, remained loyal. . . . In the midst of their enthusiasm, they made one false step. It seemed a suitable
opportunity to underline things a little for the aris- Hanno's
tocracy. They inquired, with sarcasm, whether Hanno, invited
the leader of the old party, still disapproved the war:
they invited him to let them hear the voice of Rome in
Carthage.

It was therefore from a fellow-countryman, not from
a Roman, that they heard the other side of the case. For
Hanno—according to the Roman historians—rose to
reply: and he replied.

The reply of Hanno, as it has come down to us, was
one of the most shattering passages of rhetoric that
ever were uttered in a deliberative assembly. He said
that he still disapproved of the war, and never would
cease to do so until it was ended upon satisfactory terms.
Nothing would make him cease to regret the old peace,
except a new one. "This report that you have heard,"
he said, "makes you very happy. It might make me
happy too if we were going to use it as an opportunity
of making peace, for the only use of victory is that it
gets rid of war. But if you use victory as an excuse to
plunge deeper into war, you will find it nothing to re-
joice at. And what are you rejoicing at now? You have
destroyed the armies of the enemy, and you ask for more
troops. What else would you ask for if he had destroyed Comments
yours? You have captured his bases, and you ask for Aristocratic
supplies. What else would you ask for, if he had cap- leader
tured your own? And, since we are to understand that
the political dominion of Rome is broken, and Italy in
revolt—tell me if one Latin community has come over
to us, or one Roman deserted?"

Mago admitted that neither of these things had happened.

Hanno answered: "There are still too many left: and in what mood are they?"

Mago did not know.

Hanno answered: "Have any approaches been made to Hannibal for peace? Has peace been as much as mentioned in Rome?"

Mago thought not.

"Then," said Hanno, "you are where you were when you began. Some of us remember the last war, and its changes of fortune. We were never so near victory as when we lost it for good. And if any such change should happen to you, do you think you will obtain terms in defeat that you could not get in victory? . . . If we were discussing peace, I should know what to say; but since we are only talking of help for Hannibal, I fail to see why he needs help if he is telling the truth about his victories, and I am sure he does not deserve help if he is not."

IV

The speech of Hanno had no effect. A vote was passed to reinforce Hannibal with 4000 Numidians and 40 elephants; a sum of 500 talents was appropriated to his service, and Mago was sent to Spain to raise 20,000 infantry and 4000 cavalry.

Carthage supports Hannibal

But even if Hanno made no impression at Carthage, there was probably at least one man, at another place, who took in its full value—and that was Hannibal at Capua. . . . For there were elements in the speech of

Hanno that were of deadly truth; and yet the very truth was rooted deep in error. . . . Hannibal's answer had already been made. He had made it in his famous speech to the troops after his passage of the Alps. . . . And if we compare this with Hanno's speech, we shall quickly be seized of differences deep, fundamental and irreconcilable.

True as Hanno's words may have been, and affectively as their criticism may have penetrated to the mind of Hannibal, they implied premisses which no vigorous man would for a moment grant. First and worst was the tacit assumption that although Rome was prepared to conquer or perish, Carthage was not prepared to face the alternative, but must necessarily make terms. As Hannibal had warned his men, those who are ready to conquer or die will usually conquer; and if they die, it does not so much matter. It is one of the least depressing forms of death. . . . If Hanno were right, he should at once have taken the logical step of getting off the earth. There is no room on it for men whose foothold is by permission. . . . What terms could Hanno get, that Hannibal could not better? A very little thought would reveal the embarrassing answer. . . . Carthage should never have trodden for six hundred years the path of empire, if she was to weaken now. Having trodden it, she must accept the consequences, and play the game out to its end. . . . Hannibal's position had the virtue of lucid consistency. . . . Hanno could justify himself only by rejecting all he stood for, and by being born again. . . . As he had no such intention, his attitude was essentially false. He was trying to shirk the issue.

Principles involved in Hanno's Speech

V

Position of Hannibal

Three lines of operation were available to Hannibal: and to each, the key lay in just those sensational military successes which he quite recognized to be in themselves indecisive. Cannæ had brought a large part of southern Italy over to him. While this was not enough, it had enabled him to call upon the resources of the Carthaginian State. Little as this alone would have served his purpose, it combined with the similarly imperfect revolt of Italy to give him a vastly improved position. But more even than this, Cannæ had decided Philip of Macedon to make diplomatic approaches. There was still magic in the name of Macedon, the word which Alexander had written across the world. . . . One more advantage fell in to Hannibal. In the later weeks of the autumn of Cannæ, Gelo, the son of the aged Hiero of Syracuse, died. . . . The old man himself was over ninety. He had seen the beginning of the first war: he had lived to see the battle of Cannæ. . . . The plot grew thicker when Hiero himself died, leaving Syracuse to his grandson, a boy of fifteen.

Altogether then, although no single item in the account gave him all he wanted, Hannibal at Capua could count up a reckoning which in its total was of great promise. Its chief weakness lay in its multiplicity. A power that consists of many details is liable to be imperilled by the separate failure of the several items. But Hannibal could begin the new year with a sense of having made real and substantial progress.

Rome the chief doubt

The sweep which he had made through southern Italy during the autumn had ended at Casilinum, which he invested. He had spent the winter at Capua. . . . The pause was like the interval between the acts of a drama. . . . No one could be quite sure of what was going on behind the scenes. . . . The army of the Dictator Junius, watching from Teanum, now marked the southern limit of the Roman dominion. When the curtain rose, it would at last be possible to form a true estimate of the moral effect produced upon the Romans by the events of the past few months.

VI

The Romans, busily at work upon their stage carpentering, had troubles enough. The death of the consul elect, G. Postumius Albinus, in a battle in Cisalpine Gaul, was perhaps not so great a misfortune as it looked. . . . By the careful arrangement of the government, Q. Fabius Maximus was elected in his place as colleague to Tiberus Sempronius Gracchus. . . . A third special appointment was made in deference to public opinion. M. Claudius Marcellus was invested with proconsular power. The three were to command three armies concentrated upon the line of the Vulturnus, on the borders of Campania. . . . The whole arrangement was on a great scale. Appius Claudius Pulcher was given the disgraced forces surviving from Cannæ, and sent to Sicily. The Sicilian army was brought back to Rome, while Q. Mucius Scævola was dispatched to Sardinia. Varro was sent to Picenum to raise fresh troops. The war taxation was doubled. . . . The disaster of Cannæ had only spurred Rome to more vigorous efforts. . . . Two fleets were in commission; one in Sicilian waters, the other

Rome at work

for the defence of the Italian coast. . . . Reports from the two Scipiones in Spain were favourable. They were accordingly left to look after themselves, the Senate judging that the Italian front was the principal front. . . . The stage carpentering showed signs of producing a surprise for the audience.

VII

One cheering episode encouraged the Romans during the winter. Fabius Pictor returned breathless from Delphi, and marched into the Senate house still wearing the same laurel wreath he had assumed in order to pay respect to the god. His message from the oracle was excellent. A few inexpensive religious observances had been recommended as suitable to the occasion, and then the oracle had gone on to observe that it would look forward to the substantial expression of gratitude to the divine powers which the Romans would doubtless feel impelled to make by the exuberance of their feelings when their approaching victory was realized. It ended by an uplifting exhortation to put away wanton and ungodly living.

Favourable message from Delphi

The most cynical and worldly heart might well beat higher at the thought that the keenest diplomatist in the civilized world had put its money unhesitatingly on Rome. . . . The Delphian oracle was not often caught napping. . . . There was no reason to suppose that it would be, now. . . . The Senate passed a suitable resolution, and proceeded to the next business not, we may be sure, without a deep sense of encouragement.

VIII

There had been preliminary operations early in the year. Hannibal was early afoot. Casilinum, after a desperate blockade, surrendered on terms. . . . Petelia in Lucania, similarly besieged, held out to the last extremity. The government noted both episodes for distinguished approval. Marcellus had succeeded in holding Nola against all attempts on the part of Hannibal to take the town.

Spring was well advanced before all was ready and the curtain rose. From that moment onwards the course of events was complicated.

It began with the advance of the army of Gracchus to save Cumæ. Hannibal was established in permanent lines on Mount Tifata, above Capua. The movement of Gracchus drew him down. There was fierce fighting round Cumæ; Hannibal was repulsed, and retired again upon Tifata. . . . Fabius then took up the running. He advanced between Capua and Tifata, seized Suessula, and threw a force into Nola. . . . This strange change from the whole methods and atmosphere of the earlier stages of the war was due to new tactics. There was no longer any question of meeting Hannibal in the customary open field tactics. The fighting took place on Fabian methods behind entrenchments, and on ground carefully selected.

The precise strength of the protagonists began to reveal itself.

The first reinforcements for Hannibal reached him about this time. They sailed south of Sicily to avoid the

Campaign of 215 B. C.

Reinforce-
ments reach
Hannibal Roman fleets, and landed at Locri. . . . Even so
strengthened, he failed to take Nola. . . . The danger
of basing power upon multiple foundations was illustrated at this point. A series of separate events went
definitely wrong for Hannibal. His lack of success at
Nola, culminating in this final failure, was the decisive
element in a whole series of embarrassments.

IX

The mission from King Philip, headed by Xenophanes
the Athenian, had carefully avoided the Roman Adriatic
fleet stationed round Brundusium and Tarentum, and
had landed at the famous Lacinian Promontory, where
the great temple of Hera stood. Thence it proceeded to
meet Hannibal. As luck would have it, the mission ran
into a party of Roman troops, and its members were
conducted to the prætor, M. Valerius·Lævinus, at Luceria. The head of a Greek diplomatic mission was
Adventures
of the
Macedonian
Mission hardly likely to be a chicken. Xenophanes at once explained with volubility and plausibility that the mission
was on its way to Rome to negotiate an agreement on
behalf of the king. This was good news to the delighted
prætor, who at once offered a cordial welcome. He provided the mission with a suitable escort, and with an
itinerary which would take it past all dangerous Carthaginians, safely to its alleged journey's end. So
equipped, Xenophanes had no difficulty in reaching a
point from which he could gain Hannibal's headquarters. What became of the escort we are not told.
The treaty which Xenophanes came to negotiate with

Hannibal was a very important document. Its terms were significant enough. It was contracted between Hannibal, Mago, Murcan, Barmocar, all other Carthaginian senators present, and all Carthaginians serving with him on the one part, and Xenophanes the Athenian, on behalf of King Philip, the Macedonians and their Allies on the other part. . . . No mention is made of any government at Carthage. Hannibal and his staff are regarded throughout as the Carthaginian government, just as, some centuries later, Augustus and his Friends of Cæsar might have been treated as the Roman government. If this treaty ever came into effective operation, it would obviously, of itself, constitute a very strong precedent for regarding Hannibal as the representative of the Carthaginian State. It amounted to the recognition of his status as such by no less a person than a successor of Alexander, and one of the great powers of the civilized world.

The actual heads of agreement were such as to emphasize the importance of the preamble. It provided that King Philip should protect the Carthaginians and theirs, and should be protected by them and by—this is especially to be noted—such others as might hereafter become their allies in Italy and the adjacent regions. It was a close defensive and offensive alliance. King Philip, by Clause 5, was to give such help as should be needed or agreed upon. By Clause 6 he was to be included in any treaty made with the Romans, and was to receive back all Greek or Illyrian conquests of the Romans. Finally, by Clause 9, the treaty was not to be varied without mutual consent.

Treaty between Hannibal and Philip

Such a treaty as this was better than another Cannæ; it was, in fact, the kind of triumph which Cannæ was fought to win. . . .

X

But this treaty was not yet in the hands of King Philip: and it would never become operative until it was. If wind of its existence had been obtained by the Roman intelligence service, it would be easy to understand the closeness of the watch that would be maintained along the coasts of Italy. Xenophanes was accompanied on his return by three plenipotentiaries to receive Philip's ratification on behalf of Hannibal. . . . They got away from the Lacinian promontory without mishap. As they were leaving the Tarentine Gulf the Roman cruisers caught sight of them. The cruisers were faster ships than the Greek vessel. To hove to and trust to Xenophanes' inventiveness was the only safe course. By the time the Roman officers boarded them, the Athenian was ready. He explained in the most convincing manner that they had been dispatched to Rome by King Philip, and had been sent on by M. Valerius Lævinus the prætor, but, finding it impossible to get through, had come back. All might have been well had it not been for the Carthaginian envoys. Their appearance led to questioning; and their answers betrayed an accent which was sufficient to provoke a thorough search. A letter from Hannibal to Philip was discovered. The crowning touch came with the finding of the text of the treaty itself.

The prisoners were at once dispatched to the consuls. Off Cumæ, the squadron which conveyed them

The
Macedonian
envoys
captured

was intercepted by vessels of the coast defence fleet, and brought in to Gracchus, who perused the documents, saw their serious importance, and sent them under seal by land, ordering the prisoners to be taken by sea. . . . An investigation of the affair by the Senate confirmed the importance of the discovery. A war with Macedon was indeed a serious prospect! It had, however, to be faced. . . . The Senate immediately commissioned a reliable officer to ascertain the attitude of Philip, and if it seemed to correspond with the information obtained, he was to take suitable steps to check any hostile movement on the king's part.

The Senate and the Treaty

A very good story has probably been lost to history. We do not know the circumstances in which certain members of the Macedonian mission—probably the humbler—captured the ship on which they were being brought to Rome and showed clean heels to all pursuers. When Philip learnt the events he could not ascertain the terms of the treaty, nor the nature of the proposals which had been entrusted to the Carthaginian envoys. There was no resource but a second mission. This was more fortunate than its predecessor. The treaty was ascertained and established; but the summer had passed before Philip was in a position to move. The critical moment had gone by; for in the mean time other events had happened.

XI

The news from Spain which had set the Roman Senate free to concentrate its efforts on the war in Italy had, naturally, results of a very different nature in Carthage. Mago was already prepared to start for Italy

Events in Spain

with reinforcements which would have produced a considerable change in the situation: 12,000 infantry, a corps of 1500 cavalry, and 20 elephants. He was immediately stopped. Those who had most influence upon the decisions made at Carthage were of opinion that Mago could do the greatest good by throwing his weight into the scale in Spain. . . . Before this matter was finally determined another, and a very alluring opportunity presented itself. It was almost impossible for Carthaginians, with their bitter memories of the way in which they had been jockeyed out of Sardinia, to resist the temptation when they heard that the island was ripe for revolt if adequate support could be given the native chiefs. Finally, they sent Mago to Spain, raised a new army of equal strength, and dispatched this to Sardinia. Two armies, therefore, in their combination as numerous as the whole force with which Hannibal had originally entered Italy, were devoted to comparatively unimportant side-issues, while the main theatre of war in Italy was left to take its chance. . . . Had Hannibal possessed modern means of rapid communication, he might have prevented this catastrophic decision. As it was, he probably never even heard of it until expostulation was too late.

The Sardinian diversion

But the chance had slipped before it could be seized. The retiring prætor reported to the Senate that Sardinia was in a bad way; the forces there were weak and his successor, Q. Mucius Scævola, was on the sick list. The Senate at once dispatched an officer whose constitution was more suitable to the climate. T. Manlius Torquatus arrived in time. The Carthaginian expeditionary force had been blown away to the Balearic Islands by a storm, and took some time to refit. When at last it reached Sardinia, Torquatus had changed the military situation: and a hard-fought battle ended in the total destruction of the whole expedition, and the capture of its principal commanders.

That force, landed in Italy, might have produced very different results indeed.

XII

Hannibal, therefore, was confronted by a disconcerting combination of circumstances. The Macedonian treaty had, by mere mishap, drifted so late in the year that it had brought him no effective help when help was most needed. The reinforcements from home, which might have altered the face of the war in Italy, had been diverted to Spain and thrown away in Sardinia. . . . For none of these events was he responsible. . . . The most acute intelligence could not have prevented them. Having failed to take Nola, he had the alternative of waiting until the push began again on the same terms in spring, or of keeping the initiative by means of some move which would transform the war. He chose the latter course. He struck camp at Nola and crossed Italy to Arpi on the Adriatic coast, where he would be in a new position of relation to the Macedonians. . . . Gracchus followed, and took up position at Luceria, leaving Fabius to watch the Campanian situation.

Even though he had enjoyed the worst of luck, Hannibal was very far from the end of his resources. There were two factors in the situation which from his point

Luck accumulates against Hannibal

His resources

of view were highly promising; while as far as reinforcements were concerned, with time to raise and train
them, the recruiting field of the western Mediterranean
would yield him a fresh crop of soldiers. The fighting
season therefore ended with a break-away. . . . And
now let us regard more closely the condition of the
combatants.

XIII

The first of these factors which were favourable to
Hannibal was the state of Roman finances. The gravity
of the financial situation was brought home to the
Senate when the Scipiones sent their report from Spain.
It was a very optimistic—some modern critics think it
a romantic—report. Its optimism, however, was not
without some foundation in fact. Gnæus and Publius
Scipio had certainly succeeded in drawing to Spain
Carthaginian forces the presence of which in Italy
would have been an additional embarrassment to Rome.
. . . Like most multiple bodies, the Senate was better
at detail-work than at general views. A comprehensive
grasp of a complex and widespread war is the privilege of individuals; and the individual had not yet appeared, though he was on the way. . . . Still, the
Senate could perceive the usefulness of the work that
was being done in Spain, and it was ready to continue
the Scipiones in their command, and to give them all
possible support. The problem lay in the field of
finance.

Revenue was shrinking in an alarming fashion. The
men who fell at Trasumennus and Cannæ were citizens
and taxpayers. The advantage of a mercenary army is

*Financial
position
at Rome*

that its losses do not trouble the State treasury. The greater the armies which the Romans placed in the field the more serious became the strain on the non-combatant citizens, till, as the historian observes, they looked like perishing too, though not for the same reason.

The Senate therefore decided upon what was in fact, if not in form, a War Loan. The prætor was authorized to explain the situation to those concerned, and to ask for tenders for the supply of the army and fleet in Spain on a system of deferred payments.

Three corporations, each comprising nineteen partners, appeared before the prætor on the day appointed for concluding the contracts. They were prepared to furnish the necessary supplies on long credit. Their conditions were that they should be exempted from Roman military service, as being engaged on work of national War Loan importance, and that the Government should assume responsibility for loss by storm or capture. These conditions the Senate accepted. . . .

The difficult corner was accordingly turned. Hannibal had nearly exhausted the Roman exchequer. He would need, now, to carry through the somewhat more arduous task of exhausting the credit of Roman bankers.

XIV

His other resource was less liable to Roman interference. It lay in the political situation in Sicily. The death of Hiero had brought into power a Commission of Regency comprising fifteen members who occupied the legal position of guardians to the young Hieron-

ymus. Among the commissioners were the husbands of
his elder sisters. Hiero—a man of impeccable character,
whose respectability would have passed the test of the
most exacting critics—does not seem to have suspected
the existence of vulgar ambition or unscrupulous methods in the bosom of his own family.

Adranodorus, the brother-in-law of Hieronymus, had
his own game to play. He broke up the Council of
Regency by resigning his own position and intimating
that Hieronymus was of age to reign. Effective influence at once inevitably drifted into the hands of the
small circle who were connected with Hieronymus by
family ties. Their position needed no legalizing. The
three men who thus controlled the Syracusan State were
Adranodorus, Zoippus and Thraso. As soon as this
shifting of power had been accomplished, a fresh
change in the balance began to develop. . . . That
a boy of fifteen could adequately guide Syracusan
policy was very improbable. For years to come, Syracuse would in practical fact be governed by his advisers. Now, there were cases in which minorities of
this kind had been adequately and conscientiously
superintended. But they were rare. With a triumvirate
in charge, trouble was certain. It was not long in
coming.

Among the principal questions for the advisers of
Hieronymus was the alliance with Rome. That Thraso
was in favour of its continuance might be due to his
abstract and impersonal conviction of its benefits; but
the matter can hardly have struck his colleagues in this
light. They seem to have conceived a vivid picture of
possible consequences which included the supremacy of

Syracuse (margin)

Thraso with Roman support, and their own effacement. Once this fundamental distrust was created, the rest followed by an inevitable logic impossible to resist. . . . A modern student is in no position to pronounce upon allegations which might have baffled the investigation of a judicial bench. We can only say that Thraso was involved in accusations of conspiracy against the life of Hieronymus, and together with his party suffered the consequences. The charges may have been true. But the essence of the case was that the triumvirate, thinking and feeling as they did, were drawn down by a sort of gravitational force. If we did not know the rest of the story, we might have worked it out by moral mathematics ourselves.

The alliance with Rome

There was, naturally, after this, no resort for Adranodorus and Zoippus but a policy of approach to the Carthaginians. Hieronymus was easily swayed. Hannibal at once sent two trusted representatives, Hippocrates and Epicydes, the half-caste sons of a Greek refugee who had married a Carthaginian wife. Hieronymus was anxious—or rather his advisers were—that the negotiations should be confirmed at Carthage. This, perhaps, was a mistake. Hannibal would at once look further for a permanent settlement. . . . The process of intrigue and counter-intrigue was now set going; and where and when it would come to stable rest was the interesting question.

XV

Appius Claudius, the Sicilian prætor, at once applied for a renewal of the treaty of alliance with Rome. Hier-

Cartha-
ginian
influences
in Syracuse

onymus amused himself by asking for details of the battle of Cannæ. He moreover asked why the Roman fleet had sailed to Pachynus. The envoys told him what may have been the simple truth. The fleet had sailed south in order to show that Rome would not permit a *coup d'état* in Syracuse at his expense. The boy was clever, but not clever enough to understand the substantial ground for the action of the Roman fleet. He observed that he liked looking in that direction himself.[1] It gave him a feeling of safety. In the meantime, he would give the matter his consideration. . . . Appius saw how the situation stood, and remained quietly observing the course of events.

That very powerful forces were at work against Hieronymus is obvious. He was induced to break through the quiet republican simplicity which, in Hiero and Gelo, had reconciled the Syracusans to their personal rule. According to one story, he was even induced to propose to Hannibal a change in the treaty just concluded. In return for permitting Hannibal to retain the whole of Italy, when he had got it, Hieronymus wanted the possession of the whole of Sicily. Hannibal is said to have returned ominously civil answers to this remarkable proposal. Hieronymus did not matter much.

His assassination, in the autumn after Hannibal had moved to Arpi, was an elaborately designed and perfectly successful affair; but who inspired it is a historical problem difficult to solve. Political assassination was not in those days a custom of the Romans. Nevertheless, when the confusion was over, the party in favour of Hiero's treaty with Rome was found to be in

Murder
of Hieron-
ymus
215 B. C.

[1] *I. e.*, towards Africa!

power. Adranodorus found it necessary to temporize. He had to rest content with the minor success of securing election among the magistrates who formed the new government.

The position of Hannibal's representatives is difficult to estimate. That they were taken by surprise at the turn of events seems to be indicated by their request for a safe-conduct back to Italy. Nevertheless, they did not go. They had more important work on hand. The counter-revolution which they organized had two stages. After Adranodorus had taken the lead, the conspiracy was detected, and in particularly barbarous circumstances the whole family of Hiero was wiped out. The true protagonists then appeared. The formal election of magistrates was a complete surprise. Hippocrates and Epicydes were nominated, and their election rushed through by a packed Assembly. Whether or not it would have proved valid upon a scrutiny of the votes, no power existed in Syracuse capable of compelling such a scrutiny: and the election stood. . . .

Carthaginians in power at Syracuse

XVI

A Roman fleet of one hundred ships lay at Murgantia, watching. The Senate had meanwhile dispatched one of its strongest men, Marcus Marcellus, who upon his arrival thought the situation not beyond repair. He believed that public opinion in Syracuse would still carry the treaty with Rome. To encourage her partisans, the Roman fleet visited Syracuse. This was a mistake. It gave ground to the allegations of Hippocrates and Epicydes that Rome was exercising hostile pressure. The

appearance of a Carthaginian fleet off Pachynus finally
set them free to force the situation. Acts of deliberate
hostility towards the Romans met with instant reprisals. The case was then suitably worked up by experts in the contemporary art of publicity. Reports of
horrible Roman atrocities, a little rhetorical hysteria,
culminating in Hippocrates and Epicydes throwing
themselves frantically upon the protection of the troops,
worked the trick. . . . A *coup d'état* followed. The
Romans intervened to protect their allies. Epicydes
made a defiant reply. There was then no alternative.
Syracuse was invested by Roman troops.

XVII

Sicily in
Hannibal's
hands

    The situation had been magically changed. Almost
at the last moment the Wizard had fished an incredible
success out of verging disaster. By spring, he had well-
nigh linked up Arpi, through Sicily, with Carthage.
The link still needed to be made good; but a powerful
Carthaginian armada was already preparing to leave on
its voyage to Sicily: and at Arpi the Wizard was awaiting the army and fleet which King Philip was bringing
up from Macedonia.

    He had told the Samnites to watch for the successor
to Cannæ. It seemed to be impending.

CHAPTER VIII

SYRACUSE

I

WAR with the Romans called for a cool head and a strong nerve. The higher their difficulties rose, the more their mood rose to meet it. Confronted now with the prospect of war in Sicily, as well as in Italy, Sardinia and Spain, threatened from Macedonia, where the heel of Italy ran close to the Greek mainland, impassively they increased still further their army and fleet. Eighteen legions were placed in the field. A hundred new ships were built. A special assessment was made to pay for the naval expansion. . . . The two consuls for the year were the two best men they had—Marcus Marcellus, a hard, impetuous man, who never muddled his stroke, and Quintus Fabius, that wise and genial old fellow whom nothing put off his stride.

The war grows

Events at Syracuse had not reached their culmination when the news of these vast preparations began to spread in Campania. The alarm of the Capuans showed clearly enough on which side the moral impression was being made. To the Capuans, as soon as their unbounded hopes of their future glory as the capital of Italy had palled a little by usage, there must have seemed something horrible and inhuman in the patience with which Rome accepted an expanding burden of war, increasing, growing, towering until it threatened to involve all the world in one flaming Armageddon. . . . If it were

not clear yet who would do the conquering, it was plain
that the Romans were prepared to do as much dying
as anyone else; and even a hint of this temperament is
disturbing to more emotional minds.

The appeal of the Capuans brought Hannibal over
again from Arpi. He reoccupied his old lines on Tifata.
No other very definite objective brought him. He was
marking time while events elsewhere developed. But
he filled in what might otherwise have been a blank
period by prospecting for a suitable sea-port; and since
Puteoli was within a convenient distance, he went over
to visit the famous lake of Avernus, the name and fame
of which has reached most men even today. Visiting
Avernus was as good as any other excuse for surveying
Puteoli. . . . His appearance in the field caused Fabius
to hasten to the front, travelling night and day. All the
other Roman commanders, who had been assembled in
conference at Rome, dispersed to their several commands. The army of Gracchus was ordered to move
down from Luceria to Beneventum, to watch Hannibal's flank.

At Avernus, however, a new suggestion was made
to Hannibal. A deputation of private citizens arrived
from Tarentum, who thought they could undertake to
deliver that city to him.

There were considerable advantages in making Tarentum rather than Puteoli a port of disembarkation for
allies and reinforcements. It was much more conven-
iently placed with relation to Philip, and it was much
less under the eye of Roman troops and Roman fleets
than was Puteoli. Hannibal never pinned himself down
to sieges. He would not willingly have undertaken

the serious task of besieging so great a city as Tarentum. But the prospect of gaining it on easy terms was too tempting to refuse.

To carry out this design the Wizard had to "castle," that is, to change places with Hanno, his commander in Bruttium: and he had to do it while intently watched by three powerful Roman armies.

II

The move with which he started was provided by the municipal party-divisions at Nola. The popular party was hatching a scheme to dish the aristocrats by delivering the town to Hannibal; after which, presumably, they would reign in great glory and honour under his beneficent wing. The aristocrats got word through to Marcellus. All this provided an excellent opening.

Marcellus left the mark with characteristic promptitude. To anticipate Hannibal, he left Cales and in one day reached Suessula; after which he threw a force of six thousand men into Nola. Fabius supported him by advancing to Casilinum. Hannibal's march to Nola was therefore perfectly natural. The only surprising fact—which ought to have conveyed a strong hint of something wrong—was that the Wizard arrived, according to the program, behind time. . . . The sudden appearance of Hanno from Bruttium brought Gracchus instantly to Beneventum. Hanno was in force. . . . On the presumption that the whole objective of the Carthaginians was Nola, there was nothing out of order in the desperately contested battle which followed between

"Castling" at Nola

Gracchus and Hanno. . . . Hannibal himself began a movement which, on the same presumption, would be in support of Hanno. Marcellus hastily called up all the supporting troops he could gather, and detached Gaius Claudius Nero with cavalry to cut off Hannibal's retreat. After wandering about for some time, Nero returned to explain that he could not get into touch with Hannibal. . . . And the solution of the puzzle was that the Wizard had quietly taken the road for Tarentum, leaving Hanno in Campania to bar pursuit, and the Romans to congratulate themselves on their magnificent defence of Nola!

III

Fabius
hard
pressed

Capable though Hanno may have been, the departure of the Wizard made a great deal of difference. Fabius was able to continue his push at Casilinum. Even so, he found the task rather more than he could manage. He finally had to send to recall Marcellus: and he even thought of raising the siege. Marcellus dissuaded him from such a course, on the ground that it would have a damaging effect on Roman prestige. The two together succeeded in taking Casilinum, while Gracchus held Hanno off. The fall of Casilinum opened the way for Marcellus to return to Nola, while Fabius entered Samnium and inflicted severe punishment on the country.

These events, which seemed like great and heartening Roman victories (for the fall of Casilinum rendered possible the siege of Capua) were nevertheless not followed by any startling change in the war. Hannibal knew what he was about. He had a grasp which the Romans did not, so far, possess of the situation as a whole. He could leave for Tarentum with the full knowledge that impending developments would act on his behalf. The first restraint fell upon Roman activity when the situation in Sicily called for the presence of Marcellus.

The departure of Marcellus to take command on that most threatening front left the Italian war in charge of Fabius. If Hannibal included any such factor in his calculations, he would have no difficulty whatsoever in predicting the result: the war in Italy slowed down to careful and desultory operations. This alone would have justified him in leaving Campania to take care of itself. Sicily and Macedonia were now the points of interest. . . . As regards the former, there were excellent reasons why Hannibal should not cross to Sicily. His continued presence in Italy was indispensable to the maintenance of Carthaginian prestige. The eastern front needed his personal attention and encouragement. And by all human reckoning, Marcellus had gone to Sicily on a wild-goose chase which he might cheerfully be left to follow as long as he liked.

<small>War switched from Campania</small>

IV

For the task to which Marcellus now turned his attention was not one of favourable omen. To besiege Syracuse was an undertaking which most men would have preferred to avoid. . . . Syracuse had been a trap

<small>The Siege of Syracuse</small>

and a pitfall for many good men. She had broken the
Athenian empire at the height of its power. She had
seen Carthaginian armies melt before her as Sennacherib's melted before the breath of the Lord. Syracuse had
sometimes been captured—if we can use such a word
—in the confused scuffling of civil war; but Syracuse,
turning a united front to the foe, was a fortress impregnable, virgin and intact. . . .

The consul did not need to be a bookish man to be
aware of this. The history of Syracuse, though ancient
history to us, was contemporary gossip to him. He betrayed some knowledge of the failures of his predecessors by the care he took to avoid their mistakes. As an
experienced soldier, he delivered his first assault on the
city with promptitude, and with a vigour to which the
harshest critic could have taken no exception. In five
days he had his preparations made, trusting that the
rapidity of his stroke would anticipate all possible
counter-preparations on the part of the defence. His
main attack was on the sea-wall of Achradina, where,
at the Stoa Scytice, it reached down to the deep water.

Rapidity of
Marcellus'
attack

He would probably have succeeded, had not Syracuse
abruptly unmasked a defence quite in keeping with her
history. Her great soldiers and statesmen had passed
away; but the city of Gelo, of Dionysius and of Agathocles was not at the end of her resources. She pulled
out of his quiet study a man who was neither a soldier
nor a statesman, but who in mere intellectual power
dwarfed all the former defenders of Syracuse.

This man was the great mathematician, Archimedes.

V

Archimedes does not, by any natural right, belong to this story at all. He is an unexpected and dazzling intrusion from that world of pure learning which, though it runs parallel with the secular world, and from time to time deeply affects its course, is nevertheless withdrawn utterly from its temporal interests and excitements. He had nothing to do (save by accident) with politics or war; he not improbably regarded them as unimportant and irrelevant trifles unworthy of the attention of a serious-minded man. If he ever deigned to glance at the external events which occurred among the less educated but more numerous section of the community, we may guess that he regarded Marcellus somewhat in the light of a troublesome police-inspector, and Hannibal as an intelligent but illiterate young military man who might have been better employed. . . . His life was wholly devoted to mathematical study. Any list of the half-dozen greatest mathematical intelligences which have ever appeared among men would without doubt contain the name of Archimedes. He was at this time about seventy-three years old.

Archimedes

It is by no means certain that he even appreciated with any clearness the nature of the popular excitement about which he was consulted. That he was helping two half-breed Græco-Semites to defend Syracuse in the cause of Carthage, against the friends and allies of his old friend Hiero, very likely never penetrated to his mind. He was only aware that a series of interesting mathematical problems was being submitted to him for solution; and he proceeded to solve them with rapidity and effect.[1]

VI

The traditional interest in mathematics and engineering, first started by Dionysius the elder, had descended to Hiero of Syracuse, who, by appointing Archimedes his Master of Ordnance, seems to have secured to him the means of pursuing his studies, while at the same time ensuring that some of the results should be applied to practical purposes. The war-engines which Archimedes designed for Hiero must have been among the most remarkable in antiquity. As they were intended for the defence of Syracuse, and were constructed at leisure long before the need of them ever arose, the larger were no doubt weapons of position, mounted on permanent emplacements, and they were certainly of a power which would have been impossible

The
Defence
of Syracuse

[1] The popular legend of the learned but absent-minded professor, which, in all its varieties, has given great pleasure to many generations of the unlearned, had at any rate part of its origin with Archimedes. The stories of his eccentricities are still classics of their kind. Hiero, his friend and patron, is said to have consulted him on the delicate problem whether any unobtrusive way existed of testing the amount of gold in an alleged gold crown. Archimedes considered the problem, and was getting into his bath when the sight of the rise in the level of the water, due to his entrance, inspired him with the then original idea of measuring the displacement. His sudden perception of the possibilities contained in this idea roused him to such scientific enthusiasm that he sprang out of the bath and rushed off, forgetful of the unimportant detail of propriety, crying "Eureka, I have found it!"

This is not the only tale concerning Archimedes and baths. The mythologists will have it that when he was profoundly absorbed in study it was necessary for his servants to carry him forcibly to his bath, where, without noticing the interruption, he would continue to draw diagrams with his wet finger.

For the mathematical work of Archimedes see, *e. g.* Professor W. F. Donkin's article in the *Dict. of Classical Biography,* or Mr. Tarn in *Hellenistic Civilisation,* pp. 244–255. The method of raising water by the "Archimedean screw" was one of the most useful inventions of antiquity, and is today still in regular use in some countries.

for apparatus intended to be transported and used in siege or field work. . . . These engines were the difficulty which Marcellus encountered. He pitted the best that Italian brains could think of in the way of static constructive ingenuity against the work of a Greek whose genius was for dynamics, and whose inventions had some of that terrifying air of independent but impersonal life which invaders from another planet might show.

Sixty great three-bankers, crowded with archers and slingers, moved up against the sea-wall of Achradina to clear the battlements of defenders, and to convoy four huge floating platforms, fitted with protected ladders, which followed. The ladders, raised by ropes and pulleys, were to be rested against the parapets; after which the storming troops would step straight from their protection upon the wall, and hold it while their supports followed them up. . . . The plan was a most formidable one; but it was overwhelmed by the batteries which opened upon it. The greater mechanical slings began their titanesque bombardment at long range, and as the platforms approached the smaller catapults took up the shooting, while when the assault closed in the quick-firing "scorpions" swept it with their lighter artillery. . . . The confusion and destruction were such that Marcellus was obliged to withdraw.

Roman assault beaten off

Hannibal, taking his quiet evening constitutional by the enchanted waters of Tarentum, may have wondered how the siege was progressing. . . . Archimedes, to judge by what happened soon after, was in his study calculating the length and strength of beam, and the counterweight necessary for lifting a three-banker warship. For the measures which followed must necessarily have been improvised. Neither Hiero nor Archimedes could have foreseen the precise plans which Marcellus put into operation, nor that the attack would be by three-banker warships upon the sea-wall of Achradina. Archimedes must have designed upon the spot the particular mechanical miracle which most impressed the Roman imagination.

Marcellus renewed the assault by night. It was the only way of approaching the sea-wall as long as it was defended by those terrible mechanical slings. But Archimedes was ready as soon as Marcellus. The wall had been pierced for barbettes, and "scorpions" mounted to shoot at point-blank range. And now in addition a worse terror met the assailants. Great arms swung out over the battlements and let down chains with an iron hand at the end; and the hand drove men off the forecastles by dropping enormous weights upon them, after which it seized the prow. The engineer in charge then proceeded to lift the whole ship bodily out of the sea.[1] When he thought it was high enough, he pulled a cord, released the hand, and dropped the ship back. Some fell on their sides, some turned turtle, some went straight down with all hands. . . . There was no alternative but again to withdraw.

To the credit of Marcellus, he was able to see the ri-

Second assault broken

---

[1] Polybius VIII. 4-6. Most modern readers will have no difficulty in recognizing these articles. They were obviously what we nowadays call cranes or derricks, and their employment in loading and unloading ships is so much more obvious and natural than their use in war that it is a fair question whether Archimedes had not originally designed them for the commercial port of Syracuse. He would only need to design larger ones to lift whole ships. Such cranes, worked by counterweights, were certainly used for building operations in the Middle Ages.

diculous, and even the amusing side of this very serious reverse. He had been made a fool of, as well as beaten; but the joke was so gargantuan that he laughed at it himself. . . . That Archimedes was aware of anything humorous in the proceedings is in the highest degree unlikely.

Appius Claudius, in the land attack, had fared no better. The only variation he had to report was that the mechanical hands had devoted their kind attention to individual soldiers, picking them up and dropping them in a singularly undignified as well as extremely damaging way. . . . He lost no time in calling a conference of his officers. The attack was stopped. . . . It was decided to turn the siege of Syracuse into a blockade.

Land assault fails

VII

To add to the gravity of the failure before Syracuse, the Carthaginian armada was now at hand. It landed at Agrigentum an expeditionary force of twenty thousand infantry, three thousand cavalry and twelve elephants. Heraclea also was occupied. . . . Hippocrates, seeing that matters were quiet, felt that mouths could be spared from Syracuse. He slipped out with half the garrison; and although Marcellus pursued him with energy, he succeeded in reached Agrigentum. The united forces advanced to the Anapus, eight miles from Syracuse. A squadron of fifty-five Carthaginian ships ran the blockade into Syracuse harbour. . . . That city was indeed a place of ill omen to besiegers. . . . If Marcellus ever let his mind drift upon the fate of Nicias, he cannot have felt comfortable.

Carthaginian relief forces

Rome, however, was much nearer than Athens, and possessed a much more settled grip upon actualities. A Roman fleet landed a legion at Panormus, which slipped past the Carthaginians and joined Marcellus. The reinforcement was timely help at a critical moment. The Carthaginians withdrew from the Anapus, and their fleet, finding itself considerably outnumbered by the Roman, sailed off to Carthage, where it could select its own objective. The blockade of Syracuse therefore continued. Operations degenerated into a wrangle for the smaller towns: in which the Carthaginians had the advantage, and scored, on the whole, a larger number. Marcellus held on stolidly. The Roman certainly possessed one very great military virtue—an appreciation of decisive and crucial points. He was willing to wait almost indefinitely for the moment when he could deliver a decisive blow; but he meant it to be decisive when it did come. So the blockade continued.

Marcellus holds on

VIII

Though, from Hannibal's point of view, a slow, it had nevertheless so far been a favourable year. If Syracuse held out, as he had every reason to hope, the acquisition of Sicily would gradually be consolidated into a reality, the importance of which could not be over-estimated. He would acquire a solid bar of conquest from Africa to the Macedonian coast.

The failures which he had to subtract from his successes came to him late in the year. He had not, after all, acquired Tarentum. The promises made to him proved to be somewhat illusory. . . . It was difficult

for a Phœnician to cultivate a sincere liking for Greeks.
. . . M. Valerius Lævinus, at Brundusium, had received
word of possible trouble, and dispatched M. Livius, who
reached the city in advance of Hannibal, organized a
defence corps, and prevented either the capture or the
surrender of the town. . . . Hannibal took this phil-
osophically. He withdrew without inflicting any in-
jury on the country. He still had hopes. At Salapia he
marked out winter quarters. His cavalry collected
horses from the country round. Four thousand were dis- Hannibal
tributed to his troops to be trained to service. They took fails at Tarentum
very little except horses. . . . The war in Italy was,
for the time, dormant.

His second trouble was Philip of Macedon. Philip had
set his troops and fleet in motion, and had attacked
Apollonia. The prætor, M. Valerius Lævinus, had heard
of Philip's capture of Oricum on the way to Apollonia,
and had acted swiftly. Slipping across with a small detachment ahead of all news of his approach, he had
found the haughty Macedonians indulging in a typically Greek view of the importance of a war with Rome.
His armed entry into their camp at night was—to them
—a complete but far from gratifying surprise. King
Philip escaped in his shirt. The inhabitants of Apollonia removed the siege engines into their own town for
possible future use. The damage was more moral than
material. King Philip returned home to recover his Philip
nerve. . . . His likeness to his predecessor, the great fails at Apollonia
Alexander, was certainly less striking than it might
have been.

The urgency of the capture of Tarentum was considerably diminished by this disgraceful episode. M.

Lævinus—a very efficient soldier who deserves more notice than historians have usually deigned to give him —wintered at Oricum and thus interposed a new barrier in the way of easy Macedonian co-operation.

IX

As a consequence of the failure of the Carthaginians to relieve Syracuse, the failure of Hannibal to acquire Tarentum, and the failure of Philip to exercise ordinary common sense—all of them entirely separate and unconnected failures—the war, which up to this point had been fought at an unusually fast pace, distinctly slowed down. It was perhaps time. Hannibal had from the first set a pace which was all to his own advantage, as long as he himself could control the operations; but it was too quick for the allies and subordinates who had not the Wizard's touch, and who could not always guarantee their ability to be where he wanted them, at the time appointed.

The War slows down Rapidity in war is not an unqualified excellence. Like most good things, it depends for its virtue upon its relation to circumstances. At the beginning, speed had been all important to Hannibal. For its sake he had sacrificed half his army in the passage of the Alps, and had risked even his own life in crossing the Apennines. . . . But Cannæ had changed the circumstances. . . . He had needed, since then, to amplify time, so that the ponderous machinery of events might have leisure to go through its huge evolutions. . . . If he had been guilty of any fault, it had consisted in a tendency to forget this necessity.

X

The change which now became to the advantage of
Hannibal, became also, for the same reason, to the disadvantage of Rome. The very circumstances which
had made speed all important for Hannibal had (as
Fabius for one recognized) made it all important for
Rome to delay, to fight for time, and to drag things out
to their slowest. But she had dragged them out almost
too far. In and about this year when Hannibal allowed
the war to slow down, evidence of danger began to
appear in Rome itself. The first slackening of the call
upon her power and endurance was the first moment
when they showed signs of failing. And the failure was
of precisely the most dangerous kind—it was moral.
Now, Roman power was built on a moral foundation.
It could survive a good deal more material damage without being beaten; but a failure of courage, of honesty,
of public spirit—this was something it might not succeed in surviving. If they dwindled, unity—so carefully
preserved—might go too.

That wave of spiritual unrest, with which the present
generation has been familiar, invaded Rome. Why the
gods allowed the war; why, having allowed it, they did
not terminate it in a satisfactory manner, were puzzles
which tore the heart. The generation we live in can
better than most enter into these feelings and understand the results to which they gave rise. The Roman
casualty list already ran to more than a fourth of the
total effectives; and what such a list can mean, in the
shape of ruined households, broken hearts, depressed
spirits and religious doubt, we know. . . . It is of

War strain
in Rome

course a long time ago, and at that distance men look like trees walking; but so shall we, in due time. . . . On this state of affairs the prophets with new and improved religious revelations throve apace.

A religion—whatsoever else it may be—is the outward and visible expression of an inward mental state. It is therefore an index that in times of stress the wise statesman watches closely and anxiously. Roman religion was, moreover, freely employed in reverse to control and steady the public temper. Those outward forms which are expressions of the inward state can and do, to some extent, create the inward feeling. . . . Attempts to interfere with the prophets and mediums provoked resistance. The Senate at last took serious steps to suppress them, to call in all objectionable treatises on religious subjects, and to calm the public mind. But the mere fact that such measures had been necessary was itself a proof of profound spiritual disturbance. It is not likely that the devotees of the new cults were persuaded of their errors. . . . These things marked the first experience of spiritual difficulties which were not laid to rest until Roman religion had been utterly transformed.

XI

More immediately threatening were frequent accompaniments of war—troubles with the war-contractors. The state had accepted liability for losses by storm or capture. Rumours of "coffin ships," carefully designed to be lost, were laid before the prætor, and by him carried to the Senate, which was too apprehensive of offending the contractors to take the matter up. Action had to be taken by the tribunes, who raised the subject before the Assembly. The contractors, however, brought up roughs and rushed the Assembly. When a riot threatened, the tribunes prudently dismissed the meeting, and appealed to the Senate.

The action of the contractors overreached itself. Compelled to face the awkward facts, the Senate had no alternative but to resolve that an offence against the republic had been committed. The persons responsible for using violence against the Assembly were soon in jail or in exile. But the difficulty was that they had been punished for treason, not for the civil fraud of which they had almost certainly been guilty. If the other contractors drew any moral from the episode it can hardly have been more than the expedience of not being found out.

Such episodes as these were portents more ominous than the battle of Cannæ, for it was harder to think of the appropriate remedy.

To add to the embarrassments of the government, there were two other problems no less familiar to later ages in similar circumstances. The regional magistrates attempted to enforce a peace standard of morality among the women of Rome; but apparently, after making a few examples, gave up the task. Finally, it was necessary to set up recruiting boards, with authority to comb out slackers and to enlist youths below the military age. . . . The weather was noticeably bad. On the Alban Mount it hailed continuously for two days. As no one had any scientific explanation to offer, nine days' prayer was ordered.

All was not well with Rome.

XII

We get glimpses of that which was nevertheless holding Rome together. Most of them come from the lost
saga of Fabius Maximus which doubtless is the ultimate
source of those full details and interesting anecdotes
that survive in the pages of Livy and Plutarch. In the
minor war of petty loss and gain which went on continuously in the intervals of larger operations, the consul Fabius junior took Arpi. The story of the capture
of Arpi is an excellent example of vivid minor history;
but its chief value to us lies in the character-drawing.

Old Fabius had no scruple in seeking office as often
as he could, nor in achieving it by any means in his
power.[1] He had managed to obtain the consulship for
two successive years; he managed a third year by the
expedient of getting his son in, and then acting as his
lieutenant general. The younger Fabius was as mild
an *ovicula* as his progenitor had been; but with father
to advise him he gave no cause for complaint. The old
gentleman rode into camp at Suessula to report and
join up. It was an awful moment for Fabius junior
when, in the full glory of his consulship, including
twelve lictors complete, he officially received his father.
. . . Fabius senior rode stolidly past eleven of the lictors, none of whom had the moral courage to remind
him of the etiquette of the situation. . . . Possibly his
son at last caught his eye; for Fabius junior finally summoned up audacity to command the twelfth lictor to

Minor
history

Fabius
senior and
Fabius
junior

---

[1] At his own expense, the reader will remember. The Roman magistrate got no
salary, and his term of office involved heavy costs. Fabius junior's income came
out of the same family property.

intervene. . . . He was just in time. . . . Fabius senior dismounted to approach the sacred magistrate of the republic, remarking (perhaps not wholly without severity): "I wished to see whether you remembered that you were a consul, my son."

Fabius junior does not seem to have had many ideas when the case of Dasius Altinus arose. That very slippery customer appeared in camp one night with a suggestion. He was prepared, for a consideration, to place Arpi in the consul's hand. Fabius junior laid the matter before a conference of officers. A good deal of frank speaking took place. It was observed that Dasius was the man who had originally sold Arpi to Hannibal; and now, seeing that there was opportunity for another deal, he was proposing to sell it back to Rome. He was a traitor, a man who wanted to run with the hare and hunt with the hounds. He ought to be dealt with as a deserter; he ought to be dealt with like the man who offered to poison Pyrrhus. It was then that Fabius senior offered a few illuminating comments.

He said that a good deal depended on circumstances. The task before them was to prevent their allies from going over to Hannibal; but apparently all they thought of was to make an example of repentant sinners. If, however, a man were free to secede from Rome, and not free to change his mind and come back again, all Italy would soon be Carthaginian. . . . Fabius senior advised interning the untrustworthy citizen in some safe place. When the war was over, they could discuss at length exactly how far the crime of his secession was counterbalanced by the virtue of returning to his allegiance.

Views of Fabius senior

Whether or not Fabius ever used the words put into
his mouth by the historian, those words are attributed
to him, and are perfectly in keeping with his traditional
character. . . . They throw a flood of light upon, at
least, the motives which the Romans believed to sway
the actions of the men who fought Hannibal. . . . The
cool dispassion of Fabius carried the day. Dasius was
kept under arrest; Arpi was captured.[1] . . . But the
position which Fabius took up covered more than Dasius
Altinius. It covered the whole relation of Rome with
her allies.[2]

XIII

The new
current

After its pause, the war began to quicken again. A
new current was setting in. Its first movements were
hardly visible. Perhaps the first sign of its existence was
the fact that young Publius Scipio took up his first magistracy, as curule ædile. It was Rome now which was
pressed for time; and Hannibal who could afford to spin
it out. But it remained to be seen in what form Rome
would express its consciousness that it needed to hasten.

Hannibal had not been deceived. Patience, intrigue
and promptitude at last brought Tarentum into his
hands. He had for some time been in touch with a party
within the walls. The impulse which gave him what he
wanted came, however, from the strained nerves and
imprudent severity of men who had not the dispassion
of Fabius. The representatives of Tarentum and Thurii
were kept under a light surveillance in Rome. Even a

[1] Only one life was lost. (Livy XXIV. 47.) The Carthaginian garrison was
allowed to march out with the honours of war.

[2] One hundred and twelve of the aristocratic party of Capua surrendered in
the course of the year. The Romans received them without demur.

very mild restraint got upon their nerves. They made
an attempt to escape, were recaptured, flogged, and
thrown off the Tarpeian rock.

In Greek eyes such a punishment seemed—and not
without reason—a startling atrocity. The friends of the
victims were soon in touch with Hannibal. With their
help, he surprised the city by night. To capture the
citadel with its Roman garrison was a much more difficult task. He could invest it by land; but reinforcements and supplies could always be thrown in by sea.
The prize would slip out of his hands unless he could
solve the serious problem of the citadel. He asked for
ships.

The surprised Tarentines advised him to get ships
from Carthage, for the citadel commanded the mouth
of the harbour, and their own ships were securely shut
in. Hannibal explained his plan. If they would supply
the ships, he would provide a method of getting them
to the sea. He was good as his word. He ran the Tarentine ships overland on lorries, and soon had a sea blockade in being; after which, the Roman garrison being
effectively isolated, he was free to move.

The necessity that he should preserve his ability to
strike was due to the situation at Capua. Urgent word
reached him that famine impended in Capua. The Roman armies of observation had very carefully destroyed
all the harvests, and had obstructed supplies. Hannibal
ordered Mago to reprovision the city. Mago made his
depot at Beneventum. To his indignation, the Capuans
turned up in very small numbers. After expressing his
opinion of them, he appointed another day for them
to come with adequate transport to receive their sup-

Hannibal gains Tarentum

Failure to re-provision Capua

plies. Before this day came, the consul Quintus Fulvius
Flaccus made a rapid march, stormed the defences and
gutted the depot. The stores meant for Capua fell into
the hands of the Romans. Mago retreated to Bruttium.
. . . Wild prayers for help reached Hannibal from distracted Capua. Hannibal promised to come in person.

XIV

His arrival in Campania put the Roman armies upon
the defensive. After the first engagement, in which they
lost heavily, they retired upon their lines. Hannibal
pursued the retreating army of the consul Appius
Claudius; wiped out an odd corps which he met on the
way; turned into Apulia, and inflicted a crushing defeat upon Gnæus Fulvus Flaccus—a considerable battle,
in which the Roman losses reached some ten thousand
men. . . . These were serious reverses for Rome. To
make matters worse, Tiberius Gracchus fell in a skir-
mish, and his army dispersed. Hannibal swept round
upon Brundusium very suddenly. Here, however, fresh
messages reached him from Capua. . . . The wretched
Capuans implored him to come and help them. Thoroughly angry, he told them that he had already raised
Position of the siege of Capua. None the less, he promised to come
Capua again. The envoys had difficulty in getting back to
Capua. . . . For their story was true. . . . The consuls were building a great supply depot at Casilinum
and bringing supplies up the Vulturnus. A double fortified wall was being built around Capua—an immense
work which ringed the city round with impregnable
lines of investment. . . . It was indeed hard to help

the Capuans, who seemed to have an inherent incapacity for being helped: but Hannibal was wanted.

Not only Tarentum, but Thurii and Metapontum fell into his hands this year. He had but narrowly missed taking Brundusium when he was called off. The task before him was to keep the Roman armies ineffectually before Capua until the siege of Syracuse collapsed as all previous sieges had collapsed. . . . The withdrawal of the Romans from Sicily would mean the opening of the gates for a flood of Carthaginian reinforcements and supplies to be poured into Italy. . . . The fate of the Athenian expedition was historic. That of the Roman expedition might be still more historic, for he knew how to take full advantage of it. . . .

XV

Such was the situation when the unexpected happened. The impregnable Syracuse fell.

The unexpected

CHAPTER IX

THE VORTEX

I

THE fall of Syracuse was the first fruits of the Roman
effort to force the war. Though the Romans had proved
unable to hold their own in a war of manœuvre, and
although even their obstinate endurance showed signs
of giving way under stress, there was nevertheless a
mode of fighting in which (at any rate, as a start)
their capacity for endurance could be transformed into
almost an active quality. The investment of Capua
showed that Roman commanders had realized where
their strength lay.

The struggle for Syracuse had been governed by one
military fact of cardinal importance. Rome was much
nearer than Athens. She was in a position to feed and
reinforce her besieging army with a readiness that had
never been within the power of the latter. . . . Rome,
as we shall presently see, was destined to have her "Syracusan expedition," and its doom was even now impending; but the catastrophe did not happen at Syracuse,
and its effects were not to be similar to those of the
disaster that befell Nicias.

Marcellus had not been wholly successful in establishing an effective blockade. Supplies still entered Syracuse in quantities sufficient to enable the city to hold
out. But as long as the besieging army could be maintained in full strength and health, it was ready to seize

THE HOUSE OF SCIPIO

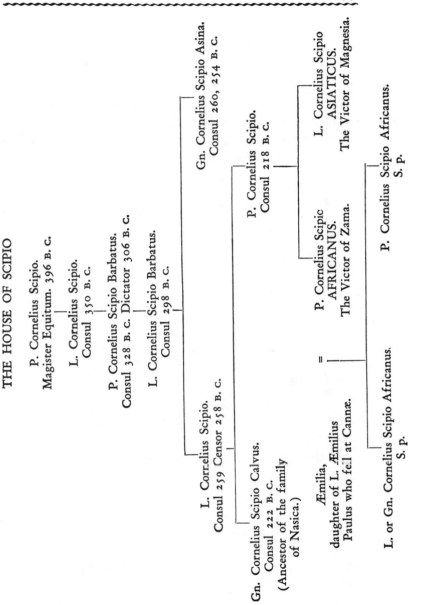

P. Cornelius Scipio.
Magister Equitum. 396 B. C.

L. Cornelius Scipio.
Consul 350 B. C.

P. Cornelius Scipio Barbatus.
Consul 328 B. C. Dictator 306 B. C.

L. Cornelius Scipio Barbatus.
Consul 298 B. C.

Gn. Cornelius Scipio Asina.
Consul 260, 254 B. C.

L. Cornelius Scipio.
Consul 259 Censor 258 B. C.

Gn. Cornelius Scipio Calvus.
Consul 222 B. C.
(Ancestor of the family
of Nasica.)

P. Cornelius Scipio.
Consul 218 B. C.

L. Cornelius Scipio
ASIATICUS.
The Victor of Magnesia.

P. Cornelius Scipic
AFRICANUS.
The Victor of Zama.

=

Æmilia,
daughter of L. Æmilius
Paulus who fell at Cannæ.

P. Cornelius Scipio Africanus.
S. P.

L. or Gn. Cornelius Scipio Africanus.
S. P.

its opportunities. Hence any calculation upon Hannibal's part that the Romans would eventually be forced
to withdraw, while true enough, depended for its fulfilment upon a vigilant defence of the city. . . . There
was, indeed, an unmistakable prospect that if the siege
were dragged out indefinitely it would collapse as part
of a general break-down on the Roman side. . . . But
this time never came. . . .

II

One of the disconcerting elements in human life is
the way in which broad reasoning can sometimes be
falsified by trifling factors almost too small to be taken
into the reckoning. The fall of Syracuse evolved from
such an assemblage of very trifling facts. Epicydes was
particularly anxious to secure the exchange of one of
The
negotiations
with
Epicydes
his diplomatic agents who had become a prisoner of
war. It was the purest accident that during the somewhat protracted negotiations a Roman officer, waiting
close in by the gates, idly counted the courses of masonry
on the wall, and multiplied the depth of the bottom
course by the number obtained. The result so surprised
him that he reported it. When Marcellus heard the report he took it seriously. The wall at the place in question must be not only much lower than elsewhere, but
capable of direct access by scaling. . . . So much history has seldom turned on the human habit of counting.

The wall, being weak, was guarded with extra care.
But here a crowd of trifles thronged to lend their help.
The blockade, partly ineffective, had permitted Syra-
cuse to be better supplied with wine than with bread. A

holiday intervened; and in such circumstances festivi-
ties are liable to be conducted with the wine rather than
with the bread. . . . Such were the antecedents of that
night after the holiday, when a picked corps of Roman
storm-troops unostentatiously brought up the ladders.

III

Epicydes could not credit his ears when the frantic
message reached him that the Romans were in. Hurry-
ing to the spot with a small patrol, he found that they
were indeed in. But their entrance was only the beginning of their troubles. Syracuse, owing to the epi-
sodic way in which it had been built, was at least three
separate cities, each with its fortified wall. . . . There
is a famous story that Marcellus, standing upon the high
ground of Epipolæ, was moved to tears when he gazed
down on the wonderful panorama below him. He had
good reason for emotion: for he had done one of those The
deeds which turn the course of human destiny. On that scaling of
ground on which Nicias and the Athenians had per- Syracuse.
ished, he had overcome difficulties greater than those
which had overcome them; for he had beaten in addition the engines of Hiero and the tremendous fortifications of Dionysius. . . . He was not a great general:
he was not even a great man. But he was a much nobler
work of God: a man who seized his opportunities.

A protracted effort was necessary to make good the
Roman footing. The strong fortress of Euryalus, built
at the apex of the triangle of Epipolæ, was the first
objective. Its surrender went far to determine the
result. Appreciating the transcendent importance of the

stake at issue, the Carthaginian admiral slipped out of
harbour on a stormy night with a squadron of thirty-
five ships, and raced for home. He was back in a few
days' time with a fleet of a hundred ships. More were
being equipped with headlong haste. Carthaginian
troops from Agrigentum were also brought up. The
reinforcement did not loosen the grip of Marcellus upon
the city. Then that calamity which once had turned
back Sennacherib from Jerusalem, and had dissolved
many a Carthaginian army of old days in Sicily, fell
upon them. Pestilence broke out—worse for the Carthaginians than for the Romans. It raged so destruc-
tively that both Hippocrates and the Carthaginian
commander Himilco perished. . . . The admiral hastened back to Carthage. He returned with a fresh fleet
of a hundred and thirty ships convoying seven hundred
transports. But the very stars in their courses fought
against Carthage. The fleet, held up by the wind, could
not—or said it could not—get round Pachynus. . . .
It is possible that something else was weighing in the
admiral's judgment: and that was the prospect of landing fresh reinforcements in a plague-stricken area. Epicydes hastened in person to him and persuaded him to
stand by, and to risk an engagement even with the Roman fleet in possession of the weather gauge. A volunteer army was being raised among the Sicilian Greeks for
the relief of Syracuse. All was not lost.

Marcellus, once he had grasped his opportunity, let
nothing slip from his fingers. He kept his fleet observing
the Carthaginians at Pachynus. All depended upon the
decisions of the Carthaginian admiral. . . . Precisely
what swayed him we shall never know. It may be that

he disliked the political opinions of the Greek volunteer
army of relief. It may be that the Carthaginian habit
of punishing unsuccessful commanders exercised its The
fatal effect in making him unwilling to run risks. . . . Carthaginians
At any rate, when the east wind dropped, instead of withdraw
steering for Syracuse he sent back the transports and
sailed for Tarentum and Hannibal.

IV

What reception he got from Hannibal—if any—no
historian has recorded. But as soon as the news was
known—together with the consequent flight of Epicydes to Agrigentum—the volunteer army opened negotiations with Marcellus. They obtained the offer of
satisfactory terms. Their next step was to establish communication with the Syracusans, and to persuade them
to share in the terms. This the Syracusans—seeing nothing else for it—agreed to do. There were immediate
difficulties with the mercenaries and the deserters from
the Roman army—the latter apparently a considerable
element in the garrison. The mercenaries, however, were
induced ultimately to listen to reason. Syracuse then
made a somewhat confused surrender. . . . Achradina,
which was defended by the deserters, was captured and
sacked. . . . Archimedes, immersed in study, was interrupted by the entrance of a person whom he did
not recognize. He rebuked the intruder and requested
him to wait. The stranger was an uneducated soldier,
who abruptly and regrettably terminated the long and
distinguished career of the most famous of ancient
mathematicians.

Marcellus expressed his regret, and took the family of Archimedes under his own protection. The mathematician was seventy-five years old.

The plunder of Syracuse was stupendous—greater, almost, the Roman historian thinks, than that of Carthage would have been. The treasury of Hiero was taken over by Marcellus for the Roman government. Marcellus also sent to Rome many of the magnificent works of art which decorated the public buildings—and apparently some of the private ones—of the city: and what the statuary of a great Greek city, in the heyday of its wealth and prosperity, must have been like, may well engage the solemn and wistful thoughts of a modern collector. . . . The action of Marcellus was historic; for it formed the first introduction of educated Romans to Greek art.

But there was no alternative. The existence of Syracuse, on her old scale of power and military importance, had proved too great a risk to be tolerated. If Rome were to survive, Syracuse must have a little less control over events. . . . From this day she began to shrink into a wealthy but still subordinate provincial city. The

task of standing as the military bulwark of Greek civilization against the Carthaginian had passed over to Rome. The Roman possession of Sicily was confirmed, and the door was closed upon the corridor between Hannibal and Carthage.

v

How hard-pressed both Sicily and Italy were becoming is illuminated by one episode. T. Otacilius from Lilybæum made a naval raid upon the African coast, and brought back a hundred and thirty cargo vessels laden with corn. He poured this into Syracuse in the nick of time. Had it not been for his good fortune, both victors and vanquished alike would have gone short. . . . And a shortage of corn in Sicily was like a shortage of coal at Newcastle.

VI

Hannibal did not accept the verdict of Syracuse as final. He sent to Sicily one of his best cavalry officers, a Liby-Phœnician named Muttines Hippacritanus, an energetic and experienced man, who joined Epicydes and Hanno at Agrigentum. Before long, the name of Muttines was known throughout Sicily. He kept the Carthaginian flag flying, and could have done much more, had he possessed undisputed authority. . . . So here was more or less of an end of one great stage of the war. The first had ended at Cannæ. The second ended at Syracuse. Rome had opened her offensive with trenches and siege engines. But could she, by these means, win a war?

In spite of the success in Sicily Rome was very far indeed from victory. She had merely, at enormous cost to herself, restored in part the previous situation. Part (but only part) of the disastrous results of Cannæ had been cancelled. . . . Yet what had been cancelled was, in a way, an after-thought, an incidental inspiration of Hannibal, evolved in the course of his preoccupation with more important matters. . . . The original scheme, the plan of Hamilcar Barca, had never been touched, altered or damaged at all. All that had sprung

Results

from it remained in full force, unreversed. Hannibal was still in Italy. The revolt of the southern provinces was still unsubdued. The thoughts of Hannibal must have reverted to the question of Spain.

Situation
in Spain
The Spanish situation had features which distinguished it from the Italian or the Sicilian. For one thing, it was much less under the control of the Senate. No annual magistrates proceeded to Spain. The two brothers Scipio seemed to have taken over the Spanish section of the war as a family enterprise. Though the Senate undertook to finance and supply their campaigns, it interfered very little with their discretion. It preferred to let well alone.

There was much to note in the campaigns of the Scipiones in Spain. By copying some of the methods of the Carthaginians, the two brothers founded the later provincial policies of Rome. They depended a good deal upon alliances with the native tribes, and learned the methods of dealing with them. Their diplomacy was as important as their actual fighting. They held the line of the Pyrenees, founded a Roman base at Tarraco, and, as we have seen, caused the diversion to Spain of Carthaginian reinforcements which should have reached Hannibal. In the dangerous year after Cannæ they penetrated far to the south of Spain; and while Sicily was in the throes of the Syracusan revolution, they were distracting the attention of the Carthaginian government by a series of adventures of the most extraordinary nature. They recaptured and rebuilt Saguntum; they all but reached the Straits of Gibraltar; and they got into touch with Syphax, one of the native rulers of North Africa.

Their dealings with Syphax set going a chain of events which did not soon terminate. Syphax was charmed with the interesting conversation of their emissaries. He insisted on retaining a Roman officer to drill his tribesmen in Roman infantry methods. Whether the tribesmen were conspicuously successful under the novel instruction perhaps does not much matter; but the proceedings were conspicuously successful in alarming the Carthaginian government. While Syracuse was falling before Marcellus, and Hannibal's Sicilian projects were collapsing, war was raging in North Africa. The suppression of Syphax and his activities was largely due to the dashing cavalry operations of a local rival, Masinissa, the young son of King Gala. The war required the presence of Hasdrubal with the Spanish army. Hence, perhaps, came some of the reasons for the Carthaginian failure to relieve Syracuse.

Effects of the Spanish Campaign 212 B. C.

The activities of the Scipio brothers thus exercised an important influence upon the course of the main war. Their operations never showed any signs of being decisive, or of reaching a definite issue; but they started a large number of tendencies and currents. Their study of the art of dealing with native tribes was so highly successful that according to Hasdrubal's report to the Carthaginian government, the mere rumour of his intention to cross the Pyrenees on the way to Italy was enough to raise revolution in Spain. Moreover, their campaigns were essays in what was, for Romans, a new art of war—that very system of free, open-field tactics and long-distance strategy in which Hannibal was a past master. They learnt it where he learnt it—in Spain.

We may confidently dismiss the idea that the Scipiones never wrote to their families. Their communications home were undoubtedly, if not frequent, at least voluminous and interesting. From them evolved directly the first part of the great Scipionic saga which succeeds the Fabian; and indirectly, through the influence which they exerted upon the growing mind of young Publius Scipio, they gave rise to both the fact and the record of the second part, the story of Scipio Africanus himself.

VII

After the suppression of the revolt of Syphax, Hasdrubal returned to Spain. His arrangements were of a particularly business-like nature. If they were not concerted in agreement with Hannibal it can be only because, in view of the situation, no agreement was necessary. The war required to be brought to a decisive issue, and touch needed to be established through Gaul with Italy. Three strong Carthaginian armies took the field. The Scipiones were ready. They took the step—novel in Roman history—of raising twenty thousand Celtiberian mercenaries to strengthen their own forces. . . .
Fall of the Scipiones in Spain Hasdrubal, an adept in all the shifts and intrigues of Spanish war, knew more of these expedients than they did; he bought off the mercenaries. The brothers were then crushed in detail, their armies destroyed, and they themselves slain. It was against Publius senior that Masinissa confirmed his fame as a leader of light cavalry.

The death of the Scipiones went far to balance the effects of the fall of Syracuse. But the incidence of the luck was singularly complicated. Had the Scipiones died a couple of years, or even one year earlier, Syracuse might never have fallen at all. The Carthaginian troops held up in Spain would have been available for Sicily: or, alternatively, Hasdrubal might have crossed the Alps four years sooner, and the career of Scipio Africanus would have been altogether diverted. As it was, fortune seemed to be playing a double game, so inclining first to one side and then to the other that one success neutralized another, and the war remained in balance, continually indecisive.

VIII

This baffling equality in the distribution of luck was illustrated in another way. The blockade of Capua was slowly strangling the life out of the defence. The news from Spain was in all probability already known when Hannibal was definitely notified that unless he could raise the siege the city must fall. He left Tarentum and advanced into Campania. Although he had a good deal to complain of in the conduct of the Capuans, the time was not one for argument. Action was called for.

His attempt to force the Roman lines was a complete failure. The Carthaginian cavalry could do nothing against the double circumvallation built round the city. The Romans sat tight and waited behind their entrenchments. To force the position with infantry would have been, at the best, a formidable task. . . . Hannibal was not in the position of a modern general who can rip up a fixed position with preliminary gunfire. To wade through the entanglements with the sword alone might have meant the expenditure of his whole available strik-

ing force. . . . To blockade the blockaders was not
impossible; but then the Romans had made it their
business to destroy all the forage in the surrounding
district, so that no considerable body of cavalry could
keep the field for any long period in the neighbourhood
of Capua. . . . The Wizard made one of his famous decisions. Leaving his campfires burning after dusk, he
set out on the road to Rome.

The
March
upon
Rome

Two ideas led him. There was the possibility that he
might, if he were quick enough, actually take Rome
unawares. While they had expected him, a march on
Rome was a useless proceeding. Now that they no longer
expected him, there was a real chance of success.
Alternatively, he counted on the pro-consuls either
abandoning the siege, or detaching a large part of their
besieging army for the rescue of Rome.[1] Crossing the
Vulturnus by a bridge of boats which he burnt behind
him, he took the road by Caiatia and Alifæ to Casinum,[2]
where he struck the Via Latina, and advanced, sweep-
ing the country with fire and sword, through the districts of Frusinum, Ferentinum and Anagnia to Labi-
cum. By Gabii he came to the Anio: and with skilful
outpost work arrived within five miles of Rome.

The city had all the sensation of the first genuine
panic it had experienced since the battle of the Allia.
The streets were crowded thick with refugees who had
fled before the advancing line of flames. The Wizard
had really arrived at last; he could be seen riding under
the walls close by the Colline Gate, examining with

---

[1] Polybius IX. 4. The rest of this episode is narrated from Polybius IX 3-7
except where otherwise specified.
[2] Livy XXVI. 7-9.

interest the mighty Rome that he had never before beheld.[1] . . . It seemed impossible to explain his arrival save upon the theory that his long-promised second Cannæ had happened, and that the army at Capua was destroyed. . . . At first there seemed a serious likelihood that his surprise would succeed. Luck, however, was adverse. The consuls had been enrolling recruits for new legions; and the day appointed for the men to report at Rome chanced to be the very day of Hannibal's arrival. He was accordingly faced by the unexpected presence of a force in the city amply sufficient for defence. The consuls took ground opposite the Carthaginian army. They had no information from Capua, and their proceedings therefore were cautious.

They looked on while the Carthaginians devastated a countryside which for a hundred and seventy-six years had not known an invader. That the work was effectively done we need not doubt. A vast herd of cattle was driven into the Carthaginian lines. The wealthy temple of Feronia was sacked.[2]

As soon as he thought that the news had duly reached Capua, Hannibal took the road again.[3] On the mini-

[1] Livy XXVI. 10. . . . Appian VII 7. 40. says that he reconnoitred Rome secretly by night with a guard of three men. Livy (XXVI. 11) tells us that he was amused to hear that the site of his camp had just changed hands at the full market value of the lands, and retorted by announcing the approaching sale of the silver-smiths' shops in the Forum! Stories of this kind, which have puzzled or irritated many scholars, are a testimony to the firm tradition that Hannibal was a good deal of a joker, quite ready to be amused by a bad joke if he could not find a good one.

[2] Livy XXVI. 11.

[3] The account of Polybius concerning this episode is perfectly clear and conclusive; but ever since men have wondered why Hannibal did not take Rome! The best though the least truthful answer is the one with which he is alleged to have snubbed some Carthaginian Nosey Parker: "What! And lose my job? No!" (Appian VII. 40.)

mum assumption, that the besiegers were detaching a part of their force to the rescue of the Roman countryside, he intended to arrive at Capua when it was too far on the way to turn back. If, then, the depleted Roman lines could not be forced, he was much mistaken. He marched by the inland roads, so that he should not meet the returning army.

The return to Capua

The consuls followed, under the impression that their heroic efforts were driving a beaten foe from their beloved city. Hannibal was too busy to attend to their views of the situation. At the crossing of the Anio they succeeded in cutting off a large proportion of the cattle. The Carthaginian cavalry, hovering about, prevented any more serious operations; and Hannibal could not trouble about such trifles as cattle. Capua was his objective. . . . Five days on the return march, the news met him. . . . The investing army around Capua had not moved at all! . . . Nothing had happened. He need not have troubled to march on Rome.

The unfortunate consuls were the men who received the full force of Hannibal's wrath. As soon as the Roman pursuers were tucked into their tents that night, he raided them with his elephants.[1] . . . When morning dawned, the Romans were ending a wakeful and disturbed night on a hill-side. . . . He left them there and marched on.

Fall of Capua

Capua, starved out, fell, with all its garrisons. The fate of the Capuans was not pleasant, and it did not fail to make a deep impression upon their friends.

[1] Appian VII. 7. 41. It was a moonless night.

IX

And yet, the best and the most that could be said of the situation after the fall of Capua was simply that matters were returning—and not completely—to their starting points. Rome, after monstrous and ruinous efforts, might now expect the arrival of another son of Hamilcar Barca across the Alps, into an Italy far less able to receive him.

There were clearly deep searchings of heart in Rome. Successful as their counter-offensive had been, it was evident that it suffered from the inherent defect of being far too slow and cumbrous. Unless a new offensive, of a very different nature, were organized, the Roman power would bleed to death.[1]

So much was obvious.

Here young Scipio enters upon the scene.

Enter
Publius
Scipio

Now, to explain the turn taken by events later on, it is necessary to shift our attention for a moment from the problems presented to the Romans by the war, and to examine instead some of its reactions.

It is easy enough to understand that the real question confronting the Romans was how to create and employ a mobile striking-force capable of defeating Hannibal in the field. The fundamental law of all war, that the object of military operations is to destroy the enemy's fighting power, was one that neither the Romans nor

---

[1] There was almost a revolution in Rome this year when the proposals for the naval levy were put forward. Ultimately, at the suggestion of M. Valerius Lævinus a voluntary subscription was adopted. (Livy XXVI. 36.) For the political result of Hannibal's devastation of Latium see *post* p. 216. (Livy XXVII. 9–10.)

any other people could escape. As long as Hannibal, howsoever many his disappointments, was unbeaten in the field, so long the war would continue to revolve in the vicious circle which the Romans were beginning, with consternation, to recognize.

Considerations

But to recognize this problem is one thing; to solve it is a totally different matter. Men may go despairingly round in a circle long after they have perceived its meaning, because they have no power to break it. . . . What we accordingly have now to notice is the way in which the reactions of the war itself solved the problem. . . . Hannibal raised up his own ghost or spectre; and the wraith of Hannibal at the head of Roman armies proved capable of beating the real Hannibal at the head of Carthaginian armies. . . . In other words, not merely the methods, but the actual personality of Hannibal could be successfully imitated.

Such an imitation or reconstitution is not a thing achieved by deliberate intention. It was not by taking thought that young Publius Cornelius became Scipio Africanus. He was moulded by the simple influence of events. Ever since he returned from the battlefields of the Trebia, while his father went on to Spain, he had been living the deeply impressionable years of early youth amid the sensational events of the war. . . . The whole of the story had reeled itself out under his very eyes: and he had been led to acquaint himself with the earlier parts of the tale, which took place previous to his own birth. . . . He had gone through the dreadful day of Cannæ itself: the day when the glorious news of Syracuse came in; the day when the gigantic shadow of the Wizard and his elephants momentarily darkened

The making of Publius Scipio

the very doors of Rome. He had read the strange adventures of Dionysius, and the picaresque career of Agathocles; he had lived, breathed, eaten and drunk the spirit and the events of the struggle of the European with the Semite. . . . Men can be profoundly affected by that which they long and steadily contemplate. . . . In the case of Scipio, this object was the personality of Hannibal. It seemed as if with every shock the mind of Scipio was twisted and slanted more and more into the likeness of Hannibal. The Carthaginian smile grew on his lips; the quick Carthaginian mentality grew in his mind—that quality which a gruff Roman took for insincerity, but which more enlightened ages call subtlety. . . . All this alone might have meant nothing; but that education in Carthaginian methods which it might seem impossible for a boy in Rome to acquire, actually came to Scipio in plenitude from the example and the experience of his father in Spain. If the campaigns of the elder Publius had no other result, at least they educated his son. The younger Publius must have absorbed practically all that the elder had to teach.

The death of his father and uncle aroused him from a kind of imaginative sleep. He awoke suddenly to realize that his dream was real. He had actually become all that he had lived over in imagination. . . . He had already, almost without his own will, slipped into the Hannibalic method—the approach to things on their unexpected, their "blind" side; the exploitation of the fact that he himself was consciously aware of details of which other men were unconscious (for Hannibal rested much of his method upon this deliberate attention to the very details which ordinary men assumed,

His awakening

or accepted, without express attention); the half-
amused, more or less benevolent wizardry by which he
achieved his ends without the knowledge of those whom
he gently tricked; a habit of impressing his friends with
the awed conviction that he possessed powers a little
more than normally human.[1] . . . No Roman before
him had ever employed—or even known—this psychological method. It was Hannibal's method. Scipio
had used it in minor matters until he felt entire faith
in his ability to employ it upon a larger scale.

As soon as Capua fell, Gaius Claudius Nero had
shipped off troops straight from Puteoli to Spain. His
commission was intended to last only until the formal
appointment could be made of successors to the Scipiones. The Senate hoped that some suitable person
would apply for the post; but when, in due official
process, the Assembly met, no one came forward. . . .

**No candi-
dates for
Spain**

Two things are certain. While the electors were waiting
and whistling, young Publius unexpectedly announced
himself as a candidate, and with tremendous unanimity
the Sovereign People elected him.

The election of Publius Scipio was so extraordinary

[1] When a man deliberately deals in facts and relations which for ordinary
men are off the field of consciousness, he will always produce upon them this
impression. Hannibal scarcely troubled to hide the element of trick; Scipio disguised what he was doing by attributing it to divine help: (not that divine
help is in itself either impossible or improbable—but he clearly did "hide his
trail" in this case, as Polybius X. 2–5 bluntly tells us). He was in the habit
of spending time in the temples, meditating and communing with the divine
powers, before making decisions or settling plans. There was nothing that anyone could object to in this; but it was a novelty for the aristocratic party to
see a private unofficial person invoking and employing powers hitherto the monopoly of the official priesthood. They seem to have been outraged at the
spectacle of young Publius "working the oracle" on his own private behalf; but
there was no rule against it. (Livy XXVI. 19.)

a fact that we can see without looking further that the granite of Roman *moral* was becoming deliquescent under the pressure of war. He was a young man of twenty-seven, who had held no higher office than that of ædile, and whose experience of warfare had been gained in the rank of tribune. To pitchfork an untried youth into the Spanish command was something unique, so far, in Roman history—and it was destined to remain unique. It could never have happened had not the Romans been willing to clutch at any straw, however frail. . . . Neither now nor at any time did the Senate—and especially its leader, Quintus Fabius Maximus—look with anything but shocked consternation upon young Publius Scipio. But (and this is the crucial point) they discovered no flaw in the auguries. No strings were pulled to prevent him from going to Spain. The Assembly had clutched at a very frail straw: and the Senate let it clutch.

Sensational election of Publius B. C. 210

The very stress of the war had therefore evoked a product of its own. Publius Scipio emerged into command not by accident, nor by fatality, but by a logical necessity similar to that natural law by which water finds its level.

And the Romans had every reason for clutching at straws. They were revolving in a vortex which could only end by dragging them down. They would go round and round in that horrible circle until Hannibal's designs were at last realized. . . . Their commissioners were even now on the way to Egypt to implore Ptolemy for corn. Hannibal had devastated the country right up to the walls of Rome; grain was up to fifteen drachmæ the medimnus, and there were no supplies in the usual foreign markets.[1]

X

The youthful Publius left for Spain amid the admiring hopes of his friends, and the hopeful scepticism of the Senate. They all trusted that with his name and his gifts he would be able to continue the traditions of the Scipiones. Plenty of able advisers on the spot were capable of guiding his inexperienced steps if he would supply the moral prestige. . . . There must have been many who patted him affectionately on the shoulder. . . . And Publius continued to be charming, and he continued to smile.

So much for Publius Cornelius Scipio the younger.

Publius leaves for Spain

While he was on his journey, Fabius Maximus (who had engineered his fifth consulship) undertook the offensive which was becoming ever more urgently necessary. Marcus Marcellus, the most active and aggressive of Roman commanders, received proconsular status to enable him to co-operate with the old man. Together they proceeded to strike that offensive blow which the fall of Capua had rendered possible.

Before leaving for the front Fabius and his colleague, Q. Fulvius Flaccus, were called upon to attend to a parenthesis shaking to the nerves of the strongest statesman. Twelve of the old and important colonies—chiefly Latin—which had suffered the worst during Hannibal's march on Rome, notified the government that no further men or money must be expected from them. They hoped that peace would be made. Seriously upset, the

[1] This was nearly three times the normal price.

consuls tried a little blustering; but they were dealing
with men as grim and as stiff-necked as themselves. As
the Latins were the main prop and stay of Rome, this
looked like the crack of doom. Most of the Senators
thought that the end had come.

The patience of Fabius calmed feeling and restored
courage. Eighteen other colonies in various parts of
Italy were sounded, and when their representatives had
given assurances of unbending loyalty, it was resolved
to express to them publicly the thanks and appreciation of the republic. The twelve defaulters were passed
over in silence, without criticism. . . . It is probable
enough that they had spoken the truth. Hannibal's
razor shaved clean.

Confronted with this default, the government dipped
into its last resources. The secret treasury in the temple
of Saturn was opened. A hundred pounds of the bullion
were put into the hands of Fabius for a special purpose
which was not specified, but which in a short time became easier to guess.

Marcellus was given the commission of holding Hannibal while Fabius advanced upon Tarentum. The
former got into touch with Hannibal at Canusium. It
was the preoccupying dream of his life to meet and beat
Hannibal in the field: and the Senate knew of no other
man better equipped for the task. The Wizard was ready
for him. Repeated changes of ground failed to shake
off Marcellus, who, after many skirmishes, at last involved Hannibal in a general engagement. Night fell
on an indecisive action. Hannibal pointed out to his
troops the necessity of a decisive battle, as they were
hopelessly immobilized unless they could force Mar-

cellus to give up his detaining tactics. . . . In the fighting which was renewed the next day, Marcellus committed a tactical error—he shifted the position of a legion in the midst of the action—and the Wizard pounced instantly on the opening so afforded. . . . Marcellus, however, hung on to his prey, and renewed the action on the day after, giving rise to Hannibal's irritated comment: "This fellow will neither let us take a rest when he beats us, nor take one himself when we beat him!" . . . As Marcellus, however, was immobilized by the number of wounded on his hands, Hannibal seized the opportunity to break contact and get free.

Marcellus retreated to Campania, and settled at Sinuessa to reorganize.[1]

The failure of Marcellus, in allowing Hannibal to resume freedom of movement, was an intense disappointment in Rome, and a matter of bitter comment. He found it necessary to return home to answer his critics.

XI

Fabius at Tarentum

Fabius, thus deprived of the help of the second army, was left alone to deal with Hannibal. He had already invested Tarentum, and was in communication with the commander of the Bruttian garrison, who undertook to deliver the town into the hands of Fabius at the first favourable opportunity. This would take a little time to mature. In order to divert Hannibal, a corps from Rhegium was detached to invest Caulonia. Hannibal, unaware of any impending treachery, and believing that Tarentum could hold out indefinitely, allowed

---

[1] So Plutarch, *Marcellus*, c. XXVI. 4. but Livy (XXVII. 20) says Venusia.

himself to be caught in this trap, and so moved upon
Caulonia in order to support the weaker point. . . .
Six days after the beginning of the siege, the Bruttian
commander notified that he was ready. . . . Fabius
did not trust entirely to him, but arranged that a general
assault should take place on the opposite side of the
town. While this was preoccupying the attention of the
defence, Fabius scaled the walls at the spot agreed upon,
and took the town by storm.

Hannibal, coming up from Caulonia, was only five
miles from Tarentum when he heard that he was too
late. He paid Fabius the most exquisite compliment that
the latter ever received: "Then Rome also has a Hannibal!" he said. . . . He rather modified the compliment
by remarking that they had lost Tarentum as they had
won it—that is to say, by treachery within the walls.
. . . It was now that a comment of a more serious nature is said to have come from him. He told his officers
that he no longer believed it possible, with the forces
at his disposal, to conquer Italy. . . . But, as we shall
presently see, although it might be necessary for him
to stand upon the defensive, he was in all probability
fairly sure that this state of affairs would not last long.

Tarentum regained by the Romans

Before he withdrew, he tentatively scattered a few
crumbs for Fabius, to see if the Roman Hannibal
would peck. He caused a letter to be sent from the city
authorities at Metapontum, offering, if their lives and
property were guaranteed, to surrender the town to
the Romans. . . . Having no reason to doubt that the
letter was genuine, Fabius replied fixing a definite date
for his arrival at Metapontum. The delighted Hannibal
at once prepared a little surprise for him when he

should arrive. . . . The old gentleman, however, was well served by his intelligence department. Before starting, he took the opinion of the Sacred Chickens, whose verdict, it is interesting to note, was adverse. All the auguries were adverse. He accordingly, with regret, felt unable to go to Metapontum. . . . When the city deputies ventured to return to hurry him up, they were promptly arrested, and a little moral pressure induced them to confess the truth.

Fabius still prudent

Hannibal retired. The honours for this deal were decidedly with Fabius.

XII

Tarentum suffered a milder fate than Capua. The city had been taken by assault; and besides the unofficial perquisites which fell to the lot of the troops in such circumstances, three thousand talents of official booty were paid into the Roman treasury. Fabius seemed to feel that this was quite enough punishment. . . . In the Senate he made a stand on behalf of the Tarentines, and his influence was sufficient to prevent the zealous advocates of vengeance from having their way. A final decision of the case of Tarentum was postponed until later, when feelings might have cooled.

He had not imitated the action of Marcellus. The officer who checked the inventory—possibly remembering Syracuse—asked him what was to be done with "the gods of Tarentum"—that is, the statues and works of art. Letting his eye rest upon them, Fabius noticed that they were all shown in militant Lacedæmonian attitudes. . . . He said: "The gods of Tarentum seem to be an angry lot: so we will leave them to their devotees."

Fabius and Tarentum

. . . He did however remove one colossal statue of his ancestor Heracles—a work of Lysippus—to Rome.

Tarentum therefore had fallen, and yet Rome was no nearer to defeating Hannibal in the field. He, too, on occasion, could employ the Fabian tactics.

XIII

Before the fall of Tarentum, Hannibal must have heard other news of another person, of whom it would have been truer to say: "Rome also has a Hannibal." *Young Publius Scipio had captured New Carthage!*

CHAPTER X

THE CRISIS

I

THE capture of New Carthage signalled the memorable fact that a new force had thrown its sword into the scale. . . . The youth of twenty-seven who arrived in Spain with his name and his smile had spent his last weeks in Rome in the task of gathering all the information Rome could yield. His landing in Spain sent an electric shock through the army. It was soon busily at work in the acceptable task of acquiring information for Publius. . . . The acquisition and communication of information has always had an indescribable charm for the ordinary human being, and the army flung itself with ardour into this new occupation. . . . Publius talked a great deal, and did not hesitate to outline the probable plan of campaign he intended to adopt. Spain was all ears. . . . Among the information which he assorted and classified was, incidentally, the exact position of the Carthaginian armies. Having learnt a good deal which he did not divulge, and divulged a great deal which misled everyone who heard it, he very rapidly and without saying a word beforehand made a dash for New Carthage, arrived there before anyone clearly realized his objective, feinted at one spot and scaled the defences at another. He had New Carthage in his hands while three Carthaginian armies looked on uncomprehending. And he continued to smile.

Publius at work

Capture of New Carthage

The capture of New Carthage was too quick and too complete to carry conviction. The world regarded it with the incredulity of an audience which has seen the performance of a conjuring trick. Granting that it was clever—was it to be taken quite seriously? [1]

II

Some time elapsed before the truth became clear, and the Carthaginians realized the full range of the weapons with which young Publius fought.

A fruitful field for the psychologist lay before him. Owing to the circumstances in which Hamilcar Barca had founded, and his successors had organized, the Carthaginian dominion in the Iberian peninsula, Spain had been taken a little too much for granted. The Carthaginian governors had almost involuntarily slipped into those faults of over-confidence which betray the rulers of a rich and backward country. They wrung fortunes out of it by means for which there was no one to bring them to book. They took too high a line with men as proud and sensitive as Spaniards in all ages have been. Worse, they indulged in the luxury of personal bickerings. These were not the methods by which they had

The Spanish situation

[1] Livy XXVI. 51. For the importance of New Carthage. See Strabo c. 147. It was the centre of the valuable silver mining district which, three miles distant, extended for forty-six miles around it. In the days of Polybius the mines produced 20,000 drachmæ of silver per day. Dr. Henderson (*Five Roman Emperors* pp. 73–74) attributes much of the later prosperity of the empire to these mines.

Had Hannibal ultimately been victorious, New Carthage would in all probability have superseded both Carthage and Rome, and become the seat of a Mediterranean empire two hundred years before Augustus. Hannibal's power was a Spanish power, directed by men who, though nominally Carthaginian citizens, were in reality cosmopolitans. That Spanish empire is one of the interesting might-have-beens of history.

won Spain. . . . And now there was a man at hand especially qualified to take advantage of such errors.

To begin with, the prisoners taken at New Carthage (a mixed assortment) [1] included an elderly Spanish woman with some young girls in her charge. The identity of this group proved interesting. The girls were the daughters of Andobales, one of the principal Iberian chiefs: the elderly woman was their aunt, the wife of Andobales' brother Mardonius. The reason for their presence in New Carthage was even more interesting. The Carthaginian governor, Hasdrubal the son of Gisco, had attempted to squeeze money out of Andobales. The latter either could not or would not oblige; and Hasdrubal had put on the screw by demanding his daughters as hostages. . . . This episode, which was a mere incident in the domestic politics of Carthaginian Spain, became something much more important when young Publius raked New Carthage into his net, hostages and all. . . . He found no difficulty in being extremely pleasant to his new captives. Pleasant manners are a profitable stock in the world of politics, and Publius had invested heavily in them.[2]

The Hostages

The wife of Mardonius was a Spanish dame who, for all that matters, might have ornamented the nineteenth century. She was quick to notice the human type that stood before her in the person of Publius Scipio.

---

[1] Publius dismissed the citizens of New Carthage, to their astonishment, back home again. The artisans and labourers he enrolled on his own pay-sheets, with prospect of future freedom.

[2] Polybius (X. 18. 3-7) draws a fine picture of Publius "nursing the babies" like any early Victorian candidate for Parliament, and distributing toys. This seems to have gone down well with everybody.

After he had given her assurances that she and her charges should be well provided for, she dropped a curtsy and expressed the hope that some of the troubles from which they had suffered would not be repeated. . . . Somewhat surprised, he assured her afresh; and to add weight to his words he called for the officers in charge, questioned them and gave them their instructions in her presence. . . . She then said that he had not quite understood what she was speaking of. He was for a moment brought to a halt; but suddenly, looking at the girls again, his alert mind caught the meaning of this bit of Spanish delicacy, and he gave her an emphatic promise that no such thing as she alluded to should happen while they were in his custody.[1]

It is hardly too much to say that the capture of New Carthage was a turning point in the war. Not only Andobales, but an even more powerful chief, Edeco of the Edetani, was profoundly impressed by Scipio's treatment of the hostages, and marked his sense of worldly prudence and friendly obligation by transferring his interest (an influential one) to the Roman side. He brought with him a large number of chiefs who usually followed his lead. The diplomatic victory so secured was worth many successful battles to the Romans. For the first time it ranged on their side a majority of the native Spaniards.

Attitude of the Spanish chiefs

---

[1] Polybius X. 18. It was at this time that Scipio's friends, having discovered the loveliest girl in Spain, affectionately presented her to him in the spirit of men presenting their commander with a beautiful white rabbit. Scipio was delighted, and expressed his warm appreciation. He reminded them, however, that white rabbits were not suitable for commanders to carry about with them during a war; so while thanking them, he felt it better to return the white rabbit to her father. She was accordingly returned, much to the admiration of everyone.

The prudent humanity and kindness, in this and in other matters, which Scipio showed after the capture of New Carthage, were the soundest statesmanship. He had doubtless picked up some of it from the shrewd old Fabius Maximus; some from the example of Hannibal; but what he had acquired so blended with his own natural good-temper that it acted like an instinct inborn. He did better than defeat opposition; he dissolved it. Time, however, was necessary before some of these diplomatic operations could mature to their fruits, and meanwhile he took up the task of drilling and equipping his army. He built workshops and set his men to work; his own constant personal presence, both in the workshops and at the exercises, stimulated the men to do their best. He was intent on the most practical business.

Methods of of Scipio

To Hannibal, not the least serious matter was the delay in the start of the Carthaginian reinforcements for Italy. We might have expected Hasdrubal to set out in the year following the death of the two elder Scipiones. He would have left Spain securely in Carthaginian hands, and there was no enemy force capable of barring his march. But several difficulties seem to have delayed him. The losses of the Carthaginians during the campaign against the Scipiones seem to have been very heavy. The enlistment and training of new men may have been necessary in order to replace the seasoned troops whom Hasdrubal would take with him. We do not know what the weather was like on the Alps that year; but we do know that Italy was badly off for grain, and, as we have seen, was asking for supplies from

Egypt: a circumstance which may have affected the prospect of military operations.[1] The Romans themselves, with two experienced soldiers in the consulship —M. Valerius Lævinus and M. Marcellus—remained idle, either holding themselves in readiness for Hasdrubal, or themselves too short of supplies to venture on more than minor operations. . . . By the next spring young Publius had arrived, and the capture of New Carthage changed the Spanish situation. Even if Hasdrubal succeeded in crossing the Pyrenees, his expedition was thrown two years later than Hannibal might justly have looked for. In the interval, Tarentum had been lost, and Agrigentum had surrendered.

Reasons for the delay of Hasdrubal

IV

Marcellus, re-elected to his fifth consulship, entered upon it with a fixed determination to wipe out the disgrace of the previous year—when he had so badly failed Fabius—and to force the issue. The need to do so was growing more and more urgent. The situation was emphatically a gloomy one, and the best that could be said was that it was gloomy all round. Hannibal could count Tarentum lost, New Carthage raided and stripped, Hasdrubal delayed. The Romans could count Hannibal still master of the open, Hasdrubal in the offing, the financial situation beyond hope, the roll of citizens alarmingly low. Etruria showed signs of the restlessness that goes before revolt. Nothing but a decisive battle could restore matters. That battle Marcellus meant to force

Marcellus

---

[1] Money (to judge by the attempt to squeeze it out of Andobales) must also have been short.

upon Hannibal. The Wizard quite appreciated the point.
. . . Such moods preceded Cannæ.

V

The Senate very evidently had its doubts. The pontiffs at first steadily refused to give Marcellus a clean bill.
The consul was determined, however, and at last they
let him go. When he faced Hannibal in the Carthaginian
lines between Bantia and Venusia, the augurs [1] still seem
to have had instructions to restrain him, for they per-
sistently found the omens adverse.

The Senate was very wise. Another battle of Cannæ
would have meant the end. Rome had stood all she could
stand. . . . The symptoms certainly were pointing to
another Cannæ. There was the same determination on
the part of the consul to force the issue, and the same
feverish enthusiasm in the camp. Hannibal remained
apparently idle. But when a Roman detachment sent
into Bruttium was trapped and cut up with heavy loss,
the temper of Marcellus reached the danger mark. He

The
wooded
knoll

moved camp close in to Hannibal, as if to watch his
very eyes. . . . Between the Roman and the Carthaginian positions there was a wooded knoll. Much discussion took place among the amateur strategists
regarding this knoll. Why had not Hannibal occupied
it? Why had not the consuls occupied it? . . . Marcellus, ready to accept any hint, went to view the knoll.

---

[1] That is, the haruspices: but the word "Augur" has become an English word
covering all the varieties of prophetical diviner. A haruspex examined the sacrificial victims for intimations; an augur observed the flight of birds. . . . The
pontiffs also assisted by raising technical religious difficulties to the departure
of Marcellus. (Livy, XXVII. 23. 25. 26. Plutarch, *Marcellus*, c. XXVIII.)

The other consul, Crispinus (possibly remembering Varro and the eve of Cannæ) accompanied him.

To watch the eyes of Hannibal it was first necessary to know where his eyes were. He had an observation post up in the trees of the knoll, unknown to the Romans, and supports were waiting over on the other side. The signal of the observer brought up these supports obliquely round the knoll. Completely taken by surprise, the escorting squadron of Etrurian cavalry broke and bolted. The consul's body-guard of forty Fregellan horse stood its ground until it saw Crispinus, mortally wounded, ride away, and Marcellus fall dead with a spear in his side. Then the survivors made off.

Two consuls and forty men slain, five lictors and eighteen men captured, were the casualties of this little Cannæ: for Crispinus ultimately died of his wounds. Hannibal came in person to view the body of Marcellus. The "Little Cannae" To net two Roman consuls at one stroke was a unique feat of arms; but Hannibal showed no signs of excitement about it. He took the consular ring off Marcellus' finger as a souvenir, and ordered the body to be arrayed and cremated, and the ashes to be sent to Rome. . . . He had wanted the army of Marcellus, not Marcellus himself. . . . It was bad luck to be given this confectionery victory instead of the substantial military success, with crushing political results, for which he had hoped. . . . A second Cannæ would have given him his heart's desire, and complete victory. Etruria would have revolted. Latium itself would have fallen away. Rome would have been isolated, and at his disposal. . . . Instead of which an ironical fate gave him the empty triumph of two consuls!

He had no reason to be particularly elated.

Far away in Spain, the battle of Bæcula had been fought. Hasdrubal had made his preparations. Young Publius, advancing to block his route, had found him in a very carefully chosen position, while the armies of Mago and of Hasdrubal the son of Gisco stood by at the distance of a few days' march, ready for eventualities. Publius at first did not see his way to fight; but after some hesitation he decided, being apprehensive of a movement by the other armies, to take the risk.

Hasdrubal had alternative possibilities before him. If he won, he could decide at leisure his policy in view of the fresh situation that would arise. If he lost, he intended to slip away north for the Pyrenees, leaving a force to mask his retreat. . . . Early in the engagement it became evident that he would not defeat Publius. The troops who were actually engaged he therefore left to hold the Romans, while he withdrew his main force, with thirty elephants and the baggage train, and set out northwards.

Hasdru-
bal's
"Break-
away"

Publius took twelve thousand prisoners at the battle of Bæcula, so that he might legitimately claim a victory of no mean magnitude. He had nevertheless failed in the principal object before him. With two other Carthaginian armies in his rear he did not care to pursue Hasdrual, remaining content to dispatch after him an observing force to watch and report his movements. He accepted the surrender of the native tribes, and spent his time in settling the district.

Hasdrubal was now on the road to Italy. Taking the westerly pass, through Roncesvalles, he wintered in Gaul. Early in the next year he crossed the Alps by

the Cenis route. Ten elephants survived the journey.
. . . The great march had been successfully accomplished, a second son of Hamilcar Barca had reached
Italy, and for Hannibal the long hoped-for, long postponed help was approaching.

Hasdrubal
crosses the
Alps

VI

The twelve years' wrestle reached its culmination
now. The decisive moment had arrived that would
determine the issue one way or the other—which way,
no man could guess. Two Carthaginian armies were
in Italy, each led by a son of Hamilcar. Their victory
now would be an absolutely decisive victory. Rome was
in no condition to recover from a serious defeat. . . .
She showed no signs of giving way: but for all that,
the arrival of Hasdrubal implied that the Roman offensive war in Italy had failed. Marcellus, its chief ex-
ponent, was dead. Fabius was too old for an active campaign. Hannibal's striking power remained intact, and
Hasdrubal (himself a commander of the first rank
among his contemporaries) was on the way to act in
conjunction with his brother. Young Publius, in Spain,
had held his ground as his father and uncle had done
before him; but he had not yet demonstrated his power
to do more.

If ever men hoped against hope; if ever they came
up to the scratch with unabated spirit when all seemed
lost—those men were the Romans. The Wizard had
tricked and battered and beaten his foes to their very
last gasp; all that remained to be seen was whether he
could deliver the knock-out blow that would finish the

struggle. . . . A man who laid money against his ability to do so would have been a rash man.

VII

There was no revolution in Rome. The reins of state were placed in the hands of no Gelo or Dionysius. The government banked on the normal processes of its constitutional action, and upon its judgment of character. The consuls for the year were men of no very sensational celebrity. . . . Passing over old Fabius, and their next best man, M. Valerius Lævinus, the aristocratic party ran for the consulship the best and most brilliant of their younger candidates, Gaius Claudius Nero. They perhaps staked partly on a belief in heredity. Nero was the grandson of that formidable old Roman, Appius Claudius Cæcus, the pontifex who in his prime had sacrificed his eyesight by rushing through the flames of his burning temple to rescue the sacred images; and the man who, in his extreme old age, had been carried into the senate house to deliver that historic speech which turned the scale against Pyrrhus, and committed Rome to the assertion of an exclusive suzerainty over the Italian peninsula. . . . Nero, whatsoever he might conceivably lack in the way of ballast, might be counted upon to be an alert and unflurried leader who would die but never give way—a robust man, embodying the very heart and soul of the Roman genius. . . . As it

was legally compulsory that the other consul should be a plebeian, the Senate fixed upon M. Livius Salinator, who had held office before, and left it under a cloud. But he was a very able man; and amid a certain

amount of heated recrimination Livius was hauled un-
willingly out of the shadows in the hope that the chance
of retrieving his disgrace would spur him to the exertion of his whole ability.

And—crowning touch!—the two consuls were personal enemies, who might confidently be expected to
work miracles for the sake of excelling one another.
. . . There was nothing more promising on which to
stake. Fabius led the way by insisting on the reconciliation of the foes. After a little difficulty, the rivals shook
hands.

VIII

The Senate fielded twenty-three legions. It did not
matter what was thrown into the scale; the last reserves of men and money might be expended without
stint, for in the event of defeat the subsequent proceedings would have little interest for the survivors.

When the news began to arrive, it was of the kind
which sends some men's hearts into their mouths and
other men's hearts into their boots. Hasdrubal cleared
the Alpine passes without opposition. He reached the
Padus and raised the Ligurian tribes. Placentia was isolated. A tremendous host took the road for Umbria.
It reached Fanum Fortunæ and the Metaurus, south of
which lay Livius Salinator with the northern army of
Rome. The wildest optimist must have felt uneasy for
Livius.

While these operations were developing, Hannibal
left Bruttium on his march north. Nero hung on to
him all the way. At Grumentum they fought inde-
cisively. The Wizard had not booked himself to come

Advent of Hasdrubal

to grips just yet; he gave Nero the go-by, and was soon on the way again. Nero followed. When they got to Canusium, Hannibal drew his lines and halted. Over against him Nero halted too.

Nero's task was to cling to the Wizard with tooth and nail; to let himself be battered into the dust, but by any and every means to act as a drag upon his freedom. He himself, probably, hardly expected to defeat Hannibal in a level fight; but he could entangle him and cripple him and wreck his designs and destroy his mobility, and keep him out of the struggle while Livius tried a desperate conclusion with Hasdrubal. . . . And at any moment might come one of those conjuring tricks by which the Wizard wiped earnest opponents out of his path. . . . But Hannibal was waiting for something. He lay quiet at Canusium while the host of Hasdrubal filled the roads from Gaul.

He waited; until one evening a round object was cast into the Carthaginian lines. It was picked up and examined, and taken to Hannibal. . . . It was the head of Hasdrubal.

IX

For the stars in their courses had fought for Claudius Nero.[1] That for which Hannibal was waiting had come a fortnight before; but the Roman pickets had caught its bearers, and it came into the hands of the Roman consul—the momentous dispatch from Hasdrubal which set the Wizard free to move. . . . The inter-

[1] Dr. Henderson, in *Eng. Hist. Rev.* 1898, pp. 417 etc.; and voting for the St. Angelo site for the battle of the Metaurus. It is to be noted that G. Claudius Nero had touched the magic soil of Spain!

ception of this dispatch was one of the crucial accidents of human history. . . . And then the divine afflatus descended upon Claudius Nero, and he was inspired. He left the usual number of camp-fires burning, and the usual appearances of his camp. Hannibal's keen eye told him no story; he did not know that Nero was already on the road to Livius with a legion and a half of picked troops. He remained waiting and watching.

Nothing, probably, but that deep-rooted sense of dignity which was an essential part of the Roman character prevented the compatriots of Nero from rolling upon the ground with agony when they realized the nature of their consul's proceedings. He was violating the law by leaving his own province and intruding upon that of another consul, and suppose Livius lost his rather uncertain temper? By leaving Hannibal unwatched he was moreover bluffing the very master of bluff, for if Hannibal once woke to the truth, the consequences might be terrible. To them, it was a highly speculative sporting venture which nothing but success—if that—could justify. Nero, with the obstinacy of the Claudian race, did nothing to lighten the strain on their nerves. From beginning to end he gambled steadily, deliberately and remorselessly on success; and all his cards turned up trumps.

It is hardly to be wondered at that when his overwrought countrymen had somewhat recovered, they consigned their saviour to private life as soon as they could, and kept him there. He might have gone on too long. The Claudians were a nuisance to Rome. Everything they did was worrying.

The risks

Nero had not merely to reach Livius: he had to reach him in fighting trim. The villagers and townsfolk were warned, and had supplies ready at every halting place on the road. Brawny peasants carried the burdens of the troops; wagons were waiting to pick up and bring on those who fell out of the march; willing hands were at the wheels. All Italy along the route was mobilized to rush the troops through. Excited veterans embraced their families and fell in behind. Hannibal was still waiting and watching down by Canusium when Nero's columns came pouring their thousands into the camp by Sena Gallica, where Livius Salinator had made his temporary headquarters. His intelligence service, which served Hannibal so well, played him false at this critical moment.

He was waiting and watching still when the consuls advanced to meet Hasdrubal. That very astute commander was instinctively uneasy. Although Nero's men had been packed neatly into the tents of those of Livius, so that the camp showed no sign of enlargement, he had an intuition that Livius had been reinforced. His trained eye noted men who showed signs of a forced march. It was reported to him that the Roman trumpets had sounded twice, instead of once, before the consular headquarters. . . . He sought to avoid a battle. But the consuls meant to fight: and fight they did. . . . Even then, Hasdrubal so arranged his dispositions that Nero was stopped by high ground, and could not get into contact with the Carthaginians. Nero's march to the Metaurus would after all have been in vain, had he not taken another terrifying decision. In the very midst of the struggle he shifted his whole force right

Nero's march to the Metaurus

across to the other wing, took Hasdrubal in flank, and
settled the issue of the day. . . . Hasdrubal had done
all that a commander could humanly do. He was no
blencher. When he saw that the battle was lost he hurled
himself into the fray and went down in the thick. . . .
So perished the first of the sons of Hamilcar Barca.

Fourteen days after he had left Canusium, Nero was
back again: and he brought with him the grim news
that Hannibal now for the first time heard, and the
only sight that the Wizard was ever to have of the
brother whom twelve years ago he had left behind him
in Spain.

Hannibal retreated into Bruttium. . . . When the
courier had fought his way through the excited crowd
into the Senate house, and the news of the battle was
announced, Rome celebrated a victory which she was
now too exhausted to follow up. The problem remained,
indeed, whether she were not so exhausted that Hannibal might even yet be the victor in a war which,
though he had not won it, the Romans had managed
to lose. . . .

X

Such an event might have been possible, save for
young Publius. It was he who took up the war where
the exhausted combatants in Italy had dropped it. From
Spain, which Hamilcar had acquired as the base for
his campaigns, and from which Hannibal and Hasdrubal had made their expeditions, came the influence
which was to carry the issue to decision.

The Carthaginian government still had reserves of
men and money. It was still pouring reinforcements

into Spain. The Romans had but one man in reserve. In the year following the death of Hasdrubal, Publius took up the running in earnest. A brilliant second battle of Bæcula, won against superior numbers, broke the Carthaginian armies; and from that time onward he began to sweep all before him. His advance southward and westward was steady and continuous, until he had driven Mago, Hannibal's surviving brother, into Gades, and had cleared Spain of enemy forces. Once he began it in earnest, the work was quick, decisive and final.

He crossed over to Africa, met Syphax, and spent some time in negotiations with that potentate.

The contact between Scipio and Syphax was not without importance. Hasdrubal the son of Gisco was also in the neighbourhood. After a little persuasion, Syphax induced the Roman and the Carthaginian to meet over a dinner table. Since their conversation was strictly unofficial, they seem to have impressed one another favourably. Hasdrubal's subsequent, half-amused verdict was that he did not think Syphax capable of resisting such a charmer as Publius. The sequel shows that he began to look about him for a competing attraction.

As the Carthaginian divined, Scipio had already begun to project his scheme for carrying the war into Africa. Before he met Syphax he had got into touch with Masinissa. It was agreed that nothing overt should be said or done at present; but when Masinissa returned to Africa he went as a secret partisan of the Romans who awaited only the right time to declare himself. . . . If Syphax had got wind of this, it would have

Publius
visits
Africa

set him against Scipio. . . . After much interesting and even friendly conversation Scipio returned from his visit to Syphax with some kind of treaty, but apparently also with the conviction that an invasion of Africa by way of Spain was not practicable; or at any rate, not expedient. . . . So he would have to submit to the critical review of a none-too-enthusiastic Senate —gain, in the teeth of its objections, a definite appointment to the command of an African war, and conduct it from a Sicilian jumping-off base.

Scipio's mission is a hint that, if he could have relied upon any element of stability in the Spanish situation he might have preferred to turn the plans of Hamilcar Barca round upon their inventor, and make Spain the base for a conquest of Africa. But it is little likely that he obtained more than very general expressions of goodwill from Syphax, who wanted much more than he was prepared to give; and, while such expressions might have their usefulness later on, they formed, when taken together with the topographical difficulties, so doubtful a ground for reliance that the plan would not work.

There were other reasons. How deep ran the ancient currents of savage unrest in Spain was shown soon after his return. The Romans themselves were touched with it. A legion mutinied on account of unpaid wages; Andobales was scheming revolt. A little of the lion-taming art by which the grim Semites had ruled in that den of splendid beasts appeared in Scipio's treatment of the country; but it was clear that Spain was hardly settled enough to be made the base for an invasion of

Effects of his visit

Africa. . . . After a very successful personal interview
with Masinissa he resigned, and returned to Rome in
time for the consular elections.

XI

His welcome was remarkably mixed. He no doubt
deserved the popular enthusiasm over the conquest of
Spain. Varro had owed his election to that pleasure
which the popular mind always feels in dramatic success and spectacular proceedings. Since the catastrophe
of Cannæ the Roman people had suffered in silence the
dreary good sense of Fabius. They did not fail to celebrate the advent of the hero who had given them that
which Varro had only promised.

The Senate, on the other hand, could not conceal its
loathing for the whole scheme of ideas of which Publius Scipio was the representative. It averted its eyes
with horror from the prospect of young Publius coming with his unctuous affability and his detestable arts
of political charlatanism, his dreams and portents, his
alleged communion with the divine powers, his nursing of babies and his sweetness to the wives of regis-
tered electors. The Senate had not warred down the
Carthaginian Hannibal in order to set up a Roman
Hannibal. In this matter the Senate had reason on its
side. It might well be argued that the political constitution which hitherto had been the secret of Roman greatness was incompatible with the kind of political in-
dividualism which Scipio embodied. One of the two
things would have to give room to the other.

The trouble was not accidental, but was inherent

Publius
returns
to Rome

in the situation. If the supporters of the political state could win the war, they were at liberty to do so. It was here that the difficulty began. The social solidarity which the political theory had given to Rome had enabled her to survive stresses that otherwise would have disrupted her dominion. But it could not easily transform itself from a power of resistance into a power of aggression. If Rome merely went on resisting, Hannibal would even yet wear her down. An offensive war needed a new type of mentality. Scipio had this mentality.

Even though the Senate were right, it was driven perforce into what amounted to the argument that if Scipio were the only man who could win the war, the war ought not to be won. And this was a losing argument. The Roman voter knew his own mind. He voted straight for young Publius.[1] It is not without significance that his colleague was Publius Licinius Crassus —one of that family of Roman Rothschilds who were always mixed up in political innovations.

Publius and the Senate

XII

The consulship of Scipio was a prolonged wrestle over the war policy. It brought into conflict the old Fabius and the young Scipio—the representatives of the school that had saved Rome from defeat, and the school that intended to lead Rome to victory. Fabius was against the plan of carrying the war into Africa. He contended that the war must be won in Italy by the

[1] The voting for Scipio during the consular elections was the heaviest poll during the war. (Livy XXVIII. 38.)

Objections
to Scipio's
policy

destruction or expulsion of Hannibal. As a contemporary of Scipio, Fabius was no doubt perfectly well
aware that he was a great admirer of both Dionysius
and Agathocles.[1] . . . These, for more reasons than
one, were dangerous heroes to admire. Neither of them
had succeeded in beating Carthage. The African expedition of Agathocles was hardly an example of solid
success. Even Regulus had failed, when backed by the
whole power of Rome at the height of her prosperity.
. . . Why should Publius Scipio be able to take Carthage if Hannibal could not take Rome? . . . Moreover,
Dionysius and Agathocles had been men who subverted
the constitution of the state. . . . This was where the
shoe pinched! This was the deep underlying motive of
the hostility to Scipio! He looked too much like an
autocrat: too much like another Spanish Dictator.

And reasons could be—and were—adduced to prove
this. It was rumoured (and when challenged by Fabius
he refused either to confirm or to deny it) that Scipio
had declared his intention of appealing direct to the
Assembly, if the Senate would not give him what he
wanted. Scipio was also charged with conduct subver-
sive of discipline and sound government. The persis-
tence with which this charge was brought seems to hint
that there was substance in it. Scipio was both then and
afterwards alleged to have condoned proceedings on the
part of his subordinates which were wrong in principle
and inconsistent with justice, and he is alleged by in-
ference to have done so for the autocrat's reason—that

Objections
to Scipio
himself

---

[1] Polybius XV 35. 6–7. Livy depicts Scipio as actually mentioning Agathocles by
name in his speech during the debate in the Senate. (XXVIII. 43.)

the loyalty of a good servant is of more value than abstract right and wrong.

But the Senate realized that if the appeal to the Assembly were made, the electors would give Scipio the authority which the Senate refused. The prudent advice of Publius Crassus induced Scipio to leave the decision unreservedly in the hands of the Senate, which, as soon as it found its authority respected, with equal prudence proceeded to give way. It was decided to give Scipio formal authority to go to Africa, if he thought it expedient in the interests of the state; but he was to raise the additional forces required for the expedition, over and above the two legions already in Sicily, by voluntary recruitment. The Senate would not authorize the conscript levy for the purpose.

With this he had to be content.

XIII

The Carthaginian government made vigorous efforts to prepare for the storm. Hannibal was reinforced, active naval operations were maintained, and Mago·organized an expeditionary force for Italy. The mind which laid the plans was obviously Hannibal's. The loss of Spain made it impossible to march through Gaul and to cross the Alps. Hamilcar's arrangements were no longer intact. It was necessary therefore to return to the alternative which Hamilcar had explicitly abandoned, and to make the expedition by sea. Mago landed at Genoa, took the town, and began to enlist Gallic auxiliaries and to make alliances with the Ligurian tribes. The development of

Efforts to frustrate Scipio

this fresh threat probably had much to do with the reluctant consent to an African war wrung from the Senate by Scipio. Nothing but an offensive would break the logic by which the war revolved continually in that vicious circle.

Another important move concerned Philip of Macedon. Although his use as an ally had been slight, he had to a certain extent diverted Roman forces; and it was worth while to take every step which would secure this end. Philip was now in negotiation with Rome. Behind this lay a long and intolerably complicated story of minor Greek politics. Behind this, in turn, lay something far more important. Antiochus, the Seleucid king of Syria, had, ever since his accession in 223 B. C., been engaged in consolidating and extending his possessions. He intended to restore the Seleucid kingdom to its old historic importance. Philip could be useful to him as an ally against Egypt: and Philip, tired of the endless, and, in the main, resultless struggle with the minor Greek powers, was inclining to throw in his lot with Antiochus. The two were projecting a plan for the partition of the Egyptian dominions in Asia. In order to be free for this scheme, Philip proposed to come to terms with the Romans.

The whole of this scheme was a matter of concern to Carthage. Not only would it set free Roman forces, but Egypt was an African power, the destinies of which engaged the active interest of the Carthaginians. A mission which went to Philip from the Carthaginian government failed to move him. He clinched his arrangement with Antiochus and with Rome.

It is easy enough to argue that Philip was singularly

short-sighted in his policy. The far-seeing mind of Hannibal could no doubt discern prospects in the future which would be uncomfortable for Philip, and reasons in the present which ought to have appealed to his sense of interest. . . . But Philip was obsessed with immediate things. Thirty years later, events had elaborately demonstrated that Hannibal was right; but it did not much matter then.

XIV

The African expeditionary force filled its ranks without difficulty. It was equipped and manned by a vast popular movement; the Etrurian, Latin and central Italian communities of their own accord poured all their available resources at the feet of Publius Scipio: timber for the ships, provisions and outfit for the troops, and the troops themselves, who pressed forward to serve. The Senate, far too wise to carry the struggle beyond a certain point, saw that it was dealing with a masked autocrat, and it took care to give him no excuse for unmasking. It went with the stream, ready to retrieve its position by quiet and unostentatious means.[1] . . . It had, of course, no objection to the success of the expedition. All it asked for was that the expedition should succeed without overturning the state . . . Scipio, for his own part, had no theories. As long as he was permitted to do his work, the political constitution did not concern him. But it was already a revolution when the first servant of the state had a task to do which he must, in the state's

Scipio's preparations

---

[1] It got up a side-show of its own, by discovering that the war would be won when the Mater Idæa was brought to Rome. The war was therefore solemnly won by this means. (Livy XXIX. 10–11. 14.) The occasion was evidently a very enjoyable one, as we can see by the story of Claudia Quinta.

service, do even at the expense of the state. It is the first hint we get that the Roman state had purposes greater than itself.

XV

The
trouble
with Cato

The fleet, tradition tells us, was fitted out in forty-five days. Publius had things moving fast when he once began them. The Senate, indeed, did not let him go without one last grasp at his coat tails. The quæstor who accompanied him to Sicily to superintend the financial side of affairs was a rising man zealously attached to the party of Quintus Fabius, on whose pattern he modelled himself—a grey-eyed, red-faced, vigorous and inflexible man, known to us by the immortal name of Cato "the Censor." Cato found a good deal to criticize, and he did not hesitate to say so. He objected to Publius on principle, because his leader Fabius objected to him. He further objected to Publius' expenditure; not (he was careful to point out) that expenditure was wrong when directed to a rational purpose, but the superfluous luxuries which Publius issued to the troops spoiled them and softened their fine Roman hardihood.

Scipio replied that he would answer for the results he achieved; but the methods by which he gained them were no one's business but his own. He added that a book-keeper as meticulous as Cato was a superfluous luxury for him. Cato thereupon resigned and went home to uphold the moral traditions of the Roman people.

A commission soon arrived to inquire into the grave allegations made in the Senate. It had taken Locri on its way. An opportunity having chanced of snatching that town out of the hands of Hannibal, Scipio had gone thither in person and outwitted the Wizard himself. As an augury for the future, and a heartener to his men, the episode was invaluable; but, like Nero, he had gone out of his province, and the conduct of his representative, Pleminius, caused urgent representations to be made to the Senate. Fabius had moved for the arrest of Pleminius and the recall of Scipio. Cato had followed in the debate with great effect. It appeared that Publius was throwing away money right and left, and wasting his time with sports and play-acting as if he were on a holiday instead of a campaign. The commissioners, having had everything frankly opened to their inspection by an amiable commander, admitted that they failed to detect any evidence in support of Cato's allegations.

The trouble over Locri

In the spring therefore, leaving behind him not the least of his victories, Publius left the Sicilian port of Lilybæum with forty ships convoying four hundred transports and thirty thousand men. The passage was unopposed. He landed near Utica; and the world watched the proceedings of the new Hannibal whom Rome had conjured up to strive with the old.

Publius gets away at last

CHAPTER XI

PUBLIUS SCIPIO AND THE STRUGGLE IN AFRICA

I

THE landing of Scipio was a portent which troubled Carthage. His first operations sent a stream of refugees to the great city, where the most frantic efforts were being made to cope with the emergency. He was almost immediately joined by Masinissa.

Masinissa   Masinissa, with a ragged regiment of some two hundred desert riders, was all that survived from the schemes which Scipio had entertained in Spain of gaining over the Numidians. But Masinissa was a host in himself—a most redoubtable sheik, and one of those strange meridionals, always so interesting to Europeans, who combine the fiercest passions with the coldest intelligence, and whose force of character, and knowledge of horses, horsemen and the tactics of the desert, rise to the level of genius. Publius could safely have relinquished all the other alliances in Africa for the sake of Masinissa.

The sheik had been "on the run" since he parted with Publius in Spain, but was none the worse for the experience. He had a torrential romance to unfold. He had been promised the hand of Sophonisba, the daughter of Hasdrubal Gisconides—one of those passionate beauties over whose charms strong men (at any rate, in Africa) flew at each other's throats. In order to undo the diplomacy of Publius, Hasdrubal, without consulting his prospective son-in-law, had bestowed the peer-less beauty upon Syphax. The love-intoxicated Syphax had thereupon sworn oaths of eternal fidelity to his charmer's country—as Publius knew—and Masinissa accordingly had flown at his throat. There was a great deal more to the tale—a long story involving the kins-men to several unrememberable degrees on each side of the sheik's family, their claims and counter-claims; Hasdrubal's attempt to assassinate Masinissa; long rides, great battles, hair's-breadth escapes, passion, murder and sudden death—none of which the modern reader could be expected to tolerate except in their appropriate medium—the "Pictures." . . . And so here was Masi-nissa, with two hundred men of the desert and what he stood up in. Publius, welcoming him in his com-paratively cold European way, may have discerned, as a student of character, that he stood up in an astonish-ing amount of ardour, ability, and ruthless resolution.

Local politics in Africa

Masinissa flung himself into the fray with relish. A cavalry corps, four thousand strong, had left Carthage to reconnoitre in force. Publius wanted it, and Masi-nissa proceeded to get it for him. The desert riders were soon worrying and skirmishing on its flanks, draw-ing it on until the Roman cavalry, waiting behind some high ground, could at a suitable moment descend upon it. Three quarters of the Carthaginian corps were killed or captured in the hard-ridden rout. The sheik had de-clared himself.

II

After his first preliminary sweep of the country, Pub-lius settled down to invest Utica, as the best base he could acquire. His siege operations were interrupted by the approach of the main Carthaginian forces.[1] Hasdrubal Gisconides, with over thirty thousand men, had waited until he was joined by Syphax with a vast host of Numidians and Mauretanians. Maintaining his blockading lines, Publius retired to the long, narrow headland east of Utica, and dug in. Hasdrubal and Syphax took positions whence they could watch him.

The situation of Publius was, to all appearance, hopeless. Interest, however, rather rose than fell in Rome. Supplies were poured in upon him; the Senate dispatched drafts to Sicily, to set him free from responsibility for the defence of the island. . . . The interest of the sporting public at home, though prolonged, was destined to be rewarded.

Publius spent most of the winter in feeling for his opening. He was particularly willing to discuss terms of peace with Syphax, who—a little uneasy in his conscience concerning the relation in which he stood to both parties—was flattered to find himself in the position of arbitrator between two great powers. Masinissa sat shrouded patiently in the background until he should be needed. The opinion of Syphax was that both parties should evacuate one another's territory. This proposition was discussed at great length, and envoys were continually passing to and fro. Finally, Scipio demanded that the Carthaginians should give a definite undertaking. After inquiry, Syphax reported that

---

[1] The numbers of the Roman expeditionary force are not accurately known. Captain Liddell Hart (*Scipio Africanus*, pp. 119–120) prefers Appian's middle estimate of 16,000 foot and 1600 horse; but by Livy's dead-reckoning Scipio must have had at least 20,000 men. (XXIX. 24. 25.)

Hasdrubal would accept the terms discussed. Publius was thereupon sorry that, although he himself was in favour of peace, his advisers objected to the details. The negotiations were with regret broken off, much to the annoyance of Syphax, whose importance suddenly disappeared; and matters reverted to the state of war.

The lamentable fire which broke out in the camp of Syphax that night caused considerable alarm, which increased when those who rushed out to extinguish it did not return again, and rose to panic when the flame spread rapidly among the reed-built huts and involved the whole camp in one disastrous conflagration. Hasdrubal's camp was roused. Its commander awoke to find that the Carthaginian camp also was burning. Hasdrubal did not take long to make up his mind. Seeing that the fires were obviously incendiary, and that there was not the remotest hope of stemming them, he gathered his gear and forced his way to safety. Syphax did the same. When the sun rose over ancient Utica, Masinissa's riders were resolutely scattering the scattered fugitives yet more widely: and no Carthaginian fighting force was left intact. . . . Masinissa must have felt great pleasure at this sudden and complete change of role from pursued into pursuer.

Publius had struck with devastating effect. His plans had been carefully laid, with the continual advice and criticism of the sheik. And this had been the reason for those artfully disguised intelligence officers who, tricked out as servants and attendants, had daily chewed straws about the Carthaginian camp in the wake of the peace envoys.

Carthaginian camp surprised

III

This unexpected reversal of the situation was a still more profound shock to Carthage. Scipio, far from being isolated at Utica, was now master of the open.

Scipio
master
of the
open

There was division of opinion in the Carthaginian Council, and some lack of definite views concerning the future. It was proposed to call upon Hannibal for help, and to re-open peace negotiations. Stronger counsels finally prevailed. Hasdrubal was authorized to gather and reorganize the fugitives, while touch was re-established with Syphax. The arrival of a corps of Celtiberian mercenaries helped to restore confidence. Within a month, a fresh army was ready for the field. It dug in at the Great Plains, and waited.

Publius, now that he had elbow room, was ready. His men were in high fettle. He advanced immediately from Utica, intending to strike before the new Carthaginian army could be welded into an adequate fighting force. After two days of light trial fighting, Hasdrubal accepted a general engagement. It was the first pitched battle fought by Scipio in Africa. He used it to test a tactical method, a variation of Hannibal's theme at Cannæ. The cavalry onslaught of the Numidian and Italian horse swept the Carthaginian wings away. The Spanish infantry, enveloped by new wings wheeled out

Battle of
the "Great
Plains"

from the rear lines of the Roman centre, fell fighting to the last. . . . Hasdrubal retreated to Carthage. Scipio, now in control of the whole country, detached Lælius and Masinissa to follow Syphax into Numidia.

By this second battle the whole situation was transformed. It was Carthage now who was fighting at bay. The Carthaginian Council had a very serious state of affairs to deal with. Various suggestions were put forward. A naval stroke at the Roman fleet was proposed; preparations for a siege; peace negotiations; and again, a call to Hannibal. It was peculiarly characteristic that the Council finally settled upon the grand expedient of adopting all these plans. It proposed to run hard with the hare, and to pursue indomitably with the hounds: and it took up the task with energy. The sub-committees entrusted with the several policies parted at the door of the council chamber.

IV

The naval stroke was the first to eventuate. Publius, advancing upon Tunis, whence Carthage was clearly visible, beheld the fleet at sea. He doubled back to Utica as fast as he could go, and he got there first. When the Carthaginian fleet, after some hesitation, put in to Utica, it was to find the Roman warships, which were totally unprepared for an action, ensconced behind a floating rampart of transports, lashed one to another. The Carthaginians managed to cut away a number of these, and towed off six—a poor result of what was to have been a decisive blow at the Roman communications. No better, however, could be done.

Lælius and the sheik had meanwhile made contact with Syphax. The new Numidian levies, in spite of the heroic efforts of Syphax, broke before the Roman infantry, and Syphax, leading a forlorn hope to retrieve the day, was captured. Masinissa lost no time in riding for Cirta and the fair charmer. It was an affecting in-

Attack on Roman fleet

terview. Sophonisba, in all her tender femininity, knelt at the feet of the conquering hero, and implored with tears that she might fall into the hands of a fellow-African, not into the hands of Rome. Masinissa, exalted to the skies, gave the lovely suppliant his royal right hand. He welcomed her touching assurances that she had been coerced into marriage with the hated Syphax. He married her that day. He was in a hurry: and he had reason to be.

Lælius, arriving hot-foot, was furious to find the ceremony over. He claimed Sophonisba as a Roman prisoner. Considering the character and temperament of Masinissa, the argument which ensued was probably a warm one. It terminated in a compromise. The matter was to be referred to Publius for arbitration. Masinissa, in the meantime, was to stick to business. He may have reflected that anyhow he had had his fling. A Numidian in love can live fast. . . . Syphax, foaming with impotent rage, was haled away to Utica, sans kingdom, sans crown, and torn from Sophonisba.

The case of Sophonisba

Syphax made the fullest use of the advantage that he was the first to arrive in Utica. To the stern inquiries of Publius, how it came about that he had broken faith with the Romans, and had even dared to pit his puny strength against Rome, Syphax made a full confession. It was the madness of love. It was the hymeneal torch, said Syphax, with meridional imagery, that had set his house on fire. Sophonisba had been the enchantress who intoxicated him to his downfall. . . . But, said the virtuous Syphax, he rejoiced in his desolation to see his loathed rival caught in the same toils.

Masinissa was young and innocent. He would soon fall captive to the songs of that Carthaginian siren.

The colouring, as laid on by Syphax, was undoubtedly luxuriant; but Publius could believe anything of a Numidian in love, and he felt it extremely probable that the prophecy of Syphax was, in broad outline, true. The report made, upon his return, by Lælius, served to confirm his doubts. Publius therefore had a private conversation with Masinissa.

What Publius is alleged to have said to the sheik is quite in keeping with his repute as a tactician. Masinissa kept his emotions and his intelligence in very distinct and separate compartments of his mind. He cooled with surprising rapidity when Publius lightly touched upon the danger of mixing up sentiment with business. Sophonisba was a Roman prisoner, and must go to Rome at the discretion of the Roman government. It would be a pity, thought Publius, for Masinissa to throw away the fruits of all that he had done for such a disproportionate reason as Sophonisba.

Publius intervenes

The sheik saw the point more quickly than he might have done if he had not enjoyed that brief intensive honeymoon. He wept; but it was only his way of re-adjusting his nervous tension. Amid a grand dramatic finale the episode of Sophonisba closed. . . . The sheik rode on ahead to Cirta, bearing with him the hemlock cup. He told her all, left her to choose whether to die his wife or to go into Roman captivity, and rode away again. . . . His sense of the dramatic did not suggest to him that the tableau would be improved if he died with her. . . . Sophonisba drank; and the curtain fell slowly upon Masinissa pointing out to the Roman officers the body of the African Helen.

Publius gently reproved him for painting the lily: but since this tropical exuberance seemed native to Africa, he indulged in a little, himself. At a solemn assembly of the army, he publicly acknowledged Masinissa as King of the Numidians, and invested him with a golden crown, an ivory sceptre, a curule chair, and an embroidered robe and tunic. . . . The sheik cheered up immensely over these significant gifts. Passionate beauties were much more easily acquired in Numidia than curule chairs.

Masinissa rewarded

V

But before the curtain had been rung down upon the romantic tragedy of Sophonisba, the Carthaginian peace envoys arrived, and the comedy began. They bowed to the very earth before Publius, with florid protestations and humble confession and contrition. The peace terms [1] which Publius cast at them ought normally to have thrown Carthaginians into a state of hysteria. The amicable humility with which the deputation took them to its bosom was itself suspicious. . . . It prepared to execute them, and to go to Rome to receive the official ratification.

The execution of the terms involved, of course, two

---

[1] These were (1) Restoration of all fugitives and deserters, (2) Withdrawal of troops from Italy and Cisalpine Gaul, (3) Cession of Spain, (4) of the Mediterranean islands, (5) surrender of all ships save twenty, (6) a supply of 500,000 modii of wheat and 300,000 of barley, (7) a war indemnity of five thousand talents. Three days allowed for consideration. On acceptance, an armistice to be arranged, pending the visit of the envoys to receive the confirmation of the Senate. (Livy XXX. 16.)

very interesting measures—the recall of Mago and of Hannibal. Hannibal was lying quiet in Bruttium; Mago's attempt to fight his way south from Cisalpine Gaul was, however, active. A hard-fought battle forced him, wounded, to fall back again into Liguria. On receiving the dispatch from Carthage, he re-embarked his Spanish and Ligurian troops for home. Luck was adverse. He died of his wounds while passing Sardinia, and a storm dispersed his transports. Mago could be ruled off the account. So perished the second of the sons of Hamilcar Barca.

Hannibal was left. He gnashed his teeth to receive the unwelcome summons, and a little of the volcanic temper of the Semite was visible beneath his impassive mask. It was necessary to go: Publius had shifted the centre of the war to Africa; but although Hannibal understood well, and may himself have originated, the plan by which he was withdrawn, under cover of the peace negotiations, to face Publius for a final contest— still it was bitter to him to leave his hopes and plans in Italy unfulfilled. The war should have been decided there. The war would have been decided there if Carthaginians could only have understood that all their efforts should be concentrated upon Italy. . . . He set about his preparations.[1]

Some confusion and disorder naturally marked his departure. He detached for garrison duty the troops with which he intended to cover the embarkation of the picked corps he designed for Africa. Those left be-

[1] Livy XXX. 20. He had expected the summons, and his preparations were in hand before he received it. Appian (VIII. 33), indicates that Hannibal did not expect the treaty to be concluded.

hind did not in all cases take their situation philosophi-
cally, and needed to be persuaded by a little suitable
violence. . . . As the ships went out, Hannibal looked
steadily back at the receding Italian shores. A very great
tale had come to a disappointing end.

The enthusiasm in Rome was not universal. Some
senators considered it a disgrace to Rome that Hannibal
should sail safely away from Italy; and they feared for
Scipio. Fabius expressed the gloomy view that the
state's last and hardest trial was at hand. The majority
were but too thankful to see the last of Hannibal on
any terms; and the Senate voted five days' thanksgiving
to the divine powers.

Lælius had accompanied Syphax to Rome. During
his visit the services of Masinissa were suitably acknowledged, and as an extraordinary compliment the consular
regalia were voted to the sheik, who had thus made a
very profitable exchange for Sophonisba. Lælius had
left again, when the arrival of the peace envoys from
Carthage caused his recall by the Senate. His presence
was desired.

The suspicions of the Senate, aroused by the departure of Hannibal, were thoroughly awakened by the
conduct of the peace envoys, who did not create quite
the impression they designed. The principle asserted by
the envoys was that Carthage had not been responsible
for the war: the whole blame rested upon Hannibal,
and as between the two governments the peace which
closed the first Punic War might be regarded as unbroken. The Senate quite declined to take this point of
view: but the really serious question was, did the Carthaginian government expect it? For, combining the

recall of Hannibal with the presentation of such a totally unacceptable basis of negotiation, the Carthaginian government might so manœuvre the situation as to
concentrate its scattered armies against Scipio in Africa,
and then throw upon the Romans the onus of rejecting
the peace. On the other hand, Scipio had certainly passed
on the terms to the Senate. Did this mean that he was
willing to allow the manœuvre? It was a conceivable
theory that Publius—a self-confident man—was actually desirous of seeing the Carthaginian armies concentrated in front of him. . . . The debate in the Senate
showed a general unanimity in these views, but some difference respecting the precise course to be adopted.
Some were for adjourning the discussion: some for re-
ferring to Scipio: some for instant denunciation of the
armistice. This was the subject on which the Senate desired to question Lælius.

The
Senate
puzzled

The latter was able to throw some light upon the
obscurity. He thought that Publius had only contemplated the withdrawal of the Carthaginian armies from
Italy after the settlement. If this were so, the apprehensions of Fabius had not been without ground. Publius had allowed himself to be outwitted by astute
Phœnician diplomatists.

Fabius was a very old man. His death at this juncture is quite likely to have been due to worry over the
dangers of the situation. The consul Cæpio was hurry-
ing into Sicily with the intention of following Hannibal to Africa, while Rome was solemnly subscribing to
the funeral costs of the man who had first checked and
held Hannibal in Italy. . . . The Senate at once obtained the nomination of a dictator, the only magistrate

who had authority to recall a consul. Any attempt to interfere with Publius, besides embarrassing his military operations, might create a serious schism in the state. At the same time, it is clear that the Senate's confidence in Publius—never very strong—had received a shock.

Prudence
of the
Senate

The Senate as a body had to restrain its individual members from any hasty action. The question was referred to the Assembly. How prudent the Senate was in this matter could be seen in the overwhelming vote by which Publius was returned as commander in Africa. A commission was dispatched to Africa to explain to Scipio the Senate's views, and to authorize him to act as he thought best. He elected to confirm the treaty.

VI

If Publius had been inclined to smile over the worries of the government at home, he was rapidly made aware of the true state of the case. His supply fleet from Sicily, caught in a gale, was blown on shore in the neighbourhood of Carthage, and was seized. The loss was no laughing matter to him. It reprovisioned Carthage at a critical moment when her supplies were short; and it was the clearest breach of the armistice. His representatives, who carried his protest, found a Carthage that had undergone a remarkable change.

The warnings which the Carthaginian government addressed to its citizens had been laughed at. Some vast orb, whose attraction far transcended that of its puny constellation, was crossing its path. It had maintained at Rome the thesis to which the aristocratic party always adhered—that the Spanish Dictator and the Govern-

Seizure
of the
supply
fleet

ment of Carthage were distinct and different powers. Now it had grown silent. It heard the envoys without comment. When they left to address the citizen assembly, the reason became plain. They faced a roaring mob drunk with excitement and hope. Only with difficulty could they gain a hearing. The Assembly wanted them held as hostages for the peace envoys at Rome. . . . The Roman representatives spoke words which were fire to the tinder of Phœnician pride.

They remarked on the wonderful change they saw from the florid persons who had bowed down with amicable smiles and voluble protestations. If (they said) the approach of Hannibal were the cause, let them remember that the man who was returning to them came as a fugitive from Italy, not as her conqueror. If Carthage, after breaking the treaty, were again beaten, what terms could she expect from Rome? They exhorted the Assembly not to push matters to an issue.

The vast orb gliding on towards Africa was far too strong. The Assembly, as one man, proceeded to tear up the treaty. . . . Hurried down to the port under the protection of anxious members of the aristocratic party, the Romans were put on board their ship and sent off. They reappeared before Publius not long after with a story of three Carthaginian triremes that, as soon as their escort turned back, had pursued them into the mouth of the Bagradas river. They had saved themselves only by running their ship ashore, and seeking the protection of Roman troops who noticed their plight. It was clear that the treaty was at an end, and the armistice denounced. Who was responsible for it

The Armistice broken

was a question. Someone had an interest in wrecking the treaty.

VII

Suddenly the great planet swam into visibility. Hannibal arrived at Leptis, and his transports landed the Italian army—the famous Old Guard of Trasumennus and Cannæ. He came, certainly not as a fugitive from Italy: and as certainly not an unsuccessful general recalled by order of his government. He came to look for Publius; and he came as a dictator who was not now confined to the province of Spain, but intended to assert his power in ancient Carthage itself. The Assembly at Carthage was electing him [1] amid uproarious enthusiasm while Publius was pulling up his tent pegs, packing, and making up the Bagradas. . . . Ahead of him galloped the express couriers who went to summon Masinissa.

Scipio
and
Hannibal

The Carthaginian Hannibal and the Roman Hannibal were in the arena at last: and all the world watched.

Publius took the lead without hesitation. He did not mean to be tied to a siege of Carthage, with the risk of being pinned there. His aim was to get into the open, where he could manœuvre. The whole of his plans must have been thought out with great rapidity. Their foundation was the fact that Hannibal was short of cavalry. This necessarily followed from his sea-voyage: he could not bring cavalry from Italy. Publius, on the other hand, had all Masinissa's Numidians to draw upon—

---

[1] Strategos autocrator—Appian. VIII. 5. 31. This is the technical term describing the status of Dionysius and other Greek dictators. The statement of Appian (though of course not the form of words), seems probable enough; but the time cannot have been earlier than this.

if, that is to say, he and Masinissa could join hands in time. The time-factor was of very great importance. Every mile up the Bagradas shortened the road of Masinissa.

The Bagradas valley was the granary of Carthage: and the march of Publius was a clean sweep. He destroyed as he went. His fleet was watching the coast, and he knew that Tiberius Nero was expected with the main Roman armada. The devastation of the Bagradas valley was the last link that surrounded Carthage with a wall of famine. . . . Hannibal, at Hadrumetum, had been negotiating with the inland tribes for cavalry. From Tychæus, a kinsman of Syphax, he obtained two thousand of the best cavalry in Africa. When the Ligurians and Gauls of Mago's army, and the Carthaginian levies, had effected their concentration, he was in command of a force more numerous than the Roman. The campaign begins

Thoroughly alarmed by the proceedings of Publius, the Carthaginians pressed Hannibal for a quick decision. He replied that he would be the judge of when to fight. But as there was nothing to be gained and something to be lost by delay, he almost at once moved. Coming up from the south-east, across the line of Scipio's march, he had on his flank an unspoiled country, whereas Scipio was taking a considerable risk in moving further and further from his base, and cutting himself off from it by a belt of devastated land. Hannibal encamped near Zama, while he ascertained the exact position and arrangements of the Roman forces.

Publius seems to have been at Naragara, beyond the Bagradas, halted. The essential information which Hannibal desired can only have been the knowledge whether

Masinissa had arrived. The Romans were keenly on the
alert, for three of Hannibal's agents were captured.
Publius, instead of executing them, ordered them to
be conducted over the camp and shown everything
there was to see. Having carefully inquired whether
they had had a satisfactory visit, he sent them back
under escort, bidding them report in full to their
commander.

Publius Cornelius Scipio was no fool; and he showed
singularly few signs at any period in his life of throw-
Naragara ing away his advantages. What he very particularly
wanted Hannibal to know was undoubtedly that Masinissa had not arrived. It is highly improbable that Hannibal attributed to him any sentimental reason for his
conduct. The communication indirectly conveyed had
a meaning, if the Carthaginian could read it aright.
What was the meaning? . . . If Publius had wished,
without putting it into words, to hint that he was at
the end of his tether, and would accept any suggestion
of a conference, he might well have done just as he did.
Without Masinissa he was at a serious disadvantage, cut
off on the edge of the desert with a superior army on his
flank. . . . Hannibal had no reason to decline any such
hint and he would have appreciated the method by
which it was conveyed. Finally, he sent across an official
request that they might meet and discuss the situation.

Publius consented: adding that he would communi-
cate to Hannibal the time and place for the interview.

VIII

Publius came across from Naragara to Margaron,
where he dug in close to water, in a favourable position.

Receiving the expected message, Hannibal moved up
and pitched about three and a half miles distant, where
water was much less accessible. His trouble in this respect was the least serious feature in the case. Far more
important was the presence of Masinissa!

Masinissa had effected his junction with the Romans **Margaron**
during the short interval between the return of the
spies and the move to Margaron; and that Publius had
known of his approach, and had been calculating upon
it, is a deduction which Hannibal would draw, if we do
not. The upshot of the whole series of manœuvres was
that Publius faced Hannibal upon the open plain, with
advantage of water and a superiority in cavalry. He
had grasped and kept the initiative throughout, and
moved the formidable Wizard where he wanted him.
. . . And to score off the Wizard in this way was a
triumph never given to any man but Publius Cornelius
Scipio.

The interview nevertheless took place. It had become
even more necessary for Hannibal to form an accurate
estimate of the man opposed to him.

A clear flat plain lay between the two camps. The
two commanders rode out, each with a small mounted
staff; and on this safe neutral ground they left their
escorts, and, attended only by their interpreters, met
face to face. For a little while they were silent, observing one another: and we would give much to know **The
personal
interview** what they observed. . . . The silence had another purpose. It ascertained the relationship in which they stood
to one another. Since Publius did not open the conversation, it became clear (as Hannibal by this time had
guessed) that he was not making any appeal for peace.

Hannibal does not seem to have revealed by any flicker of eyelash or turn of phrase his perception that he had been hoodwinked. He accepted with inscrutable courtesy the position in which he stood: and he began to speak.[1]

The official account of the interview which Publius Scipio handed to the world for publication depicts Hannibal beginning with smooth, very courteous phrases. In reading them we are chiefly conscious of the deep warm pile of the velvet glove that covered the iron hand of Hannibal, and the thinner cuticle and sharp nervous European grip of Scipio. . . . Hannibal regretted that Carthage and Rome, two great empires which had each their natural boundaries, ever allowed themselves to seek possessions outside those limits. But having begun by fighting first for Sicily and then for Spain, they had now gone so far that Rome first and **Hannibal's remarks** Carthage next had been in serious danger. They ought to find some means of composing their differences. He himself was ready because he had learnt by experience the changeability of Fortune, and how by slight turns of the balance she played see-saw with her children. . . . Publius, being new to the game, and having been up all the time so far, might not think that he would ever be down. But he, Hannibal, instanced himself as an example: after Cannæ he had been master of Italy almost up to the gates of Rome, and now he was trying to secure the safety of his own country. Let him mark that, and not be too sure of himself: let him take the wise man's course—which is the safest course. Scipio had

---

[1] Compare Sulla and Mithridates. Plutarch. *Sulla.* c. XXIV: and *Sulla the Fortunate.* p. 228,

nothing to win by victory, and all to lose by defeat. Finally, he suggested, as terms, the cession by Carthage of all the lands in dispute, including the Mediterranean islands, with an undertaking never again to claim them. These terms, he thought, gave security to Carthage and honour to Rome.

Scipio, according to his own account, replied that the Romans had not been responsible for the wars in Sicily or in Spain. The Carthaginians were the aggressors in both. No one (he continued, with equal untruth) was better aware than he of the fickleness of Fortune. But (ceasing to address the Roman public, and turning to the consideration of Hannibal's remarks) though the proposed terms, if made before Hannibal had left Italy, would probably have been accepted, the case was changed now that Rome had gained command of Africa, and had forced him to evacuate the peninsula. Hannibal was suggesting terms which were less favourable to Rome than the recent treaty which had been torn up, and he could not accept them. Scipio's reply

The two commanders thereupon parted without arriving at any agreement: at any rate, without any agreement that they cared to report to their respective governments.

It is very improbable that Hannibal expected his proposed terms to be considered for a moment. He had offered a gold brick, politely counting upon its rejection. And for this he had very serious reasons. His battle-tactics had always been based upon his estimate of the mentality of the opposing commander. The interview afforded him an opportunity of gauging the character and intelligence of Publius Scipio. Faced by the crit- Problems as to the interview ical battle upon which all depended, no knowledge had ever been more necessary to him than this: and Scipio had been very willing that he should have it. But although he, no less than Scipio, fully intended to fight, nothing in honour prevented them, if they so desired, from a little unofficial conversation on other subjects. . . . If we know nothing whatever on that probability, we may remind ourselves that that is all those two very astute men ever intended us to know.

IX

At daybreak next morning the armies took ground. The interview between the two commanders had had its effect. Neither attempted to take any liberty with the other. The marshalling went off quietly. It was a very serious preparation for a very serious struggle. . . . Any surprises would come later on.

Hannibal, though weak in cavalry, was stronger in elephants than he ever had been in Italy. He had over eighty, which he set in front of his first line [1]—the Gauls and Ligurians of Mago's army. His second line was composed of the African and Carthaginian levies. Some way behind these he drew up the Spanish infantry— his own trained and tried veterans. The Carthaginian cavalry, and that of Tychæus, he assembled on the wings.

Unsensational as this arrangement appeared, it presented some very difficult problems. The elephants were an attacking arm which definitely placed the tactical

Battle of Zama

[1] The reader will bear in mind that elephant tactics were tank tactics. A modern tank is only an improved mechanical elephant.

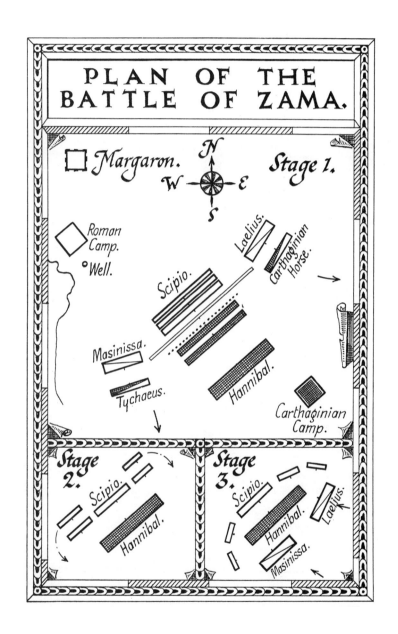

PLAN OF THE BATTLE OF ZAMA.

Margaron.

Stage 1.

Roman Camp.

Well.

Scipio.

Laelius.

Carthaginian Horse.

Masinissa.

Tychaeus.

Hannibal.

Carthaginian Camp.

Stage 2.

Scipio.

Hannibal.

Stage 3.

Scipio.

Hannibal.

Laelius.

Masinissa.

initiative in the hands of Hannibal.[1] There were recognized methods of repulsing them; but if a definite decision were to be reached this day, the method must be one which did not hinder the chief power of the Roman infantry—its mobility on the field. Moreover, no methods of staking the ground were possible to Scipio: the equipment was lacking, and could hardly be improvised upon the spot. He therefore set out his infantry not, as was the usual rule, in echelon, but in file of maniples, so that straight lanes ran through. His light troops he ranged in front, with very careful instructions as to their procedure. The Italian cavalry under Lælius were massed on the left; Masinissa's horse on the right. . . . These dispositions seem to have been completed while both commanders attentively studied each other's tactical scheme, and made the final adjustments.

The tactical arrangements

x

The first casual skirmishing of the Numidian horse was followed by the signal from Hannibal; and the

---

[1] Some modern writers have mistakenly imagined that elephants were useless in war. This was very far from being the case. Mr. Tarn (*Camb. Anc. Hist.* Vol. VI. p. 408-409) observes,. concerning the Indian elephants against which Alexander fought: . . . "There is conclusive proof of the desperate nature of the battle with the elephants—its effects on the minds of the generals (as seen later) and especially on that of Seleucus, who actually fought with them. When King, he ceded whole provinces in order to obtain enough war-elephants." See also p. 504, the battle of Ipsus, where the elephants of the allies turned the scale against the otherwise superior forces of Antigonus. . . . But these African elephants at Zama were imperfectly trained, and some were apparently new to their business. (Appian VIII 9.) Even if Scipio were unaware of this, Masinissa, who was qualified to know, might have passed the hint. . . . What the Romans thought of elephants may be judged by the terms of the peace treaty (*post* p. 274) by which the Carthaginians were definitely prohibited from training them.

The
elephants

elephants began their onslaught. It was a tremendous one. The light troops broke and bolted with the ferocious beasts among them. Their first move, however, was met with a blast of trumpets and bugles from all the assembled instruments of the Roman legions. The uproar—no doubt as cacophonic as experienced musicians could manage to mix it—sent the less trained elephants careering back towards the Numidians who were already in contact on the southerly wing. There Masinissa's men, with little to learn about elephants, saluted them with a shower of darts. They did not long endure these banderilla tactics, but rushed madly in among the horsemen of Tychæus; and Masinissa gave the word to charge. In one rush he had the whole mass going, and Tychæus, elephants and Masinissa disappeared like a whirlwind into the distance.

The light troops, meanwhile, pursued by the rest of the elephants, poured back into the lanes between the Roman squares, which held tight to their formations. Had the Romans been drawn up in their customary echelons, they would probably have been broken. Coming up over the trampled wreckage of the light troops, the elephants had to face the unnerving trumpets and weighted javelins of the legions. They were not well-trained enough for that. Some of them, taking the line of least resistance, hurried along the lanes out into the

The
cavalry

open at the Roman rear, where no more is heard of them; others ran back and wandered along the Roman front till they came to the cavalry wing, where they were saluted by a fresh storm of spears, with the result that they bolted into the Carthaginian cavalry. Lælius

followed upon their heels; and he, elephants, Carthaginians and all were soon emulating Masinissa into the
distance.

XI

The advance of the Roman first line must have been
fairly prompt. Hannibal either had no opportunity for
manœuvre or, as is probable, he had other intentions.
The massed ranks of Gallic and Ligurian troops,
strengthened with Mauretanian archers and Balearic
slingers, at first held fast, but after a severe struggle
were broken, and thrown back upon the Carthaginian
and African foot. These, warned beforehand, refused
to break their ranks or receive the fugitives, but stood
steady in rank. The Roman first line, coming up over
ground littered with slain and slippery with blood, was
completely repulsed. Publius ordered his second line to
advance. It hesitated a little, but went in, and the Carthaginians were broken. The "Old Guard" would not
receive the fugitives, but stood with lowered spears
until they had dispersed. When they had gone—and
their position was a trap from which few could escape
—the Romans, badly damaged, confronted the fresh
army of Cannæ, more numerous than themselves, and
veterans as well trained and equipped.

The tactics of Hannibal at Zama were new to him,
and were based upon a profound respect for the lessons which Publius Scipio had learned at Cannæ. His
aim throughout had been to wear Publius down by hard
pounding, and then to confront him with an over-

The
infantry
battle

whelming superiority of strength.[1] This he had successfully done. The situation of Scipio, when the army of
Cannæ was unmasked, was no enviable one. With inferior forces,[2] half of which had been broken, he faced
fresh troops of historic invincibility. . . . If Tychæus
and the Carthaginian horse could keep Lælius and Masinissa running for a short time more, the latter might
return to find the Roman army no longer in being.

Publius did not flinch. In the pause which ensued he
re-organized and re-arranged his forces, consolidating
his old first line, and wheeling out his second and third
lines to the wings, to overlap Hannibal. He carried out

The Ace his movements unhurriedly. . . . The Wizard made no
attempt to move, or manœuvre or counter-attack in the
face of Roman infantry. He stood perfectly steady;
and he was the best judge of his own wisdom.

When the Roman infantry closed upon the Spaniards
the real struggle began. Owing to the attitude of the
Senate during the year of Scipio's consulship, it was no
ordinary levy that he commanded, but picked volunteer
veterans of the Spanish campaigns, and not a few of the

[1] G. Veith claims the tactics of Hannibal at Zama as the first use on record
of the true reserve "intended definitely to speak the last word." The tactics
invented by Xanthippus and developed by the Carthaginians came to their last
logical end at Zama; for Hannibal himself had invented the method of counter-
ing them. (*Heerwesen und Kriegführung der Griechen und Romer* (1928) pp.
295–297.)

[2] Livy says otherwise, but does not make out his case. Appian alone gives any
actual numbers for the armies. By his account Hannibal had 50,000 men; Scipio
had 23,000 foot and 1500 horse (which is round about the normal figures for
four legions) besides Masinissa's men.

According to Veith (*Schlachtenatlas*) Scipio had 23,000 Roman foot and
2400 horse, as well as 6000 Numidian foot and 4600 horse. Hannibal's first line
was 12,000 strong; his second, about equal; 4000 horse were on the wings; so
that if Appian's figure of 50,000 be correct, the third line was 22,000 strong. If
Scipio's Romans had not lost a thousand men when they met the Spaniards, one
can only feel surprised.

actual survivors of Cannæ, whom the Senate had allowed him to take from their exile in Sicily. The contest between these men and the Spanish infantry was
bitter, desperate and unflinching. But it was not a level
fight. The Spaniards were fresh, as well as more numerous. . . . If both commanders had not their hearts
in their mouths when it became clear that the day was
turning in favour of the Spaniards, they were "either
more or less than men." . . . A very short time, possibly, would have seen the Roman line dwindle, break
and roll up: when the whirlwinds sprang up again in the
desert, and back, only in the nick of time, rode Lælius
and Masinissa.

The verdict was given! It was Cannæ again. The
Spaniards mostly fell or surrendered where they stood.
Those that got away out of the slaughter would have
little chance against the Numidian horse on the level,
open plain. . . . In this way the battle of Cannæ came
home again on its victor.[1]

The Ace trumped

XII

Hannibal, with his staff, reached Hadrumetum in
safety. He waited there a few days, till he knew the
feeling of his countrymen. Then they sent to recall
him to Carthage, and he went.

That impassive, enigmatic mask, which throughout
his days of success had concealed the thoughts and emotions of Hannibal, hid them no less closely now. He
arrived at Carthage as clear, as decisive and as self-
controlled as if he had been the victor of Zama. In re-

---

[1] Polybius XV. 14 (9). gives the Carthaginian losses at over 20,000, and nearly
as many prisoners.

ply to questions he told the council that there was no alternative to surrender.

To the very humble deputation which accordingly waited upon him, Scipio gave no direct answer. He invited a conference at Tunis. There, after he had dryly let the Carthaginian envoys sing their song, he presented his terms. They ran as follows:—(1) Autonomy for Carthage, and full possession of her African territory, (2) Surrender of all fugitives and deserters, (3) Surrender of all ships of war save ten, and of all elephants. No more elephants to be trained. (4) No war, either in or out of Africa, without the consent of Rome, (5) Full restitution to Masinissa, (6) Full maintenance for the Roman forces until the ratification of the peace, (7) A war indemnity of ten thousand talents of silver, to be paid in equal annual instalments over a period of fifty years, (8) One hundred hostages to be delivered, over fourteen and under thirty-one years of age. And finally (9) No treaty or armistice to be considered until the transports and cargoes were restored.

The new Peace terms

When these terms were laid before the citizen Assembly at Carthage, one enthusiastic die-hard, shocked at their nature, rose amid general agreement to advocate their rejection. Before he had gone far, Hannibal had risen to his feet, thrown him off the rostrum, and faced the Assembly.

To the emphatically expressed disapproval of the meeting at this breach of decorum he began by a brief apology. "I left Carthage when I was nine years old. Thirty-six years have given me a tolerable acquaintance with the art of war; but my education in civic procedure you must attend to. My action is reasonable in the spirit, if not according to the letter; for when I think of the way in which we should have treated Rome in a like case, I cannot conceive how any rational man can do other than thank heaven for such terms as these." He then spoke at length in demonstration of the necessity of accepting the treaty: and he brought the Assembly over to his view.[1] . . . From his subsequent actions we can guess the full import of that view. He had not lost hope. Calmly and lucidly he foresaw the possibility of rebuilding the power of Carthage.

Approved by the Carthaginian Assembly, the treaty was referred by Scipio to Rome. It did not pass unopposed.[2] The Senate at length referred it to the Roman Assembly, which gave the Senate authority to conclude peace, and nominated Publius Scipio to negotiate the terms. The treaty was therefore ratified, and put into execution.

The Treaty ratified

XIII

But this treaty was, as we have seen, carried through the Carthaginian Assembly only by the influence of Hannibal; and it was carried through the Roman, and forced upon the Senate, only by the influence of Publius Scipio.[3] It was their treaty. . . . And we are left wondering what more took place, during that interview

---

[1] Polybius (XV. 19) Livy XXX. 37. Appian also bears testimony to Hannibal's influence in the matter. (VIII. 56.)

[2] Livy XXX. 40. 43. Appian VIII. 56–64. Appian says that Scipio threatened to promulgate the treaty on his own authority if there were delay—which shows at least the kind of tradition current concerning Scipio!

[3] "Kid" Hasdrubal nearly wrecked the treaty by insisting that the Carthaginian government was not responsible for the war. Other envoys smoothed over the difficulty; and the Senate began to perceive that it was dealing with a domestic controversy in Carthaginian politics to which it might be wise to give a little diplomatic encouragement. (Livy XXX. 42.)

before the battle of Zama, which we shall never know until all secrets are revealed. As Livy hints, Publius could make what he liked of it, since there was no one to check him; and over Hannibal's share in it lies a silence deep as the grave. . . . It is certain that there was afterwards a curious sympathy and mutual understanding between the two great commanders; and if they, knowing that one of them must be defeated, did not secretly settle their terms before the battle of Zama was fought —it looks at any rate very like it.

Was there a secret agreement before the battle of Zama?

XIV

Where the shoe pinched was seen when the first payment of the war indemnity was arranged. . . . The cumulation of bitter disappointment, wounded pride and hope deferred affected men in various ways. The aristocratic party in the Council wept when it was clear that special taxation must be imposed. It was then that Hannibal laughed.

Hannibal laughs

"Kid" Hasdrubal, their leader, asked him whether he intended to insult them on the miseries of which he had been the cause.

Hannibal made it clear that his laughter had been of a harsher kind. He said: "I laugh because you weep over the least of your misfortunes."

XV

But Publius returned to Rome the greatest man that had trodden its stones since Tarquinius Superbus; and there were those who thought the likeness close.

Peace

CHAPTER XII

ANTIOCHUS MEGAS: AND THE STRUGGLE
IN ASIA

I

HANNIBAL, in Carthage, was almost as much a stranger as he would have been in Rome. He scarcely knew more of one city than of the other. Nothing held him to Carthage save the accident that he was born there, and that her language was his childhood's tongue. . . . He was a cosmopolitan, a citizen of the great Mediterranean civilization, uninterested in its local differences, and unable to see it save as essentially one beneath all its familiar varieties. . . . For his fellow-citizens of the aristocratic party he had neither admiration nor sympathy. Though he retained his authority, it was natural enough that after Zama and the treaty which followed it he should not wield the undisputed power he had once exercised. . . . His policy, therefore, though it may have shown an imperturbable hope and faith, was the natural outcome of the ways in which he habitually saw the world.

Hannibal in Carthage

The situation after the treaty of peace was emphatically not one to give him any reason for despair. Rome had all her troubles before her. Moreover, the investigation into the resources of Carthage, which he set on foot as soon as peace was restored, seems to have been very encouraging. The commercial prosperity of the city had scarcely been injured. With prudence and good ad-

ministration, Carthage might recover herself more
quickly than Rome. The airy fabric of Carthaginian
credit and financial prosperity was likely to survive
while Roman fields lay untilled, and the brute material
of the earth waited for hands to restore its fertility.

His interest was directed particularly to the east:
whither ours may for a moment follow it.

II

Now while Hannibal was besieging Saguntum, crossing the Alps, fighting Cannæ, and going through all that
long adventure which (for the time being) ended at
Zama, events of a serious nature had been taking place
in the eastern Mediterranean. Antiochus of Syria, as a
direct descendant of Seleucus Nicator, had determined
to restore the empire of Alexander.[1] Whether or not
his confidence of success were well grounded, no one
could question that his growing power would at least
sway the balance of affairs in the Mediterranean. Much,
of course, would depend upon the circumstances in
which it was brought to bear; and to affect these was
the object of Hannibal.

Antiochus had already exercised a good deal of in-

---

[1] The empire of Alexander had included Macedonia, a hegemony over Greece,
Asia Minor, Syria, Phœnicia, Palestine, Egypt, Mesopotamia, Persia, Turkestan
and Afghanistan. The idea—let alone the prospect—of this vast area falling
beneath a single rule would considerably disturb a modern statesman. By 202
B. C. Antiochus had "recovered Asia Minor, conquered part of Armenia, made
Arsaces of Parthia tributary, defeated Euthydemus of Bactria, and penetrated
the Cabul valley." (Tarn, *Hellenistic Civ.* p. 20.) The final success of Antiochus
of course involved the shifting northward of the Indian trade route, so that it
should run (as it did in the grand old times of Babylonian and Athenian greatness) overland by Mesopotamia to Asia Minor and Europe instead of by the Red
Sea to Egypt and North Africa. These were highly practical issues, in which
every peasant and camel-driver had an active interest.

fluence upon the course of events. He had been responsible for King Philip's change of attention from
the west to the east. His full weight was beginning to
tell just when, after Zama, Hannibal was searching for
a third party to counterbalance the prospective supremacy of Rome.

The death of Ptolemy Philopator of Egypt in 205
B. C., and the accession of Ptolemy Epiphanes, a minor,
made it certain that great alterations in the political
balance would soon be in progress. They began by the
alliance between Antiochus and Philip for the purpose
of dividing up the Asiatic provinces of Egypt. The
landslide was now started. . . . The Egypt of the Ptol-
emies was not the backward minor state with which the
modern observer is familiar. She was among the most
civilized, the richest and the best organized states then
existing, holding almost a monopoly of the Indian trade
(which Antiochus wanted for the Syrian overland
route); a centre of learning, and a great sea-power. A
war in which Egypt was involved might pull the roof
in upon the Mediterranean politics of the day. . . .
Astute Egyptian diplomatists ensured that it should not
fall upon them. They gracefully placed young Ptolemy
under the guardianship of the greatest of the western
powers. They selected the Roman Senate.

The vast and somewhat conventional powers concerned took a little time to get going over this tremendous business. It was only in the year after Zama that
Philip crossed to Asia and began his attack on the Greek
cities. The campaign was soon passing down the Ægean
with some of the effects of a cyclone. Rhodes declared
war. The fleets of the Rhodian League soon put another

complexion upon affairs. King Attalus of Pergamus, a Roman ally, was involved. . . . Rome made diplomatic overtures.

Philip's action had, as its first result, his own isolation. He had proved an extraordinarily bad diplomatist; for after failing to support Hannibal when he could have done so without danger, he had embroiled himself with Rome, alienated Egypt and offended the Greek cities: and he had put his trust in Antiochus—an ally who was certain, sooner or later, to assert his own claim to Macedonia. The crisis came when two Macedonian partisans illegitimately intruded into the Eleusinian mysteries. Philip may have been right in considering that their execution by the Athenians was an excessive punishment for what he asserted to be an unintentional offence; but until its unintentional nature was clear he was unwise to invade Attica. . . . The Athenians, with the support of Egypt, appealed to Rome, and Rome was drawn into the maelstrom that began to circle around King Antiochus.

Rome drawn in

III

The Senate, seeing that it must either protect its friends or openly abandon them, prepared for war. The Assembly heard the suggestion with horror. There was nothing it wanted less. The strain on the temper and finances of Roman citizens was too much. Earnest propaganda was necessary before it could be persuaded that the Senate was not actuated by sinister motives. The argument employed was Hannibal. When the Assembly heard the contention that there was no choice between peace and war, but only between fighting Philip in

Macedonia or fighting him in Italy, it gave way. The parallel with Saguntum and the remembrance of Pyrrhus were too much for the electors.

That Carthage had not been crushed; that Hannibal still stood quietly waiting in the background, biding his time, were thoughts never far from the surface of men's minds. While the preparations for war with Philip were being pushed forward, such feelings were revived by disturbing news from the north. The unrest in Cisalpine Gaul, which for a generation had been smouldering, dying down, and leaping up again, sprang into a blaze that might have been the herald of a new conflagration. Three Gallic and several Ligurian tribes combined under the command of a Carthaginian officer of Mago's army, named Hamilcar, who had been left behind—probably wounded—when Mago sailed away. A force forty thousand strong sacked Placentia, crossed the Padus, and marched on Cremona. The garrison shut the gates and sent an express for help. It reached an unhappy prætor who, with only some five thousand men under his command, was helpless.

A Carthaginian in Cisalpine Gaul

The Senate was not disturbed. It sent out orders for the reinforcement of the prætor's army, and it sent a commission to Carthage to demand the recall and surrender of Hamilcar. The Carthaginian government protested that it could do nothing but sentence him to exile and confiscate his property.

Hannibal, still the commander of the Carthaginian army, and in virtue of that fact still dictator, had to bear the responsibility for Hamilcar. It is possible that the aristocratic party suspected him of having a finger in that pie. At any rate, he vacated the post, and after

Hannibal resigns from the army

an interval joined the Judicial Board [1] which was the stronghold of Carthaginian aristocracy. It is not probable that he was welcome there; but his status and influence must have made indisputable his right to a seat.

IV

The operations of the first year of the Macedonian war gave the Romans no cause for enthusiasm. Philip's elation found some reflection in Carthage, where the failure of the Romans raised hopes which increased the influence of Hannibal. Any satisfaction which the aristocrats had derived from their victory of the previous year was wiped out with the payment of the first instalment of the war indemnity.

First instalment of the war indemnity 199 B. C.

It was paid in silver. The quæstors who weighed the bullion, dissatisfied with it, reported to the Senate. Assay proved that the metal was fully a fourth below standard. The disgraced Carthaginian envoys were compelled to borrow from Roman bankers to make good the deficit. The Senate was by no means hard upon them. It restored a hundred of the hostages, with the good-humoured promise that the rest should follow if Carthage fulfilled her treaty obligations.

But the tolerance of the Senate (which was not free from suspicion of bias in favour of Hannibal's political enemies) does not seem to have been imitated at Car-

---

[1] Cornelius Nepos, *Hannibal* c. VII. This author (whose account differs from that of Livy) certainly drew upon the writings of Sosilus, Hannibal's Greek secretary. Livy is probably the better authority for the proceedings of his own countrymen, but any statement of Sosilus concerning Hannibal deserves respect. Cornelius Nepos, in saying that Hannibal became "prætor" (in which Livy agrees) no doubt means that he joined this Judicial Board of one hundred. From Livy XXXIII. 46, it appears that he became one of its presidents.

thage. Hannibal immediately came back to power, and he was not long in obtaining authority to probe into the roots of the scandal.

His first actions brought him into collision with the power of the Judicial Board. Attempting to question one of the officers of the treasury, he found himself treated with defiance. The man was an adherent of the aristocratic party, and expected to become a member of the Board. It was not safe, however, to defy the old disciplinarian of the army of Cannæ. He promptly had the man arrested, and produced before the Assembly.

On the address which Hannibal then delivered to the citizens of Carthage a great deal hung. It embodied one of these constitutional crises which determine the fate of nations. In order to understand it, we may review the case he had to make.

As far back as the time just precedent to Gelo and the battle of Himera there had been a clash of political principles at Carthage. The trouble lay in the continual *The Judicial* effort of the Phœnician aristocracy of Carthage to re- *Board* strain and prevent the individual discretion of its great commanders. From contests of this kind there is no escaping. We can illustrate it by the similar contests that were waged at Rome, and that in later ages found their consummation in Cæsarism. The Romans succeeded in keeping their control by normal constitutional means: but at some time after the revolt and fall of Malchus, the Carthaginians established the Judicial Board of one hundred members now in question, the aim of which was to control the military commanders.[1]

This Board was one of the most effective instruments

[1] See *ante* p. 12–13.

ever invented for such a purpose. But its power grew until it became the real governing body of Carthage, and the whole of Carthaginian life passed under its scrutiny. As a purely negative force, its purpose was not active government, but the prevention of action. It exerted a power to stifle, not a power to act. . . . The effect of such a body became clearly visible towards the end of the first Punic War. It was a paralysing, an inhibiting effect, strangling every effort to introduce new ideas or new methods, defeating every original or independent personality. We have seen how Hamilcar Barca treated the problem. He founded a dictatorship in Spain outside the circle of regular government. Hannibal had inherited this dictatorship. His return home brought him face to face with the old problem. . . . Carthage was no longer a single commercial city; it had become the centre of a dominion embracing many various peoples. Were the imagined interests of men too stupid and too cowardly to take large views so to act as a brake upon the strong and the foreseeing? Was Carthage—like some kind of madman—to die by holding her breath? . . . This was the case Hannibal put to the Assembly. Which were they to have—the selfish cowards, or the men of bold ideas and vigorous action? Would they at any rate die fighting, or die of inanition?

The Assembly had no two minds. He had not come to his peroration before he saw the current of opinion setting fast for him, just as that of the Roman Assembly set for Scipio. He concluded therefore by putting the motion that the members of the Judicial Board should no longer be irremovable, but should submit themselves

Influence of the Board

annually for re-election. It was carried. When he
stepped down from the rostrum, it was as a new Her- It is
acles competent to turn out the Augean stable of Car- elective
thaginian domestic government.

Even Hamilcar had never won such a victory as this.

v

Had the course of the Macedonian war continued
favourable to Philip, Hannibal's return to power might
have been permanent: but a change took place when
Titus Quintius Flamininus, a soldier of the school of
Scipio, was appointed to the command in Greece. By
dint of acting with courtesy, tact and intelligence,
Flamininus left behind him a name which speedily came
to rank among the minor immortals. The smaller Greek
states were almost pathetically grateful to find a Roman
who acted as if he understood them. Antiochus, busy
with the conquest of Palestine, did not send the help
that Philip might have looked for: and in this critical
moment, Philip fought the war alone. At the battle of
Cynoscephalæ, Macedonia, which had risen to the
hegemony of Greece, overthrown Persia, and extended
its rule to Bactra and India, came to a sudden and ca-
lamitous termination: and for the time being she disappeared from history.

Though one hope of Hannibal had thus gone, the Fall of
game was still far from being played out. The fall of Macedonia
Philip rendered it only the more certain that Antiochus
would now be obliged to try conclusions with Rome.
Philip had always been a fool. Antiochus might prove a
more capable statesman. He had, at least, the material
resources for the task.

Since Hannibal had never, at any time, possessed military force sufficient to achieve his objects by that means alone, war had never for him been anything but a method of exercising political leverage on those who did. Even if, in the short immediate sense, he had not been successful, there still remained the possibility of exercising that leverage in another way, without the intermediation of war. A great league of Mediterranean powers would face a Rome which was very far indeed from being the Rome of twenty years ago. From this point of view it was no paradox to contend that even after Zama Hannibal's war-making might have achieved its intended object. . . . If such a league could be formed, the military power of Carthage could rapidly be reconstituted. . . . Finally, an inconclusive, mutually exhausting war between Rome and Syria would leave Carthage in an extremely favourable position.

Prospects for Hannibal

Attalus of Pergamus had already appealed to Rome for protection; and although the Senate was slow in taking up the matter, Antiochus was sure to act, if the Senate did not. Thrace and Macedonia were integral portions of the empire of Alexander; Greece was a political appanage of Macedonia; and Antiochus would not fail in any event to assert his claim to them. To count on a war between Antiochus and Rome was therefore perfectly safe. And whether Antiochus turned out to be a faithful and intelligent ally, or whether he proved another Philip, Hannibal stood to gain.

This was sound reasoning: but there were matters in which his reasoning was not so sound. It might have been wiser for him not to have challenged the position of the Carthaginian aristocracy. Hamilcar's

policy might have paid him better—had there but been
another Spain.

VI

There were others who could perceive these things.
The Senate had to face the unwelcome fact that it could
not slip out of a war with Syria. To allow Antiochus Difficulties
before
Rome
to make good his claims to Macedonia and Greece, and
to confront Rome with a great power stretching from
the Adriatic coast to India, was not to be thought of.
No great intelligence was required to see that in such a
case Carthage would become once more a pressing danger. So far from the war having ended at Zama, it
looked as if Zama had but closed a chapter, and that the
tale would reopen with more formidable omens. . . .
In such circumstances, Hannibal's foes were sure of a
hearing in Rome.

VII

It was perhaps not at first certain whether they could
adduce sufficient ground for Roman intervention. The
defeat of the Judicial Board had opened the way to a
thorough survey of the financial resources of Carthage.
The investigations brought to light a considerable
amount of highly interesting evidence. The fact that
Carthage was immensely rich must sometimes have puzzled those of her sons who wrestled with the unaccountable truth that she often had no money. Hannibal's
investigation solved this strange problem. It revealed
peculation and incompetence upon an immense scale.
The Semitic gentlemen who had attempted to pass off
upon the Roman quæstors bullion a fourth under stand-

ard, and who had wept at the idea of fresh taxation, were robbing the treasury and wasting its money right and left. Hannibal undertook that the war indemnity should be paid from the current resources of Carthage, without the imposition of fresh taxes; and he made good his word.

While this was hardly a crime, it was not much more pleasant hearing to the Senate than to those whose peculations had been stopped. The Senate had undoubtedly intended the war indemnity to be a crippling burden, and, at the time when it was calculated, it no doubt so appeared to be, in proportion to the financial resources of Carthage.

The difficulties attending a war with Antiochus made more urgent still such preliminary diplomatic action as could be achieved. The Romans were still comparatively new to foreign wars. Sicily, Spain and Africa they had undertaken, the two latter only through the individual enterprise of Publius Scipio; and, with even smaller forces, the mainland of Greece. But to fight Antiochus on his own soil meant an enterprise such as no Roman army had ever attempted. The first necessity therefore was to exhaust every available means of reducing the power of Antiochus before-hand: and action against Carthage might be held to come under this head.

The decision to intervene at Carthage was not immediately nor unanimously reached. Publius Scipio for long opposed, as below the dignity of Rome, any attempt to take sides in Carthaginian politics, or to help Hannibal's domestic enemies to hound down a great man. But Scipio himself had not perfectly clean hands. He, too, belonged to the tiny but terrible party of the

cosmopolitan autocrats. What turned the scale was the
assurance that Hannibal was in touch with Antiochus.
It was at length decided to send a commission to Africa
to lay before the Carthaginians the allegation that Hannibal was in communication with an enemy of Rome.[1]

VIII

Hannibal had either a guilty conscience (as his enemies suspected) or an unusually good secret service (as
his friends may believe). He had no doubt as to the
purpose of the commission: and he was fully prepared.
During the day before the commissioners had their first
official audience, he showed himself carefully in public.
At dusk he went to the city gate. There his horse met
him. Ordering his two servants to await his return, he
rode out, as if for an evening gallop.

Flight of Hannibal

That night and the day following he rode a hundred
and thirty miles [2] through Zeugitana into Byzacium,
striking the coast at his villa between Acylla and Thap-
sus. A ship was waiting, and bullion was ready packed
for transport. He was at Cercina before the next night.
Phœnician ships were in harbour. He was recognized,
and hailed with enthusiasm; too much enthusiasm for
his purpose. He therefore invited the ship's officers on
shore; and told them to bring their sails to make an

[1] Was he? Publius Scipio does not seem to have thought so; and Livy
(XXXIII. 47) hardly writes as if he believed the allegation. But evidently the
likelihood was somewhat striking for the reasons given in the text: and the disbelief of Scipio, otherwise important, was discounted by the sympathy that
always existed between him and Hannibal.
[2] This does not seem very fast riding: but it is improbable that he could
lay a chain of relays without being detected. He rode one horse all the way, and
did not stick to the high roads.

awning against the sun. Sailors do not seem to have
changed much in some characteristics with the lapse of
ages. . . . When they awoke, late next day, the Wizard
had gone like the morning mist; and as it took them
time to get their sails back on board the news reached
Carthage later still. His ante-chamber had been
thronged with disturbed partisans. When it was realized that he was not to be found, the wildest rumours
were current. It was believed that he had been mur-
dered by the Romans. By the time the ships from Cercina had revealed the truth, the Wizard was far away

on blue water on the easterly passage. Two fast ships
were sent after him. They did not find him.

His foes relieved their feelings, and placated the angry Romans, by confiscating his property, razing his
house, and declaring him outlaw. They also, apparently,
provided the commissioners with a quantity of sensational fiction calculated to divert attention in Rome
from their customary failure to deliver the goods. . . .
The commissioners went home to report that a great
conspiracy had been unearthed. The Macedonian war,
the coming Syrian war, a revolt of Carthage, and many
events that never happened, were part of the Wizard's
plans. . . . It may have been so. . . . But he was more
accustomed to take advantage of the opportunities
kindly provided by others.

IX

So closed his attempt to govern and to restore Carthage. The blow was directed at him from Carthage
itself: the fate of Malchus had befallen him: and when
we see the mentality which sacrificed, from such mo-

tives, her only hope, we need look no further for the causes which led to the ultimate collapse and disappearance of Carthaginian power.

Those who betrayed him could no doubt have adduced reasons and motives with the colour of plausibility. The party which entertained the conviction that the safety of Carthage depended upon avoiding pride and ambition, and upon concentrating upon the humble task of making money, must have had a singular conception of the view taken of commerce by such men as the directors of the Roman state. . . . Commerce is a political fact. . . . As long as man is a political animal, commerce will be the method by which the mutual relations of men are established and expanded. Control of money and exchange is so indissolubly connected with the control and government of men, that the two gravitate together into the hands of those who exercise the greater political activity. The gift for marketing is a form of power; and a form of power can never be a fact politically neutral. . . . Hence, only a profound misconception of the very elements of the case could ever lead men to suppose that a commercial system could in any sense be maintained without all those other activities which we specifically distinguish by the word "political." [1]

Political philosophy of his enemies

The exile of Hannibal thus implied that Carthage relinquished the one power which could hold her commercial interests together, and the one purpose—that is to say, government—for which those interests were ultimately valuable. And the fall of Carthage, when it came, was the conclusive proof that the whole idea upon

Its implications

[1] This is the meaning of Hannibal's speech, Livy XXX. 44.

which the Phœnicians had originally based their proceedings, and from which they had only half-heartedly
and inadequately departed—the idea of a non-political
commerce—was an illusion. . . . The rich man who
possesses no political significance may exist in Utopia
—but nowhere else.

X

Hannibal's welcome at Tyre was very different. He
was honoured as the most famous and distinguished of
her sons. He basked in a little refreshing admiration for
a few days, and then went on to Antioch. The king had
left for Ephesus, but his son continued the friendly
welcome to the great Carthaginian. Following to Ephesus, Hannibal found the king, who embraced him as a
messenger from heaven. So far, all was hopeful. The
king already saw the world at his feet.

It would be hard to believe that the Roman diplo-
matists had quite meant this.[1] They had hoped to see
Hannibal finally suppressed—certainly they had not
intended to throw him into the arms of Antiochus.
They were more successful in their other operations.
Designs When Publius Scipio gained his second consulship in
of the the ensuing year, he had schemes for naming Mace-
Senate donia a consular province—with, of course, at the back
of his mind an idea that it might fall to him. . . . The
Senate interfered to prevent this. Its own Cosmopoli-
tan Autocrat was accordingly shelved, and had no op-

---

[1] The natural ally of Carthage was Egypt, whose control of the Indian trade
was invaluable to her. Carthage certainly did not want to see this trade diverted
to the overland Syrian route and the Greek cities. The interests of Hannibal
and Antiochus were therefore not identical; a fact which must be very carefully remembered in all that follows.

portunity of fighting any more battles of Zama, while the Senate proceeded to carry out a coup of another sort.

The suppression of Macedonia had been achieved by the policy identified with the name of Titus Quintius Flamininus—that of detaching the republican city-states of Greece from support of the Macedonian monarchy. While Philip's military power was derived entirely from Macedonia itself, the financial resources which alone could enable him to fight a considerable war were drawn from the Greek states. Hence the diplomacy of Flamininus practically decided the result before the military issue was fought out. . . . Flamininus, with the support of the Senate, played his game squarely. Not only did he restore the sovereign autonomy of the city-states of European Hellas, but he intervened on behalf of the Asiatic Greek cities. . . . The aim of the Senate was now to preserve the influence so acquired. If Antiochus could win over the city-states, the coming war would be fought close to Italy, perhaps, ultimately, even on Italian soil. If they could be kept solid for the Roman interest, the war might be fought in Asia. The Senate therefore decided upon a singularly bold step. It instructed Flamininus to withdraw the Roman garrisons from European Greece, and thus to carry out his policy to the logical end.

Roman troops withdrawn from Greece 194 B. C.

The ardent political idealists of Greece could scarcely believe their senses. Their enthusiasm and gratitude are touching, even over this long retrospect. When Flamininus mentioned that he would like to take home with him all Hannibal's Italian prisoners working in Greece as slaves, they rushed to oblige him, and were delighted to foot the bill. . . . No honour, perhaps, was ever better deserved than the three days' Triumph of Flamininus. He left behind him a land indeed at his feet— but with thanks; and the captives who marched in his procession were not foreigners enslaved, but his own people set free from servitude. . . .

There was no danger. The astute statesmen at Rome were counting—and did not count in vain—upon human nature and the force of circumstances. With their determined idealism and their system of confederate leagues, the city-states were in no position to hold their ground against a centralized military monarchy such as that of Antiochus. When the pull came, Antiochus might assert as loudly as he liked that he came to free them from the crushing tyranny of Rome. They would draw instinctively towards the powerful protection of the republican Roman state which had not merely proclaimed their freedom, but withdrawn its troops.

Object of the step

XI

Against this shrewd calculation, the advice of Hannibal was founded upon an equally shrewd judgment of the military situation. As a military expert, he laid before Antiochus his own plans. He asked for a fleet of one hundred decked ships, and a striking force of ten thousand infantry and a thousand cavalry. He proposed to touch first at Carthage, where he thought he had the ground fully prepared; and then he would land at some point in Italy, the identity of which he withheld. The king could meanwhile enter Greece and hold himself ready to co-operate as and when circumstances directed.

This information came to the astonished Senate from Carthage itself. A mission arrived from the aristocratic party with a somewhat confused and unsatisfactory story. It was alleged that, in accordance with the foregoing plan, Hannibal had dispatched to Carthage a man named Aristo, a Tyrian, fully instructed with the details necessary to bring him into touch with the Barcid party. This man was detected. As nothing had been committed to writing, it was impossible to bring these allegations to the test of proof. The Barcids, vehemently denying the statements made, pointed out with reason that if Tyrians in Carthage were arrested on flimsy suspicions, there would be reprisals against Carthaginians in Tyre. The aristocratic party, however, determined to denounce the affair at Rome. . . . Apparently they could not see that they injured themselves as much as they injured their opponents. The Senate, a good deal disturbed, answered by declining to support Carthage against the aggressions of Masinissa. . . . It seemed the wisest course on general principles to embarrass Carthage.[1] . . .

Hannibal's war plans

For all that, the allegations were probably true; and we may find some confirmation of their substance in the significant way in which the diplomatic situation was spun out by Antiochus. Envoys were coming and going: Titus Flamininus, sitting as chairman of a committee of foreign affairs in Rome, rejected the contention of Antiochus that he had an hereditary claim to Macedonia. The envoys asked for time to report; and

---

[1] Livy, XXXIV. 61–62. The Senate sent a commission of inquiry, headed by Publius Scipio, to investigate the allegations against Masinissa. Publius took good care to do nothing that gave satisfaction to Hannibal's political enemies.

there was delay, and consideration, and all the usual
methods of filling in time. A Roman commission was
appointed to interview Antiochus personally. If Hannibal's plans had been discovered and frustrated, there
was reason for this, and for the distinct decline of his
prestige in the eyes of Antiochus.

**The plans
frustrated**

Antiochus made every effort to secure his own position. He made young Ptolemy his son-in-law; Ariare-
thes of Cappadocia he similarly attached; while he
offered Eumenes of Pergamus a third alliance. The
Ætolian League made overtures to him—which turned
his attention still further from Hannibal's plans. The
Roman commissioners, on their way to meet Antiochus,
were instructed to turn aside to make sure of Eumenes.
They had other instructions also. Reaching Ephesus in
the king's absence, Publius Villius paid particular attention to Hannibal, whom he constantly visited. His
aim was to discover, if he could, Hannibal's intentions,
and at the same time to reassure him concerning the
attitude of Rome towards him personally. As nothing
is recorded of his results, it is to be supposed that they
were nil.[1]

---

[1] Livy (XXXV. 14) says that Claudius Quadrigarius, on the authority of
Acilius, declares Publius Scipio to have been one of the commissioners: and that
he had interviews with Hannibal. Livy himself, however, gives the names of
the commissioners as P. Sulpicius, P. Villius and P. Ælius. The importance of
this point is that on it depends the credence we give to the famous story of the
interview between Scipio and Hannibal. They discussed great generals. Hannibal,
in reply to a question, named Alexander as in his opinion the greatest; Pyrrhus
as the second; he ranked himself as the third. Scipio is reported to have said:
"And what if you had beaten me?" Hannibal answered: "Then I should have
called myself by far the first." Scipio was delighted at the skilfully turned
compliment.

This is a good story; and there is nothing in it inconsistent with what we
know of Hannibal. Plutarch (*Flamininus*, c. XXI.) adds the detail that in their
walk Hannibal took the lead, Scipio raising no objection. (Hannibal, as senior,
had the right to do so.) If we could rely upon the statement of Acilius, some

Eumenes, however, was only too glad to ally himself Delay with the Romans; and the interviews of Villius with Hannibal had one indirect result—they shook his status with Antiochus. A conference between the commissioners and the king had no result, except to make him abandon the attempt to negotiate. An interview between Minnio, his principal adviser, and the commissioners only led to a further warm exchange of views. Publius Sulpicius Galba, a bluff man, was very emphatic in pointing out the insubstantial nature of the king's claims. They were, in fact, attempts to find adequate justification for the political unification of the east. The sound prosaic arguments of detail were all on the side of the Romans. As no compromise could be reached, the Roman commissioners withdrew. The real issue was whether the breach with eastern Mediterranean was to come under the control Antiochus of an Asiatic or a European government: and that was not a question capable of being settled by argument.

XII

To the council which the king summoned for the final decisions, Hannibal was not invited. That the councillors almost fought one another in their zeal to advise war was its least serious feature; far worse was the kind of advice tendered. Alexander the Acarnanian ad-

important deductions might be drawn from it concerning the military models studied by Hannibal, his friendly relations with Scipio, and his personal character. But was Scipio at Ephesus this year?

The story does at any rate testify clearly to the view taken of the relation between Hannibal and Scipio by men who lived a very few generations later. If it is not true, it may be "as good as true." . . . Another suggestion is conceivable. The story, if it has any basis at all, must have come from Scipio. Can it be one of the suppressed details of the interview before Zama, slightly amended?

vocated, and apparently carried, the plan of landing in Greece, depending upon help from Philip of Macedon in the north, the Ætolians in the centre, and Nabis of Sparta in the south. Hannibal was to go to Africa in order to divert the attention of the Romans. . . . He probably got wind of what was happening, for he managed to obtain speech with Antiochus while the council was breaking up.

Pressed to the point by a direct question, Antiochus said that he had been unfavourably impressed by Hannibal's repeated interviews with Villius. . . . This was probably not the whole truth; but Hannibal accepted it as if it were, and told Antiochus the story of the oath his father Hamilcar Barca had administered to him, as a child. Talking to an oriental despot of the type of Antiochus is a delicate business. Hannibal probably took a carefully calculated risk when he ended upon a harsh note. He told Antiochus that that oath had driven him from one land to another, seeking its fulfilment. If Antiochus needed help against Rome, he, Hannibal, was ready. If not, he would seek a place where he was wanted.[1]

Antiochus was in the mood to find this kind of talk acceptable: and he once more smiled upon Hannibal. But he did nothing more than smile.

The opportunities that Antiochus was throwing away with such plenitude can be illustrated by the plans attributed to him in Rome. War-time rumours were ac-

---

[1] This story (Livy XXXV. 19. Polybius III. 11. See *ante* p. 70) must be distinguished from the circumstances of its narration. It was no doubt true; but Hannibal was colouring his own feelings to suit Antiochus. It does not necessarily follow that Hannibal really possessed an anti-Roman "complex." He was far too cool a man to be swayed by obsessions.

tive. He was said to be intending to send a fleet to Sicily; and a special defence force was actually raised against the danger. The Senate sent a commission headed by Titus Flamininus to the Greek cities, to keep them steady. It had not miscalculated. The only element in Greece that Flamininus could not hold was the Ætolian. The latter grandly, in the spirit of the *Skibbereen Eagle,* declared war. When he asked for a copy of the declaration, they surpassed even that celebrated organ by telling him that they would hand it to him on the banks of the Tiber!

It may possibly have been the news of this episode that inspired Hannibal to the third exhibition of bad temper he gave in the course of a fairly lengthy life. The philosopher Phormio had held forth somewhat exhaustively in a lecture at which he was present, on the principles of command in war: and Hannibal was asked to express an opinion. He said: "I have heard many old fools in my time: but never such a ridiculous old fool as this." . . . And so Phormio achieved immortality!

Hannibal disappointed

He fought in vain against human stupidity and human vanity. The king bungled his first steps. Antiochus could not even capture the Asiatic Greek cities. The ships for Hannibal's African expedition were not ready. The Ætolians then raised the question whether it ought to be made. Having involved themselves with Rome, they stopped at nothing in order to get Antiochus between themselves and the Romans. Antiochus liked to hear their declarations that Greece was only waiting to fall upon his neck. In view of this alleged enthusiasm —which was the figment of their own interested fancy —they urged him not to divert a ship or a man from

Greece. Hannibal, they argued, was a dangerous adventurer working entirely for his own hand. The general result of his campaigns would, no doubt, consist of a series of sensational victories in view of which the importance of Hannibal would go up like a rocket, and the importance of Antiochus—and his advisers—would come down like a stick.

Greeks were not Greeks for nothing. The hellish ingenuity of this argument lay in its element of truth. Antiochus—and his advisers—suddenly decided that Hannibal need not go to Africa.

The African expedition cancelled

XIII

Worse remained. Antiochus crossed the Ægean from Imbros and landed at Demetrias, with a force of ten thousand infantry, five hundred horse, and six elephants. . . . To the horrified Ætolians he apologized for the smallness of his force; his enormous hosts, he assured them, were on the way. As it was inadequate even for an occupation of Greece, let alone a war with the Romans, the Ætolians hesitated. Ultimately they joined him. The enthusiasm of Greece was conspicuous by its absence. At Chalcis, some inquiring interest was expressed in the identity of the mysterious Greeks he had come to "liberate." The Bœotians hedged. The Achaian League, swayed by a sarcastic speech from Flamininus, refused to have anything to do with Antiochus. The winter was wasted in these useless proceedings.

At last, at a council held at Demetrias, Hannibal spoke out. He informed the king that the only hope was to gain the alliance of Philip of Macedon. His own

view was, and had always been, that the war should
be carried into Italy; and if he had had his way, the
Romans would not how be hearing of the capture of
Chalcis, but of war at their own doors. He advised the
immediate calling up of all the forces the king could
raise, the dispatch of a fleet to Corcyra, to watch the
crossing from Brundusium, and of another to the Campanian coast. He wound up by remarking that even if he
did not know everything about war, he did know how to
fight the Romans.

Antiochus
in Greece

None of these recommendations was put into force,
except that the army and fleet from Asia were sent
for. After pottering about after small local alliances,
Antiochus managed to offend Philip, who at once got
furiously into touch with the Romans. Various communities protested against the presence of Antiochus in
Greece.

In spring the Roman consul Manius Acilius Glabrio
crossed from Brundusium at his leisure, without opposition. Antiochus was developing a fresh respect for
Hannibal, all of whose pessimistic predictions were
coming true. The Ætolians turned up with a very small
contingent. . . . Antiochus accordingly retired upon
the historic pass of Thermopylæ. We are not told that it
was Hannibal who advised this simple step, and perhaps it was too obvious to call for the exertion of
genius; but he could certainly have done no better.

Behind the entanglements he built at Thermopylæ
he did not think he could be easily dislodged, and the
Romans had no great hopes on that score. It was left
to the terrible "Censor," Cato himself, to inflict the
last disgrace. Antiochus could not even hold Ther-

Antiochus
expelled
from Greece

mopylæ! Picked like a snail from a shell, he and his staff reached Elatia, got safely to Chalcis, and escaped by sea. Very little of his army escaped the Roman pursuit.

XIV

Hannibal was the only person who dared to tell him the cold truth. When it became obvious that the king thought the war over, Hannibal told him that, far from this being the case, the only cause for surprise was that the Romans were not already in Asia. Antiochus bestirred himself to do what he could.

A more formidable competitor than Acilius Glabrio was by now on his way to deal with the main armies of Antiochus. Publius Scipio had not been successful in his efforts to gain the eastern command; the Senate, utilizing the prestige of Titus Flamininus, had seen to this. Too prudent to press his own claims further, Publius ran his brother Lucius for the consulship, got him in, and proceeded to conduct him personally to the east, where Lucius, on the whole, competently carried out the task of signing the official orders laid before him by his brother. Indecisive sea-fighting was still worrying up and down the Ægean. Publius therefore took the land route by the Straits.

By this time Antiochus had altogether lost the offensive. His efforts had to be directed towards preventing Publius Scipio from entering Asia. The operations of the fleets would decide whether the passage of the Straits could be made. Hannibal hastened southward to use his influence in raising a Phœnician fleet.

After successful operations in the north by the Ro-

Publius Scipio goes to Asia

man admiral, to clear the way for the land army, news came that the Rhodian fleet had been entrapped and beaten by the Syrian admiral Polyxenidas, who was free to move. The Roman fleet hurried to the spot; but Polyxenidas promptly immobilized it by retiring into harbour at Ephesus and waiting. . . . The arrival of Hannibal from Phœnician waters would enable the combined fleets to fight the Romans with the certainty of success, and to hold the Straits. But Hannibal was held back by the wind. Rhodes had time to recall and concentrate her ships. Cruising off the Pamphylian shore, on the watch, the Rhodians at last heard that Hannibal was at Side. He was in force, having thirty-seven battleships, including three seven- and four eight-bankers, as well as ten cruising three-bankers—forty-seven ships in all. Against this the Rhodians had only thirty-two four-bankers, and four three-bankers; and their crews had a long sick-list.

Hannibal brings up the Phœnician fleet

Coming up in column of sail, the Rhodians unexpectedly ran into the Phœnician fleet as it rounded the point of Side. Hannibal, leading the van, was bringing his ships into line of battle, standing away from shore so that his rear ships would take the position nearest the land. Into this situation the Rhodians fell unprepared. The Rhodian admiral, Eudamus, leading the column, at once turned to starboard, out to sea, signalling the following ships to turn likewise as they came up, and take their places in the line. He went so fast, and took up his own position so quickly, that a serious gap was left. The battle opened by the engagement of Eudamus and five ships with Hannibal's wing. Then came a long line of unengaged Phœnician ships; and all the Rhodians were crowded close to land opposite the Phœnician right wing. They soon began to take their correct positions, each turning and sailing out after Eudamus. But the temporary crowding of the Rhodians on the landward wing had an expected consequence. Assailed by an overwhelming force of Greek rams, the Phœnician wing was shattered. An immense moral impression was created at the outset by a smaller Rhodian ship at one stroke ramming and sinking a Phœnician sevenbanker. Eudamus, hard pressed and signalling for help, was soon rescued by the approach of his victorious left wing. Hannibal had no alternative but to break off the engagement.

The Rhodians did not pursue. Their sick crews were exhausted. They stopped for lunch. Eudamus, at any rate, appreciated what had happened, for during the interval he called from his conning tower to his ship's company: "Up and look at a wonderful sight." . . . They crowded forward, and saw the huge Phœnician galleys towing off their crippled companions. . . . So Hannibal never reached the Ægean.

XV

The failure of Hannibal to effect a junction with the fleet at Ephesus compelled the latter to fight at a disadvantage. At the battle of Myonnesus the Romans captured or sank forty-two ships, and established their supremacy in the Greek seas. The route for Publius Scipio across the Straits was open.

Antiochus lost his head after the battle of Myonnesus and the failure of his land operations. Not only did he withdraw his main armies south to Ephesus, but he

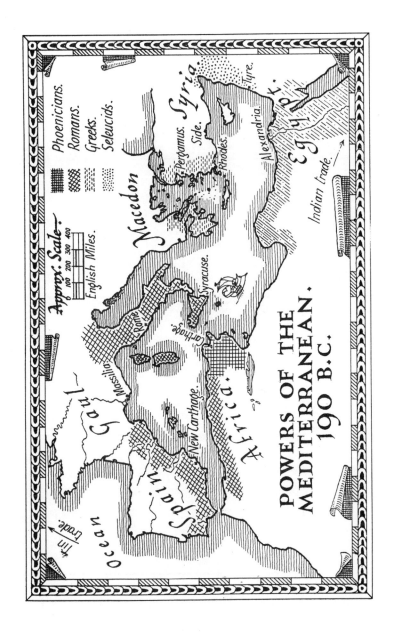

Phoenicians.
Romans.
Greeks.
Seleucids.

Approx. Scale.
0 100 200 300 400
English Miles.

Tyre.
Pergamus. Syria
Side.
Rhodes.
Alexandria.
Indian trade.

Macedon

Egypt

Syracuse.

Rome
Carthage.

Gaul
Massilia

Ocean

Spain
New Carthage.

Africa.

Tin trade.

POWERS OF THE
MEDITERRANEAN.
190 B.C.

evacuated the great fortress of Lysimachia on the
Straits. Publius was even more pleased at this than at
the naval victory. The immense supplies abandoned in
Lysimachia were very acceptable to the Roman army;
and Eumenes of Pergamus had made every necessary
preparation for the crossing, which was a trimphal procession instead of the desperate struggle anticipated.

Overtures to Scipio were rejected. The terms laid
down by Publius were impossible for the king to accept.
But their very enormity was intimidating. The demand
was made that Antiochus should evacuate Asia Minor
and retire beyond the Taurus. The mere suggestion
seemed to threaten that he would be compelled to do so.

The battle was fought at Magnesia on the Hermus,
north-east of Smyrna, in the autumn of the year. Publius did not condescend to honour the harmless festivity
with his presence. He was indisposed, and resting; while
Hannibal, we may guess, down in Pamphylia was re-
packing his bullion and consulting the list of possible **Battle of**
employers who might consider the application of a mili- **Magnesia**
tary expert with capital to put into the business. . . .
Quite inferior people fought the battle of Magnesia.

When it was over, Antiochus sent envoys instructed
to accept any terms offered. Publius, in his lordly way,
replied that they were the same as before. . . . So
Antiochus paid the expenses of the war, and departed
over Taurus, on his way to disappear from history.

XVI

Two years later the Roman armies and fleets had
withdrawn from Asia, and left the country to its own
independent governments, which became on various

terms allies and connections of the Roman state. The hegemony so established became by degrees a government continually increasing in its effective control. . . . The battle of Magnesia gave Rome the dominion of the eastern Mediterranean as that of Zama had given her the dominion of the western. . . . The life's work

End of the Asian War of Hannibal was over. He had created the Roman empire. . . . And through Publius Scipio, whom he had evoked into being, he had created the Roman emperors.

XVII

The Wizard, after Magnesia, hardly waited for the news that his own surrender was included in the peace terms. Long before anyone could give effect to so difficult a provision, his ship was hull-down on the horizon of the Pamphylian Sea.

CHAPTER XIII

LAST NEWS ABOUT HANNIBAL

I

HANNIBAL tarried at Gortyna in Crete, on the southern slopes of Mount Ida, until he could find some definite work to do. Crete, once the home of Minos and the centre of his power, was in these days as wild a nest of corsairs as the cays of Yucatan became in later times; and the fate was a strange one which sent the last great suffete of Carthage into such company. . . . The Phœnicians had seen the glory and fall of Minos, and now they were following him into the shadows. . . .

Hannibal in Gortyna

But Gortyna had its own disadvantages. Hannibal's bullion did not long remain a secret. It attracted the hungry interest of gentlemen among whom the tenth commandment was yet unrevealed religion. Not the least famous of the ruses which legend attributed to the Wizard was the story of how he filled many pots with lead, "salting" them with a little gold and silver on the top, and officially depositing them for safety in the temple at Gortyna. The city warmly welcomed the deposit as a guarantee of good faith; and the strict guard it kept over Hannibal's imaginary treasure—so strict, that he might have found some difficulty himself in penetrating it—was unspoiled by any knowledge that the real bullion was contained in the cargo of brass images which lay carelessly stacked on a piece of waste land near his house. . . . Apparently there was little demand in Gortyna for Phœnician brass images; for no interest was taken in them.

At last he got into touch with King Prusias of Bithynia, and entered his service. The scene when the Gortynians solemnly confiscated his deposit has not, unfortunately, been recorded for the sympathy of later ages. . . . For some years he remained the military adviser of Prusias, and conducted his campaigns against Eumenes of Pergamus. Prusias himself was a man without very great brains, or courage, or resource; and such an assistant as Hannibal was invaluable to him alike in war and in diplomacy.

Hannibal's presence in Bithynia seems to have been unknown among the senatorial party in Rome, though in other quarters—probably the Scipionic circle—many persons were aware of it, and deliberately refrained from taking any steps to harry a man who was now growing old, and who was no longer a serious menace to Rome. The Cosmopolitan Autocrats remained a loyal little party to the last.

The Senate, in due course, intervened to remove the causes of friction between Prusias and Eumenes. It was one of Prusias' envoys at Rome who, at dinner with Titus Flamininus, let the cat out of the bag. Titus reported to the Senate his information that Hannibal was in Bithynia, and as this fact might explain much, he was authorized to demand Hannibal's surrender.[1]

Without venturing to defy the Senate, Prusias protested against being asked to break the law of hospi-

[1] Cornelius Nepos, *Hannibal*, XII. His account seems more natural and probable than Plutarch's version that Flamininus acted upon his own responsibility.

tality. If the Romans wanted Hannibal, he suggested that they had better take him themselves.

II

Thus, seven years after the battle of Magnesia, the event came which Hannibal had long foreseen and provided against. He was at Libyssa, on the shores of that long inlet which runs up from the Propontis to Nicomedia. A servant, watching from the gate, reported that unaccountable armed men were visible. Hannibal at once sent him to survey the other approaches. . . . All were picketed. . . . Sure now that the strangers were no accident, and that every avenue of escape was closed, he drank the draught that he habitually kept ready against emergency.

"This," he said, "will save the Romans from the worry of waiting for the death of an old and hated man. But Titus Flamininus is not a worthy descendant of the men who warned Pyrrhus against the poison prepared for him."

So, as if he had opened a door and walked out of the world, went Hannibal. . . . Public opinion in Rome was divided. There were not wanting those who regretted his end. He was in his sixty-fifth year. Death of Hannibal 183 B.C.

Publius Scipio died the same year, at the age of fifty-three. The man and his shadow disappeared together. Cato and the purists had demanded the account books of the Asiatic campaign. Publius deliberately tore them up before a crowded Forum, and left an ungrateful city which pretended to care more about methods than about results. But the leaven worked. He was the first of a succession of mighty individualists who thought more of results than of methods.

III

As if he had opened a door and walked out of the world. . . . Whether to silent and eternal dissolution or whether to the judgment of God, still we, ignorant of what that judgment may be, have for our own sakes to reckon him up and estimate the man. Was he a meteor flitting across the night of human history without purpose or meaning?—or one of those powerful luminaries which run in definite orbits, and exercise a definite influence? Not without cause, men have lingered with interest over the story of Hannibal. He both fascinates our interest and puzzles our understanding. That he was a very great man, we can see. But what else was he? What was his meaning?

His character

As a private individual, there is singularly little that we can bring against his character. As far as we can judge from the reports that have come down to us, he was a quiet, well-living man of perfect integrity, who hardly ever lost his temper; who never, apparently, got drunk,[1] and whose attitude towards women astonished his contemporaries. Whensoever he is depicted speaking, his enemies put acute and often epigrammatic good sense into his mouth. We hear of him wholly from his foes, and we hear little evil of him. There cannot be many men of whom we could say as much.

The two charges brought against him by the Romans

[1] He never drank more than a pint of wine at a time. (Justin XXXII. 4.)

were those brought generally against Carthaginians as a people—cruelty and love of money.[1] . . . The latter might be no more than the surprise of men, still predominantly landowning and agricultural, at the customs of a community much more developed in financial and commercial organization. But it comes through Polybius, a Greek, who was no stranger to the ways of a commercial people: and it is the accusation which is still brought against those close kinsmen of the Phœnicians—the Jews. . . . Polybius discussed the point with Carthaginians and with old Masinissa, who gave him his own views on the subject of Phœnicians and money. We can gather that they were interesting and vivid.

Money was the only form of wealth that can have had much meaning for Hannibal: we need not doubt that he was careful with it, and that he expected fractional sums to be accounted for. No anecdotes of his careless generosity have survived. That he was honest, we may infer from his financial reforms at Carthage, when it might have paid him better to share in the spoils. He seems to have owned land in the province of Byzacium; but he can scarcely have taken much interest in it. We cannot quite imagine him as a country squire. . . . He was cut off by a great gulf from the world of men like Fabius, whose wealth and interest were in land.

The charge of cruelty also is one which is made against Carthaginians as a race, and we therefore have

[1] Polybius IX, 22–26. Some details of the accusation of cruelty are collected in the speech of P. Lentulus given in Appian VIII. 63. Both charges incidentally were brought against the Romans themselves, as is made clear by Mr. Tarn, *Hellenistic Civilisation*, pp. 20, 71 and 97.

difficulty in distinguishing the degree to which it is an accusation against Hannibal personally. There is nothing in his record similar to the ferocity with which Hamilcar suppressed the revolt of the mercenaries. Polybius, in defending him, suggests that the charge is one which arose out of the acts of his subordinates rather than out of his own personal actions. . . . But the charge nevertheless has ground. A man who did so much damage to Italy [1] must have ordered many things which, if we knew them in detail, would revolt us to the point of indignation. It is hardly conceivable that he had not that indifference to death and suffering which is quite consistent with a cool and even an appreciative intelligence. . . . We may conclude that he shared with his fellow-Carthaginians a considerable degree of obtuseness to these things, and that he was in his private personality a man dominated by calm and calculating reason, which might be helped, but never deflected, by emotional sympathy.

The charge of cruelty

IV

These two charges of avarice and cruelty practically exhaust the list. [2] In neither case are they very distinctly underlined. The whole tenor of the picture [3] drawn of

[1] Diodorus (XXVI. 36) remarks that Hannibal almost depopulated Italy: which, though an exaggeration, is not a gross one. See Greenidge, *History of Rome*, Vol. I.

[2] Livy adds "a more than Punic faithlessness": but this is hardly borne out by the facts. (XXI. 4.)

[3] No absolutely authentic portrait of Hannibal exists. The author has to thank Mr. Harold Mattingley for pointing out the two Carthaginian coins from which are reproduced the heads of "Hannibal as Hercules" shown in the frontispiece. There is good reason for believing that the heads on these coins may represent Hannibal; they are contemporary in date; and they are in themselves of great beauty and interest.

him would seem to indicate that such features were
rather less noticeable in him than in his countrymen.
. . . He seems hardly ever to have performed any action merely for enjoyment. The anecdotes which are
told of him very seldom refer to his private actions.
Most of them are stories of the sometimes playful and
usually quite amiable humour [1] which must have been
a marked feature in his character as a man. The two
things which survive the impersonality which surrounded him are the ingenuity of his actions as a leader,
and the peculiar kind of thing he used to say. He was
a surprising man, who, even if he could be relied upon,
had a habit of realizing expectations in a totally unexpected manner. . . . The distinctive feature of Hannibal was originality. The one thing that no man could
do was to tell beforehand precisely what he would do
or say. Whensoever the world guessed, it guessed
wrong.

*Person-
ality of
Hannibal*

This liability to guess wrong is one to which the
modern critic is equally subject. . . . We might, with
good reason, think that Hannibal's intelligence was of a
purely practical kind. He left not a single speculation
on record: scarcely a hint of any spiritual experience.
And yet this silence is not entirely satisfactory. We cannot rely upon it. The unexpected man whose career was
one unbroken sensation to his contemporaries might
have one last sensation to spring upon us. He might in
these matters have something unexpected to say: as un-

[1] Carthaginians, however, seem to have had a much more modern—and even
"American"—type of humour than Latins or Greeks. Before they started to
cross the Alps, Hannibal's council discussed the commissariat. One member
remarked: "Well, we shall have to eat one another." Hannibal replied that he
did not think they would come to that. . . . And this was put forward by
Romans as serious evidence of cannibalism!

expected as the crossing of the Alps or the battle of Cannæ.

Few men can have conserved their energies with more dispassionate care than Hannibal. For the main object at stake he could take great risks, as he did when he crossed the Alps and the Apennines: but he never took a useless risk, and he never threw away any power, moral or material, that he possessed. . . . He showed, in these things, all the economy of the Semite.

His economy

V

But the private personality of Hannibal is the least part of him. His importance was in his function as the representative of Semitic power in the Mediterranean, and as its greatest protagonist. The day is long gone by when we could think of these vast tides of human energy as set going by private ambition or as changed by individual effort. Statesmen and soldiers are only the pilots of the ship; the waves neither rise nor are still at their bidding. Of this principle the story of Hannibal is an illustration. If any single man could have changed the current of history, he would have changed it. . . . But he did not change it: or at any rate, he did not change it in the obvious way he proposed.

The sense we have that Hannibal was a brilliant individualist is not deceptive. He did not trudge genially in a crowd, as Fabius did. He spent most of his life in sole and despotic command of an army which was devoted to him, and which willingly made at his request the most astonishing sacrifices. When, in later life, he had to struggle with hostile colleagues, he could not do

it. He was unable to wear down hostility and shepherd His limitations
the reluctant. His greatness was in the inspiration
which, if laboured or truncated—if not executed exactly as conceived—is useless.

In this he was a typical Phœnician, only able to put
forth his full power in isolation. With a certain kind of
communal life he was never at home. His chief colleagues were his own brothers, attuned to him by family likeness and long association. He never seems to have
got free from the necessity of this ready-made likemindedness. His close and personal relationship with
other men was not a bond he could artificially create
by a process of discussion and accommodation. Even
his relations with his army, personal and intimate as
they were, were not produced by any such means. They
were the relations of a generous and wise, but exacting
employer with his "hands." [1] . . . What Hannibal
could have done with an army like the Roman army is
a problem over which it is interesting to speculate.
The strong probability is that he could not have han-
dled an army of fellow-citizens with votes and opinions of their own. The mere necessity of adjusting his
mind to theirs would have paralysed it. . . . He was
one of those men who are good masters but bad equals.

And such was the psychological history of the whole The essential problem
Phœnician race. What was really at issue was the type
of mentality which should govern mankind. We have
seen the story told. We have seen the fierceness of the
struggle, the exhaustive nature of the test which tried

---

[1] All the principal authorities notice his excellent relations with these "hands."
Polybius XXIII. 13, XI. 19. Diodorus XXVI. 36. Justin XXXII. 4. Livy XXI. 4.
Allowing for some copying, the tradition seems a firm one. He never had any
trouble with his men.

every link to breaking point, the absoluteness of the proof. . . . The Carthaginian power was entirely and radically destroyed, and over its dust was erected the rule of men whose power lay in mutual accommodation.

The significance of Hannibal thus lies in his representative character. The Hannibalic war was a dividing line in human development. Before Hannibal, it was by no means certain that the political mode of organization would govern the future of the human race. It was still possible that human society might evolve on other lines; that common blood-relationship might be a stronger bond of unity than common thought and feeling; that those who agreed in the spirit might be overcome by those who agreed in the flesh; that, in fact, the only way to produce likemindedness was to be born alike. The Hannibalic war settled this problem. It proved, by the extreme test, that a greater power and a firmer unity was forged in the Forum and the Senate than could be achieved out of the resemblances of family likeness, and the dynamic energy of individual genius.

VI

His setting greater than himself   The interest of Hannibal cannot be made to depend entirely upon a study of his psychology. It is quite true that the hints we get from ancient historians are intensely suggestive, and even provoking in making us realize what we have for ever missed. If we knew as much of Hannibal as we do of Napoleon, the Carthaginian might not suffer in the comparison. But no such detailed account of Hannibal is possible. He remains a brilliant sketch. What we lose here, however, is compensated for by the greater opportunity we have for seeing him "in the large." Our eyes can wander freely over the vast outlines of a whole world, in which the distracting minor detail has been softened and lost, and only the important major facts are left. We can range, without disturbance, over the spectacle of a collision of vast forces which are perfectly visible. The interest of Hannibal consequently lies in his setting: the relation he bore to the world in which he lived. . . . Not a single scandal relieves the reader from the strain of observing great events.

VII

The political power which withstood and destroyed Hannibal was, as we have seen, composite. It was **The Roman State** founded partly on an aristocratic administrative tradition, and partly on a constitutional democracy. These two elements played their part in the contest. The aristocrats were the men who held Hannibal in the early days when the populares, left to themselves, would have gone under. But it was the populares who struck him down. By electing young Publius Scipio over the heads of the Senate, the Assembly proved the value of that constitutional power which at need can go outside the beaten track of customary practice.

Even in this, the composite nature of the Roman political state was illustrated. Though the Assembly elected the commander who ended the war, that commander was in his private person an aristocrat. Where the plebeian Varro failed, the patrician Scipio succeeded.

The superiority of the Roman political system over the Greek is emphasized when we compare the stories of Dionysius and Agathocles with that of Scipio Africanus. The latter needed no formal dictatorship, nor required, for his effective functioning, to subvert the constitution. Battered as Rome was, she emerged intact from the long contest, recognizably the same in character and system. This alone was enough to exalt the Roman state beyond all its rivals. A constitution which could survive a test which had destroyed all others was clearly a force to which all others must conform. And this was the actual result. The Roman system drove its competitors out of the field. Of them, little survives. The subsequent development of humanity was on the model which Rome provided.

We may draw some deductions from the different parts borne in the war by the various elements in the composite Roman state. The experience of Carthage also casts a side-light on the whole problem with which the world was struggling. In the series of steps by which the process of unification was carried out in the Mediterranean, practically all the powers were groping for something they had not got—a creative function within the state which could guide their action. They were all conscious, in varying ways, of the difficulty that their action was blind, or at any rate was carried out by elements more or less amateur and unspecialized for the task. The Greeks and Carthaginians in turn had recourse to dictatorship in the hope of finding in that expedient a specialized creative political function capable of carrying out the changes necessary. . . . But Rome faced the Carthaginians with a political "ar-

Its survival

rangement" which was destined to be the true solution. In the Hannibalic war we see it in germ in this difference between the parts played by the aristocratic and the popular parties. The former we will consider in a moment: but the latter needs all the more emphasis because it was a crude beginning, needing to pass through a whole series of transformations before it assumed its final shape.

The relations between Scipio and the Assembly were the beginnings of a new political institution. Without overriding the normal processes of the state, he established an unofficial link with the Assembly which was the first step towards personal government. The future of this relation was conditioned by its beginning. It was from the first based upon the support of the electors. It was not a dictatorship like that of Dionysius; it was not external to the state, like the position of Hannibal; it was not a tribal monarchy like that of Alexander; it had not—and never acquired—the nature of the monarchy possessed by Antiochus. Dictatorship, as a normal function, was fading out of Roman practice precisely at the moment when Scipio introduced the new idea.

From these relations of Scipio and the Assembly sprang ultimately the creative office which carried Mediterranean civilization to its due consummation. Its pedigree is clear. Necessity invented Hamilcar; and Hamilcar begat Hannibal; and Hannibal provoked Scipio; and Scipio suggested Sulla, and Sulla created Cæsar; and Cæsar trained Augustus; and from Augustus sprang the principate; and from the principate the later Roman and north European monarchies, which founded the modern world. This personal government, depending first upon an assembly, then upon a military guild, and later upon a curia, court, or, in its latest form, a body of tenants-in-chief, was radically different from earlier monarchy, and bore from beginning to end the stamp of its origin. It was the creative office which the political state specialized to meet the needs of its evolution.

VIII

The failure of the Greek and Carthaginian methods was due to the fault that they overrode instead of supplementing the normal processes of a political state. The difficulty was to arise again later in circumstances not necessary here to detail. . . . Against this, the Roman Senate formed a strong barrier. The old aristocratic element in the Senate was the active force in moulding opinion and determining policy. From their ranks came most of the successful commanders and statesmen; and they were resolute from the first in conciliating, in persuading, in guiding and even in tricking public feeling into the preservation of the normal political action of the state.

If, therefore, the aristocratic party exercised none of the extraordinary functions which are performed by travelling outside the beaten track, it rendered them possible by acting as a kind of gyroscope continually restabilizing the state as the balance of forces changed. . . . For the most part we are in the habit of picturing to ourselves a violent contrast between the idea of discussion and mutual agreement, and the idea of

Function
of the
aristocracy

aristocracy. The one (we think) is "democratic"; the other, built up of irresponsible command and servile obedience. We think of aristocracy as the contradiction of the political state. . . . But this view is not borne out by the facts. Discussion and agreement are often the last things that a crowd of men can manage. What it can easily achieve is common action under a collective emotion; and this is so far from being discussion and agreement that it is often their polar opposite. Among the most alarming things in life is a crowd under the influence of an unreasoning collective emotion.

One of the aims of a statesman is to break up the crowd, to prevent it from acting under collective emotion, and to get it to reason, and to reach a likemindedness born not of sympathetic feeling but of rational agreement. This was the function of the Roman Senate under the leadership of Quintus Fabius. Again and again the Senate was called upon to get things away from the sphere of enthusiastic emotion into the sphere of cold reason. . . . We do not see old Fabius telling the people to eat grass, nor haughtily issuing commands to the lower classes. . . . We see him smiling steadily, arguing patiently: and we see him getting his way by an enormous patience and a monumental good sense. . . . Yet if any man was an aristocrat, in the narrowest sense of the word, that man was Fabius.

The Senate under Fabius

Aristocracy is as much a political institution as democracy is. The notion of an aristocrat as a man who issues arrogant commands is a tradition of barbarism, not of civilization.

IX

Theory of
aristocracy

The modern world has tended partly to lose altogether the remembrance of what aristocracy is, and partly to think that the particular kind of aristocracy it chances to know is the only kind there is, or ever was. But within its own limits [1] aristocracy is susceptible of immense variety. For it is a political function rather than a type of character. An Aristocracy is a body of men who can act as a common denominator in a state composed of differentiated and specialized types; and a race might in the human sense continue to be great, and even increase in the distinction of the character it produces, and yet cease to be an aristocracy because it has ceased to command the common allegiance of other types of men.

But the type of character that is embodied in any aristocracy is nevertheless interesting and illuminating. The characters of Fabius and Scipio are essential elements in the story of Hannibal. We can, of course, reduce that story to the brief formula that Hannibal was a man of genius who was overwhelmed by the mass of the commonplace men against whom he fought.

Genius of
Hannibal

. . . But men of genius are not overwhelmed by the mass of the commonplace. They circumvent it and dissolve it. It is because of this power that they are men

[1] Its own limits. An aristocracy can be either gentile or feudal. To be an aristocracy it must cultivate and produce from its own resources the type of man it requires: that is, it must be hereditary. It is an order of men within a political state: that is, it is not the whole state. It must be a distinct body: but if it is entirely closed it is a "caste." A body which co-opts its individual members is not an aristocracy but an oligarchy. The qualification must not be the possession of wealth but the exercise of function. An aristocracy may be based upon either money or land, but land is, for various reasons, the more usual.

of genius. What a man of genius cannot rely upon doing is to defeat men with another kind of genius. . . . Rome produced two men of genius to counter Hannibal. One—Quintus Fabius—was a great man of the aristocratic type. The other—Publius Scipio—was a great man of the autocratic or monarchical type. Both were men very peculiarly and especially adapted to the processes of a political state. As simple individuals, neither of them could compare with Hannibal. As living parts in the political machine, they were capable of collecting and transmitting forces that destroyed him.

X

The men who directly profited by the fall of Carthage were the wealthy plebeians—the bankers and commercial men who were the controlling power of the Assembly and the popular party. At the old landed interest throughout Italy the war struck a deadly blow from which it never recovered. The change in the political balance was no doubt not immediate. Cato shows us the bridge over.

That remarkable man, as he grew older, developed the character which made him the embodiment of the Roman tradition, as it was fixed and perpetuated by the war. . . . Himself a plebeian, with most of the instincts of the reformer and the puritan, he added to his natural qualities those which he imperfectly learned from a passionate admiration for the aristocratic party led by Quintus Fabius. The blend had some immortal characteristics. It was unbending, incorruptible and consistent to the point of meticulousness: it sought,

Effects of the Fall of Carthage

even if it did not achieve, some central ground of
realism where expedience was not judged merely by the
feelings. The result, curious in its way, gave shape and
perpetuity to a mood of transition which might otherwise have perished. Since he sought to deal with social
problems without shirking their moral difficulty, his attitude led him to solutions which were consistent at the
expense of their human feeling. He was traditionally
made responsible for the destruction of Carthage.

Not all Romans agreed with that policy. Its chief opponent was a Scipio. But there was no longer a direct
descendant of Publius Scipio Africanus to witness it.
Fate had a stranger irony in store when she brought it
about that Scipio Æmilianus, the great-grandson of the
consul who fell at Cannæ, should superintend that
tragedy.

The Landed and the Moneyed classes

On the awful day when Hasdrubal's wife, the embodied spirit of Semitic Carthage, after denouncing her
cowardly husband, had hurled her children into the
flames; when the Roman labour-corps was raking the
fiery ashes and tangled ruins out of the path of the
legionaries; when the last Carthaginians were dying as
the last Romans would have died in the Capital, had
Hannibal reached it; Scipio Æmilianus seized Polybius
by the hand and spoke immortal words of fear lest this
nightmare should return to haunt the deathbed of
Rome.

But it had other effects. It placed the Roman in
the shoes of the Carthaginian; it made him the heir of
the financial and commercial supremacy of Carthage;
and he took over the liabilities as well as the assets of
his predecessor.

XI

The change weakened the moral foundation of the
Roman state, as the Romans themselves believed. It was
by no desire of theirs that power slipped into the hands
of a moneyed instead of a landed class, and transformed
Roman civilization more into the likeness of the Carthaginian civilization it had destroyed. But the process was
inevitable, because even apart from other causes it was
impossible that the influence of the landholders of central Italy could permanently retain its power in an expanding state. The conquest of Carthage and the acquisition of the East altered the proportion of things. . . .   Rome suc-
The commercial interests could extend their activity   ceeds to
                                                          Carthage
over the whode Mediterranean world; but the landholders could not extend in the same way. . . . The
war, by weakening the landed interests, very possibly
cut out of Roman history the political struggle that
might have occurred between the two classes had this
development been more gradual. When, half a century later, the small farmers did revolt against the
moneyed men, many of the old aristocratic families
sympathized, and even shared the struggle: but the latter were already broken as a compact force, and could
contribute nothing but individual leadership and assistance.

The growth of the moneyed power was thus not a
tragic accident but a natural stage in the evolution of
the Roman State, growing direct out of the necessities
and conditions of its development. Rome did suffer
from the diminution of that stabilizing force which
the old aristocratic influence represented. The age of

the civil wars betrays unmistakably that some saving function had failed within the state. It is impossible to conceive such men as Fabius sharing in the rage of civil

Loss and gain

strife which convulsed the Italy of later generations, and deluged Rome itself with blood. . . . But if it were not a tragic accident it was a tragic necessity. . . . At intervals men reasonably stand aghast at the conditions of their own progress. It seems to be built up on blood and contest; it seems to be achieved by sacrificing what was already gained. The ultimate result may make the intermediate difficulties worth enduring. But to justify the means, the end must be singularly splendid. The instinctive belief of mankind is generally that it will be so: and this belief has to be taken into account.

XII

Another factor also had a share in the growth of the moneyed power. While a landed aristocracy starts in the political race with an advantage over other classes, in as much as the very exercise of its function teaches it the rules of government, it is seldom or never the originator of creative ideas concerning the use of wealth. In every civilization, however, there is a stage at which the question of the utilization of wealth becomes the dominant problem; and it is this stage which gives commercial oligarchy a significance all its own.

Material wealth

The Roman aristocracy, in its prime, never had any particular gift for consuming. It had no art, no literature and no luxury. We should err if we thought that it had therefore no brains. It had singularly acute and

profound powers of thinking. It hoed its turnips while
meditating upon the mysteries of Law. Its meditations
on this head have outlasted the Colosseum and the
Mausoleum of Augustus.

But jurisprudence, after all, is nothing but a system
of relationships. The things it relates are the concrete
actualities; and the old Roman aristocracy, good as it
was at the establishment of relations, never showed
much gift for producing things to be related. . . .
Left to its aristocratic inventors, life would have remained about as interesting as a volume of Euclid. It
was the commercial man, the stout plutocrat, who
clothed the abstract relations with the vulgar gorgeous-
ness of material well-being. The plutocrat walked in
purple and fine linen—to the indignation of the aristocrat and the fury of Cato—and handed out the endow-
ments to the artists and the literary men who gave the
tale of his vices and weaknesses a long life, and his gifts
a short one.

The expansion of the commercial and financial interests of Rome was thus marked by an influx of cul-
ture and luxury which were alien to the old aristocratic
tradition. . . . Scipio and his circle were the first to
adopt the new fashion; a fact which is not without its
significance.

Function of commercial oligarchy

XIII

To defeat a man is to become like him. . . . There
is some recondite law of the human mind which forces
the critic to do the thing he criticizes; and this perhaps explains why men, when they have fought to the

death to destroy some hated thing, insensibly begin to take on its colour and assume its vesture. . . . The defeat of Hannibal and the destruction of Carthage had this effect. For good and evil, the spirit of Hannibal haunted Rome; for good and evil, the moral atmosphere of the great African mart accompanied Rome on her march through time. The curled and bewhiskered seamen were still lounging the quays of the Mediterranean when Columbus signed on his crews. The Phœnician vocabulary and phonetics, it is said, were long traceable in Africa and Spain. However that may be, the very visage and mentality of the Phœnician lingered on; and when Cortez and Pizarro had hewed out new conquests in lands of which Carthage had never heard, the swarthy, gold-ringed man with his touch of Tyrian purple was among the foremost of the human eagles who gathered to explore and exploit.

Indestruct-ibility

INDEX

Dictatorship, Spanish, 68, et seq., 73.
  Greek, 15-27.
  Roman, 104-125, 128, 259-260, 319.
  Carthaginian, 262, 284.
Dion, 22, 23, 51.
Dionysius (The elder), 18-22, 213, 242.
  (The younger), 22-24.
Drepanum, 44, 56.
Duilius, Gaius. (Consul), 38.

Ebro (River), 71, 76-77.
Ecnomus, (Battle of), 40.
Egypt, 3-4, 244, 278-280, 292 f.n.
Elephants, (War), 28, 29, 42, 43, 65-67, 80-83, 90, 97, 210, 268-271.
Engines, (War), 19, 180-183.
Ephesus, 292, 296, 303, 304.
Epicydes, 169, 171, 198, 199, 200-203.
Ercte, (Mount), 53.
Eryx, 53, 59.
Etruria, 96, 227.
Etruscans, 9, 11, 17, 20-21.
Eudamus, 303-304.

Fabius Maximus Verrucosus, Quintus, (father), 104, 105-125, 126, 138-139, 157, 190, 216-221, 233, 247, 259, 321, 322, 323, 326.
  Quintus, (son), 146, 190.
  Pictor, 68, 85, 102, 141, 158.
Fæsulæ, (Fiesole), 98.
Fanum Fortunæ (Fano), 111, 233.
Flaccus, Gn. Fulvius, (consul), 194.
  Q. Fulvius, (consul), 216.
Flamininus, T. Quintius, 285, 293-4, 295, 299, 300, 302, 308.
Flaminius Nepos, Gaius, 92-101.
Forli, 97.

Gades (Cadiz), 7, 238.
Gelo (Dictator), 15-17.
  (son of Hiero), 156.
Gerunium, 118, 119, 120, 131.
Gisco, 59-64.
Gortyna, 307.

Great Plains (Battle of), 252.
Greeks, 9, 10, 16, 17, 49, 293, 300.
Grumentum, 233.

Hadrumetum, 273.
Hamilcar (Carthaginian officer), 281.
  Barca, 45, 53, 56-7, 61, 63, 67 et seq., death, 71, 223, 243, 298.
Hannibal (Barcides), (birth), 58, accession to command, 74; methods, 213, et seq.; interview with Scipio, 265; a cosmopolitan, 277; flight, 289; outlawed, 290; character, 310-314; a representative man, 314-317.
  "The Rhodian," 44 f.n., 56 f.n.
Hanno "the Great," 60, 65, 153-155.
  (Carthaginian general), 175-176.
Hasdrubal (Barcides), 79, 205-206, 226, 230, 231, 233, 234, 236; (death), 237.
  ("Beau"), 69, 71-73, 76.
  (Carthaginian Cavalry General), 120, 137.
  (Gisconides), 224, 230, 238, 248, 250-252.
  ("Kid"), 275, f.n.; 276.
Hebrews, 2, 3.
Herennius, Q. Bæbius, 127-129.
Hiero, 130, 156, 167.
Hieronymus, 167 et seq., 170.
Himera (Battle of), 17, (city), 18.
Hippocrates, 169, 171, 200.

Indemnities, War, 56, 57, 68, 78, 85, 256, 282, 288.

Judicial Board, 13, 283-285, 287.

Lacinia (Promontory), 160, 162.
  (Temple), 84, f.n.
Lælius, Gaius, 252-255, 258-259, 269-273.
Lævinus, M. Valerius, 160, 227, 232.
Leptis, 262.
Libyssa, 309.
Lilybæum, 21, 44, 56, 59, 202, 247.
Livius Salinator, M., 232, 233.

OTHER COOPER SQUARE PRESS TITLES OF INTEREST

AUGUSTUS
The Golden Age of Rome
G. P. Baker
378 pp., 17 b/w illustrations, 8 maps
0-8154-1089-1
$18.95

HISTORY OF THE CONQUEST OF MEXICO &
HISTORY OF THE CONQUEST OF PERU
William H. Prescott
1330 pp., 2 maps
0-8154-1004-2
$32.00

AGINCOURT
Christopher Hibbert
176 pp., 33 b/w illustrations, 3 b/w maps
0-8154-1053-0
$16.95

THE DREAM AND THE TOMB
A History of the Crusades
Robert Payne
456 pp., 37 b/w illustrations, 11 maps
0-8154-1086-7
$19.95

THE LIFE AND TIMES OF AKHNATON
Pharaoh of Egypt
Arthur Weigall
320 pp., 33 b/w illustrations
0-8154-1092-1
$17.95

T. E. LAWRENCE
A Biography
Michael Yardley
308 pp., 71 b/w photos., 5 b/w maps
0-8154-1054-9
$17.95

GENGHIS KHAN
R. P. Lister
256 pp., 1 b/w illustration
0-8154-1052-2
$16.95

THE WAR OF 1812
Henry Adams
New introduction by Col. John R. Elting
392 pp., 27 b/w maps & sketches
0-8154-1013-1
$16.95

WOLFE AT QUEBEC
The Man Who Won the French and Indian War
Christopher Hibbert
208 pp., 1 b/w illustration, 4 b/w maps
0-8154-1016-6
$15.95

MAN AGAINST NATURE
Firsthand Accounts of Adventure and Exploration
Edited by Charles Neider
512 pp.
0-8154-1040-9
$18.95

Available at bookstores; or call 1-800-462-6420

 **Cooper Square Press**

150 Fifth Avenue
Suite 911
New York, NY 10011